THE CULTURAL-HISTORICAL DEVELOPMENT OF VERBAL THINKING

Horizons in Psychology
Series Editor - James Wertsch

Cultural-Historical Development of Verbal Thinking　　　Peeter Tulviste

Learning in Children: Organization and Development of Cooperation Actions
V.V. Rubtsov

Meaning and Categorization　　　Rebecca Frumkina and Alexei Mikheev

Psychophysiology of Visual Masking　　　Talis Bachmann

THE CULTURAL-HISTORICAL DEVELOPMENT OF VERBAL THINKING

Peeter Tulviste

Translated by
Marie Jaroszewska Hall

Nova Science Publishers, Inc.

Nova Science Publishers, Inc.
6080 Jericho Turnpike, Suite 26
Commack, New York 11725

ISBN-1-56072-006-9

Book Production Manager: Barbara Maki
Graphics: Elenor Kallberg and Janet Glanzman White

Library of Congress Cataloging-in-Publication Data

Tul'viste, P.
  [Kul'turno-istoricheskoe razvitie verbal'nogo myshleniiā.
English]
  The cultural-historical development of verbal thinking / Peeter
Tulviste ; translated by Marie Jaroszewska Hall.
      p. cm.
  Translation of: Kul'turno-istoricheskoe razvitie verbal'nogo
myshleniiā.
  Includes bibliographical references and index.
  ISBN 1-56072-006-9 : $39.00
  1. Psycholinguistics--History. 2. Cognition and culture.
I. Title. II. Title: Verbal thinking.
BF455.T7613 1991
401'.9--dc20   91-39140
                                                                      CIP

© *1991 Nova Science Publishers, Inc.*

Printed in the United States of America

CONTENTS

Preface

It is a pleasure and a distinct privilege to be permitted to write a few words of introduction to Peeter Tulviste's monograph about the relationship between culture and thought. My special feelings about this work go back to a Sunday afternoon in the spring of 1963, to the spacious study of Alexander R. Luria, a study lined with books in many languages and cabinets filled with files containing data and manuscripts from various projects Alexander Romanovich had carried out over his long career.

While we were sipping our tea, Alexander Romanovich took a thick folder from one of the cabinets and told us about an interesting line of research he had carried out thirty years earlier among the village people living in remote areas of Uzbekistan. It was then that I first learned of people whose responses to logical syllogisms are a central topic in the current book: "All the bears in Novayazemlya are white. My friend Ivan want to Novayazemlya and saw a bear. What color was it?" I smiled at the simplicity of the question. Why of course, I thought, the bear is white. What's the issue? Luria's subjects replied quite differently: "I have never been to Novayazemlya; it was your friend who went there, ask him."

An anecdote to amuse a visiting American post doctoral student, and soon forgotten. I returned to the United States and took up my career where I had left it the previous year—studying mechanisms of learning among white rats and college sophomores.

When, unexpectedly, I was sent to Liberia to study the difficulties that tribal children experience when they enter American-style schools, I vaguely recalled Alexander Romanovich's anecdote. We began to correspond about that long-ago project, but in those days communication between Soviet and non-Soviet scholars was frought with difficulties which were not reduced by the vagaries of international mail service. Anxious to get a more complete understanding of what Alexander Romanovich had been doing in Central Asia and why, I struck a bargain with him. I would spend a summer as a volunteer helping to organize an upcoming international congress of psychologists if he would spend an hour a day with me going over this cross-cultural data so that upon return to Liberia I could attempt to replicate and extend them. In the meantime, I gathered as complete a set of materials on the topic of culture and thought as I could, and sent it off to Moscow.

During the summer of 1966, true to his word, Alexander Romanovich would meet with me daily to go over his materials. I learned that when the work was first reported it had met with an angry reception, which explained why it had not been published previously.

But times had changed for the better, and in a few years Alexander Romanovich pulled together those of his materials that he could make sense of and published them, first in an article, then in book form. I, for my part, carried out replications and extensions of the Central Asian studies and studied the theoretical rationale upon which they were based. I urged Alexander Romanovich to follow up on his own innovative studies, but he was already elderly and preoccupied with other matters. However, he had an able student, an Estonian named Peeter Tulviste, who could carry on this line of work.

The reader will encounter here the fruits of Peeter's work of more than a decade—a far ranging scholarly review of the extant literature on cultural variations in human thought processes and descriptions of carefully planned experiments. The central issue posed by this work is clear: How are we to interpret the heterogeneity of human thought revealed by cross-cultural comparisons? Are there fundamental differences in human thought as a function of the culture into which one is born and are such differences, if they are shown to exist, rankable in terms of developmental level? In crude but direct terms, do "primitives think like children?"

Peeter's answer to the former question is yes—there are fundamental qualitative differences in human thought attributable to the cultural environment. His answer to the second is no, cultural differences do not imply cultural deficits. In place of a single "mentality" divisible into its "primitive" and "civilized" variants, Peeter finds heterogeneity not only within as well as between cultures, but heterogeneity within individuals in every culture depending upon the form of activity in which they are engaged. To be sure, the industrial revolution has brought new forms of activity and new forms of intellectual activity into existence. In this sense, people who have undergone a modern education have additional intellectual tools associated with science and bureaucratically controlled life which are either lacking, or found only rarely in pre-industrial societies. But these new intellectual tools can be considered "better" only in a conditional sense, related to the activity which engendered them in the first place.

The conclusions that Peeter reaches are by no means beyond dispute. There are deep methodological problems associated with cross-cultural research as his probing analysis indicates. Nor is there general agreement about what constitutes evidence for a fundamental and broad change in thought processes in contrast with a superficial or narrow change. Readers will have to make up their own minds about the difficult matters discussed in the pages to follow. However, they can rest assured: They will come away with a firmer notion of how to think about cultural variations in thought and full of admiration, as I am, at the range and acuity of Peeter Tulviste's scholarship.

Michael Cole

Introduction

If one asks a professional psychologist why, in psychology text books, one can find numerous answers to questions which an ordinary person interested in psychology would never think to ask and which seem third-rate in importance while "really important" questions about mental life usually remain unanswered, two circumstances are cited in response: psychology is a young science, and the human mind is a complex phenomenon.

Neither argument seems convincing. The prehistory of psychology as a science began in antiquity. If, however, we limit ourselves only to experimental psychology, then in 100 years, other sciences attained significant success in resolving their basic problems. On the other hand, we can scarcely be justified in claiming, for example, that visual perception, where scientific psychology has made significant progress, represents a simpler phenomenon than, let us say, determining motivational processes. There must be some other reason for the fact that in psychology, phenomena that are of interest to the ordinary man or to other human sciences are little studied.

It is easy to see that psychology refused to study these phenomena when it became an experimental science. This was the price it had to pay for being "scientific." N. Chomsky, one of the most prominent modern linguists, writes: "Modern linguistics shares the delusion—an accurate term, I believe—that the modern 'behavioral sciences' have in some essential respect achieved a transition from 'speculation' to 'science' and that earlier work can be safely consigned to the antiquarians. Obviously any rational person will favor rigorous analysis and careful experiment, but to a considerable degree, I feel, the 'behavioral sciences' are merely mimicking the surface features of the natural sciences; much of their scientific character has been achieved by a restriction of subject matter and a concentration on rather peripheral issues. Such narrowing of focus can be justified if it leads to achievements of real intellectual significance, but in this case, I think that it would be very difficult to show that the narrowing of scope has led to deep and significant results" (Chomsky, 1972, p. xi).

Of course the solution lies not in a return to that state of affairs which prevailed in psychology a century ago. We know that great hope was placed on experimental psychology because the status quo was never satisfactory. The turn to experimentation was indisputably an important and positive event in the history of psychology.

Moreover, restricting the sphere of phenomena studied in psychology as a result of resorting to experimentation was, it seems to me, not the only, and even not the main problem. A much more negative role was played by the fact that in the two decades preceding Wundt's founding of the first psychology laboratory, investigators of the mind, influenced by the works of Spencer,

1

Darwin and others, began to consider man as one of the animals. Together with the evolutionary approach, which gave psychology a strong boost toward development and gave rise to whole branches of psychology, the idea spread that the human mind could be <u>explained</u> in the same way as the mind of any other animal: through hereditarily set structures of the brain and adaptation to the environment.

Many phenomena in human psychology actually can be explained in this way. In some well-developed areas of psychology, the successful application methods from physiology and physiological and biological reduction created the illusion that at some time it would be possible to explain the whole human mind in this way. When better encephalographs are developed, when we learn how better to read the genetic code and apply better mathematical methods, when we recognize more fully what is taking place "in the head," that is, in the brain, then we will explain all the phenomena of the human mind.

It seems to me that it is specifically here that the basic delusion lies. Success in explaining so called "lower" mental processes can be explained by the fact that when these are studied, an explanatory principle adequate to the material being studied is applied. But it cannot lead to success in the study of so-called "higher" mental processes no matter how perfect the means and methods of study used. Exactly for this reason, and not because of the complexity of the mind, the internal world of man and higher, specifically human mental processes have been less easily explained thus far than phenomena which psychophysics and psychophysiology are studying. These phenomena are determined mainly by physiological and common biological factors, which, naturally, must serve as a basis for their explanation, while the human personality, the overwhelming majority of its ways of behavior, thinking and memorizing, conflicts, needs, feelings, etc., are not generated by nature, and for this reason, are not subject to being explained through natural— common biological and physiological—factors.

In short, common conceptions that may have arisen under the influence of evolutionary theory nudged investigators to apply to the human mind the explanatory principle that was well-grounded and productive in the study of the mind of rats. Naturally, it was successful in the investigation of mental processes common to rats and to man, but the processes that are absent in rats thus far beg explanation. The latter processes owe their emergence to culture and history (which are also lacking in rats). Consequently, they must also be explained through culture and history, through facts not of biology and physiology, but history, sociology, culturology, semiotics, ethnography, and cultural anthropology. The basis for turning to these data is not the inapplicability of experimentation as a method for investigating the higher processes, as Wundt assumed, but the simple circumstance that every phenomenon must be explained through the causes that gave rise to it.

We have known for a long time that in man, together with hereditarily transmitted species memory and individual memory, there is still a third, specifically human type of memory: culture. Methods of behaving, needs, skills, and knowledge are transmitted through culture. Man needs a comparatively short time for these to be fixed. It is exactly from this that the possibilities of history flow. Rats are now doing the very same things that they did hundreds of thousands of years ago while man and his activity during that time have changed substantially and continue to change. These circumstances are well known to investigators of culture, but have thus far rarely been seriously considered by psychologists.

Within psychology, the concept of the social, cultural, and historical nature of higher mental processes in man was formulated more than 50 years ago in the works of L. S. Vygotsky. As a methodological principle, it is mentioned in psychology texts and in theoretical and experimental studies. Authors, however, usually forget this principle when they attempt a direct explanation of the mental processes. Thus far it has the status of a catchword rather than a real, applicable, explanatory principle. One is easily convinced of this in reviewing any textbook of general psychology or the psychology of children and comparing the number of physiological facts cited (indispensable, of course) with the number of references to sociological, cultural, or historical data.

For psychologists, the brain, heredity, maturation, adaptation, etc. continue to be as if "more real" and more substantial from the point of view of explaining the mind than society, culture and history. A. R. Luria propagandized the idea going back to Vygotsky that to explain the individual mind, it is necessary to go beyond its boundaries, beyond the boundaries of the "head," and to explain what is going on in the "head" through sociocultural processes. In his last works, he maintained that culture and activity determine both the higher mental processes and the corresponding physiological systems of the brain. He proposed creating a new science for the study of this problematics "psychological physiology". This idea provoked no enthusiasm among psychologists and representatives of other humanitarian sciences. Many, on the other hand, are fascinated by the functional asymmetry of the hemispheres. This is fascinating material for study, but here too, in their attempts to explain both the mind and culture through the physiology of the brain, psychologists and culturologists characteristically strive to "anchor" in the hemispheres the types of mental and cultural phenomena described in these sciences.

It is obvious that in the absence of an adequate explanatory principle, the result of studying one phenomenon or another may be only its description, not its explanation. This specifically is the situation with the study of the higher mental processes no matter which phenomenon we consider: verbal associations, syllogistic reasoning, formation of concepts... The influential works of Piaget, as we know, are distinguished for the subtlety of their descriptions, but also for the weakness of their explanations. Many critics of Piaget, including some of his followers, agree that his use of general biological categories—adaptation, assimilation, accommodation—can scarcely explain causally the intellectual development of the child. After it was established by many comparative studies of Piaget's phenomena in children and adults from various cultures and cultural groups that two of the four presumably universal stages in the development of intellect in the child—the stage of concrete and the stage of formal operations—simply do not appear in many people in many cultures, it became obvious that cultural factors play a much more substantial role in the development of intellect than Piaget assumed.

For a better explanation of the higher mental processes, of their emergence and development, psychology at present lacks a satisfactory theoretical concept of their connections with culture. Even in the seemingly most "cultural" branch of modern psychology—in comparative cross-cultural psychology, in which data from sciences studying culture are frequently taken seriously—there is a striking absence of any kind of productive concept of culture itself and its role in the formation of higher mental processes that would elucidate the higher mental processes. According to a common assumption, cultural factors only "have an effect" on higher mental processes that exist "per se," determine some of their features, and activate or actualize one process or another. Culture is not considered as giving rise to these processes, as a factor that generates them. In general, it is assumed that the biological unity of man ensures his psychic unity while culture is capable only of adding various, sometimes quite unexpected and exotic features to mental processes. From the point of view of causal explanation, little has changed since the time when attempts were made to deduce differences in the human mind from hypothetical differences in the brain structure of peoples of different races and ethnic groups—as we know, the existence of such differences has never been proven. Present-day investigators assume that identity of the brain ensures identity of the mind, including higher mental processes. In both cases, the brain appears as the cause, and the mind, as the effect, that is, both then and now, the explanatory principle is the same.

This book was written with the conviction that in their complexity and variety, the higher mental processes in man must be explained through culture and history. This conviction is no more than a general assumption that permits deducing concrete hypotheses that may be subjected to testing. One such hypothesis is considered in the book. It pertains to verbal human thinking, its changes in history and its features in people of societies currently existing in the world.

The following problems are discussed in the book: Are the processes of verbal thinking in people of various currently existing societies the same or not? What are the differences? What causes them? Was the thinking of people who lived at different historical times the same or not? Does thinking change when society or culture changes? Why is "our" verbal thinking the kind that it is?

It seems that these problems are interesting in themselves. However, their diverse solutions are interesting also from the point of view of solving certain more general and basic problems of the psychology of thinking.

First, the study of historical changes and cultural differences in verbal thinking will help to clarify the role of biological and sociocultural factors in determining the units and operations of this kind of thinking. If psychological patterns of thinking are due to physiological and general biological factors, then these patterns must be identical in general in all people regardless of sociocultural conditions. If, however, substantial differences are found in comparative studies of thinking in people of different cultures and cultural groups, then these indicate the significance of the conditions in the establishment and development of verbal thinking in the individual.

Second, the method of cross-cultural comparison sometimes makes it possible to establish the role of one concrete sociocultural factor or another in the determination of thinking. The variability of currently existing societies in the world permits a study "in pure form," for example, of the role of schooling in the formation of verbal thinking. For this purpose, we need not isolate a group of children from school and from the possible indirect effects of "school" learning and skill. In many countries, only some of the children attend school while the others are given traditional home schooling. Another example: a child entering school learns reading and writing there as well as specific "school" or scientific knowledge. Under the usual conditions, it is impossible for this reason to test the well-known hypothesis as to whether training in reading and writing as a separate factor has substantial influence on thinking: for example, does it make thinking abstract. S. Scribner and M. Cole studied thinking in the Vai ethnic group in Liberia which has a unique system of writing, the teaching of which takes place outside school and is not accompanied by the learning of scientific information (Scribner and Cole, 1978, 1981). Here it was possible to study the significance of teaching reading and writing as a separate factor in the formation of thinking.

Third, experimental data on the thinking of people in various presently existing societies may be used for reconstructing the course of the historical development of human thinking in the past. In many developing countries, sociocultural changes are taking place at an accelerated rate at present, similar in certain respects to changes that occurred in other societies very long ago. Psychologists have perhaps only for a short time been given the opportunity to study experimentally the effects on the historical development of thinking of such factors as the spread of new types of economic activity, scientific knowledge, schooling, literacy, mass media communications, etc.

Finally, fourth, the data from comparative studies of thinking open new prospects for a causal explanation of the ontogeny of verbal thinking.

Obviously, knowledge concerning the effects of one sociocultural factor or another on thinking may be applied in explaining the development of thinking in the child where it is frequently difficult to detect the determining role of biological and sociocultural factors.

Such, in short, are certain of the possibilities of applying the results of a comparative study of human thinking in different cultures and cultural groups for solving problems in the psychology of thinking.

The title of the book, "Cultural-Historical Development of Verbal Thinking (a Psychological Study)" requires certain elucidation. The words "cultural-historical" indicate both the subject of the study and the tradition in psychology to which this book belongs. In it we are speaking not about the general evolution of thinking, not about its phylogeny or ontogeny, but about the development that human thinking experienced and continues to experience in the course of the cultural history of mankind affected by cultural-historical factors. The book represents an attempt to apply to problems of historical changes and cross-cultural differences in thinking the ideas of the so-called cultural-historical psychology developed in the 1920's and 1930's by L. S. Vygotsky and advanced later by A. R. Leont'ev, A. R. Luria and other followers of Vygotsky. The basic idea of cultural-historical psychology, as we know, is that the so-called higher mental processes must be explained not by natural factors, but by the cultural-historical factors that determine these processes.

The problems discussed in the book emerged in the middle of the last century under the influence of the idea of evolution, and their investigation was undertaken under the aegis of genetic (developmental) psychology. In modern cross-cultural psychology, the idea of development is not popular. We have come to speak not about historical changes, but about cross-cultural and intergroup differences in thinking. It is easy to see that the reason for rejection of the historical approach toward these phenomena lies beyond the limits of psychology. If comparative psychology arises from the circumstance that different species are on different rungs of the evolutionary ladder and child psychology deals with children of different ages, then an historically oriented cross-cultural psychology would obviously have to be based on an historically oriented ethnology. Although in recent times, there has been a return in ethnology to the idea of the historical development of culture and its separate components, the influence of cultural relativism is stronger and calls forth—in counterbalance to the self-satisfied Europocentrism of classical evolutionism— a consideration of all societies as different, but equal and, in this connection, precludes considering some cultures as less and others as more developed. Without analyzing the weak and strong points of these approaches, let us note that in psychology, as in linguistics and other humanistic studies, both synchronic and diachronic approaches to the phenomena under consideration have a right to exist. We are interested mainly in the cultural-historical changes in thinking, in the coming into being in one society or another of new types, units, and operations in verbal thinking. For this reason, in the title and in the work itself, we are speaking of the cultural-historical <u>development</u> of thinking and not of the ethnopsychology of thinking. In studies done thus far, differences in thinking between subjects attending school and those not attending were more serious than any other differences regardless of how different the societies we were dealing with were. Schooling is an historical, not ethnic factor, of course. It seems to us that rejecting the idea of development reduces the potentials of cross-cultural psychology. Either only variations of certain processes are studied or the question must also be posed of the historical origin of these processes, of the reasons and mechanisms of their coming into being and developing.

In the book, we are speaking not of social consciousness, but in the thinking of the individual in different cultures and cultural groups; about changes through history not in the content of thought, but of the thinking processes themselves. For this reason, the book belongs to the psychology of thinking, and not to its sociology or ethnology. We will touch on social consciousness and on the content of thought only to the extent to which this is required for explaining the development of processes of thinking and their unique forms in people in different cultures and cultural groups.

Finally, <u>thinking</u> in this book is treated somewhat more broadly than it sometimes is in the psychology of thinking. We know that in psychology, thinking is considered primarily as problem solving. Although in definitions of thinking, the subject matter is problems <u>in general</u>, in psychological literature, common sense and scientific thinking are sometimes contrasted with other types of thinking (artistic, religious) that are regarded as "forms of consciousness." It seems obvious that within the framework of psychology, such a distinction is not appropriate. This inappropriateness is perceived, for example, in the study of thinking in cultures that do not have clear boundaries between religion and science, religion and art, etc.

Obviously human thinking is never wholly verbal. At the same time, at a certain level of abstraction, it is admissible and reasonable to digress from consideration of interactions between verbal components of thinking and its sensorimotoric and visual components.

The experimental data used in this book were obtained in various presently existing cultures and cultural groups. Most often, the results of American or European children or adults are compared with the results of children or adults of so-called traditional cultures or groups, or comparisons are made within a single culture of the results of groups that had and had not experienced the effect of certain cultural factors (schooling, city life, participation in "new" types of economic activity, etc.). Cultures or cultural groups are designated as traditional if there is no "modern" type of economic activity, science, schooling, or literacy. They are distinguished by an attachment to traditions, as distinct from those cultures and groups that are characterized by constant sociocultural changes. Earlier these cultures and groups were frequently called <u>primitive</u>, but this term implies an unpleasant and unjustified judgmental aspect. In ethnographic literature, the term, "<u>archaic</u>," is used, with various reservations, for these cultures. In order to avoid repeating these reservations constantly and to avoid such difficulties as, for example, the need to distinguish in specific cases between archaic and feudal societies, we will stay with the term, "<u>traditional cultures</u>," which, from the standpoint of purposes pursued in the comparative studies of thinking, is quite adequate. Not very long ago, such terms as "<u>savages</u>" or "<u>natives</u>" were applied to these cultures. A most paradoxical term was used by the German investigator, K. Weule, whose book was titled, "Die Kultur der Kulturlosen" ("The Culture of the Uncultured") (Weule, 1921).

Difficulties also arise in designating those cultures and cultural groups that are distinguished by "modern" economy, presence of science, school, literacy. We will call these groups "modern" for lack of a better term, but this designation is obviously unfortunate because even the traditional cultures which were studied exist in modern times and are a part of the modern world.

In setting forth old conceptions, in order to preserve their shades of meaning, we will sometimes use old terms without quotation marks for various types of cultures.

In the <u>first chapter</u>, we will consider the most significant old and modern theoretical conceptions of the historical development of thinking, some of which belong to ethnology and others, to psychology. We will present the basic positions of authors of these conceptions, attempting in this way to find in them answers to two questions that may be asked of anyone who studies historical changes and cross-cultural differences in thinking: Why has thinking changed through history (what is responsible for cross-cultural differences)? What is it that changes in thinking in the course of the historical development of a society (of what do the cross-cultural differences in thinking consist)? We will compare the positions of various authors and consider how well grounded their responses to these two questions are.

In the <u>second chapter</u> we will discuss certain theoretical problems of the historical development of thinking: the problem of determination of thinking by activity in various cultures and its development; the problem of heterogeneity of thinking in any culture, in any individual; the problem of typology of verbal thinking; the problem of the origin of reflection in thinking and control over the course of thought. Consideration of these problems will allow us to formulate our hypotheses on what promotes historical change and cross-cultural differences in thinking and what these consist of.

On the basis of these hypotheses, in the <u>third chapter</u> we will attempt to analyze certain significant differences in thinking, discovered in experimental studies, between subjects attending school and those not attending school. We will consider differences in solving simple syllogistic tasks and in the results o experiments directed toward the nature of units in verbal thinking. Then we will consider the question of what specifically induces changes in thinking in school. Finally, we will focus on the problem of correspondence between the character of thinking and verbal texts and thinking and self-consciousness.

In the <u>fourth</u> <u>chapter,</u> differences in thinking found in cross-cultural and intergroup comparative studies will be compared to the differences established in studies related to the hypothesis of linguistic relativity. Consideration will be given to problems of the connections between historical changes in thinking and changes in language and in the use of language.

Peeter Tulviste, 1991

CHAPTER 1

Theoretical Conceptions of the Historical Development of Thinking

In the second half of the last century and in the first decades of this century, quite a few purely speculative works were published on the assumed differences between thinking in traditional societies and in educated European societies. Since the mid-1960's the picture has been reversed: a greater number of experimental studies have appeared which have not been supported much of the time by seriously developed theoretical concepts about why human thinking in various cultures and cultural groups must be different or the same, what the differences are, or the mechanism of change in thinking as the result of one set of cultural factors or another. At one time, Huizinga, speaking of historical science, said that ten fools are more ready to answer than one intelligent person is to ask. As early as the mid-1970's a similar situation arose in cross-cultural psychological studies, and since that time, certain authors openly ask the questions listed above and other general theoretical questions and risk hearing Huizinga's saying paraphrased in its primordial form. It has become obvious that the accumulating experimental material in itself will not answer these questions.

Before deducing any kind of positive ideas, it would be wise to review existing theoretical concepts of the historical development of thinking. Keeping in mind the words of Chomsky quoted in the introduction, we will consider not only modern, but also old theories. In all authors, who represent the most varied ideational trends, we will seek answers to questions as to the reasons for changes, differences, and universal qualities of verbal thinking and what these are. Since we are interested here in the change through history of verbal thinking, we will not specifically consider applying one of the influential modern concepts, the theory of Piaget, to problems of the historical development of thinking.

1.1. H. Spencer and the Problems of the Evolution of Human Thinking. The idea of evolution, which entered into psychology with H. Spencer's Principles of Psychology (first edition, 1855) even before the publication of Darwin's Origin of Species, gave rise, together with child psychology and comparative psychology, to the psychology of "primitive peoples." Spencer was the first to collect and systematize a large body of information from travelers and missionaries about the customs, beliefs, folklore, and sayings of savages in order to show that human thinking, like everything that exists, develops.

The work of Spencer differs from speculative works of philosophers of the 18th century, which outlined the progress of the human mind, first by the richness of empirical material. J. Kennedy calculated that in the third edition of Principles of Sociology, which discussed mainly problems of the evolution of thinking, there are about 2500 references to 155 works (Kennedy, 1978, p. 94). Another factor that distinguished Spencer's works from 18th century works was his concretization of concepts of what it is that specifically changes in thinking during its evolution and why and how this happens. Finally, as distinct from authors of the 18th century, Spencer "biologizes" the process of the development of thinking, introducing concepts of hereditary transmission of abilities which determine the possible level of development of human thinking in one society or another.

Spencer deduces the need for evolution in thinking from growth and increasing complexity of the environment and, correspondingly, of human experience. As society developed, "supra-organic products" accumulated (material adaptations, knowledge, customs, esthetic objects) that embellish and complicate the "natural environment" of the individual. "...As a result of gradual growth, development, organization and consolidation of societies, experiences come into being and thinking capacity develops through the assimilation of these...The development of higher mental capabilities went *pari passu* with social progress, simultaneously as its cause and as its result" (Spencer, 1876-1877, p. 103). "The accumulation of experience is sufficient to explain the development of all rationality, beginning with its simplest forms" (Spencer, 1876, Vol. ", p. 187).

Thus, the cause of the evolution of human thinking lies in the accompanying historical development of society, the complication of the natural and social environment of the human habitat, which leads to complexity of perceptual experience. Differences in the thinking of people belonging to different societies may be explained by the difference in the degree of complexity of their environment. Here Spencer understands experience as an exclusively individual phenomenon: each person alone, independently of others, comprehends the world and generalizes his perceptual experience in concepts.

What specifically changes in human thinking in the course of its historical development? Being an associationist, Spencer (1876-1877, p. 110) had no doubt that "the laws of thought are identical everywhere and ... a conclusion deduced by primitive man is a rational conclusion from the data that he had." Conviction of the universality of patterns of the mind and its development was so strong at that time that another renowned evolutionist, E. Tylor, wrote: "The assumption that the laws of the development of reason were different in Australia and England during the time of cave dwellers and during the time of builders of houses of iron is no more soundly based than the assumption that laws of chemical compounds during the carboniferous formation were other than they are in our time. That which existed will exist" (Tylor, 1939, p. 92). Correspondingly, Spencer assumed that "as soon as the initial idea is presented, the whole remaining series of ideas will follow from it completely logically" (Spencer, 1876-1877, p. 251). According to Spencer, however, evolution (understood by him as a movement from a vague, incoherent homogeneity to a definite, coherent heterogeneity through constant integration and differentiation) is based, first, on the relation between thinking, perception, and action, and second, within thinking itself, on ideas (concepts) (1). Among "primitives," concepts were few, concrete, and changed little. This is explained by the fact that their experience was limited in time and in space and distinguished by its monotony. Simple concepts are formed as a result of association of scanty perceptions which do not convey all the complexity of the real world. In the formation of concepts, not the essential, but the obvious properties of objects and phenomena are the basis for their classification. Specifically, primitive beliefs are engendered by obvious similarity of things. For example, people see how a tadpole turns into a frog; the idea arising as a result of this observation of transformation in conjunction with the observation of the similarity between man and a hyena (both have four extremities and laugh!) generates the belief in the possibility of a person being transformed into a hyena (Spencer, 1876-1877, p. 128) (2).

Like any "aggregate," concepts tend toward integration accompanied by differentiation. General, abstract concepts arise in the following way: among obvious properties and relations, there are also those that are substantive at the same time. Functioning as "unconscious hypotheses" and being associated as experience is extended by ever new observations, they are confirmed and bring order to the "chaos of primitive knowledge" (Spencer, 1876-1877, pp. 135-136). From observations of numerous cases of cause-effect relations, abstract ideas arise about cause and effect, etc. "... During human progress, common ideas may arise only to the extent that social conditions make new experiences more numerous and more various..." (Spencer, 1876, Vol. 4, p. 220).

Thus, according to Spencer, both abstract and concrete concepts arise according to the same sensualistic plan, in the course of man's individual accumulation of sense experience. Abstract concepts differ from concrete, not according to their nature, but according to their greater volume and because they unite objects and relations more on the basis of their substantive rather than their obvious traits. Converting concrete concepts into abstract ones in the course of development of a society seems to Spencer to be a slow and gradual process: "...We have a history that shows us that progress in its trend toward concepts of the most significant complexity and the greatest generalization makes very slow steps, that is, proceeds through natural growth" (Spencer, 1876, Vol. 2, pp. 186-187).

Since, according to Spencer, concrete and abstract concepts are formed and function according to universal laws of association inherent in all people, it would be natural to assume that any man, if he finds himself in a rich, complex environment, will form abstract concepts and will attain a high level of development of thinking in this way. Here, however, Spencer introduces the idea of innate abilities. Ascribing Lamarck's evolutionary ideas to man, Spencer describes the developmental mechanism of man's psyche, and specifically, of thinking, as follows. The development of society complicates the environment of the individual, and the correspondingly more complex experience engenders in man more complex and higher mental abilities. "Just as the intellectual abilities themselves are products of accumulated experiences which formed the brain apparatus corresponding to them, in exactly the same way, ideas developed through these abilities during the individual life are products of personal experiences to which certain small changes correspond in inherited nerve structures" (Spencer, 1876-1877, p. 104). These "small changes" are transmitted hereditarily and they make it possible for succeeding generations to adapt more easily to the ever more complex environment. From this it follows that a man belonging to a society with "uncomplicated" experience, due to the limitations of his innate abilities, cannot master any large number of complex ideas or a large amount of information.

It is easy to see that the Spencerian explanation of the causes of evolution in thinking rests on two assumptions: it assumed that civilized society is more complex than primitive society and that the function of human thinking consists in adapting to the environment.

The claims concerning the "simplicity" of primitive cultures were never actually proven. F. Boas noted already that various aspects of culture exhibit different developmental tendencies with respect to simplicity and complexity. Boas (1926, pp. 107–108) wrote: "An important theoretical consideration shook our faith in the correctness of the evolutionary theory as a whole. One of the substantive characteristics of this theory is that civilization in general developed by a transition from simple to complex forms... Recently, we have begun to admit that human culture does not always develop by transition from the simple to the complex, but that two tendencies intersect with respect to many aspects: one, toward the development from the complex to the simple, and the other, toward the development from the simple to the complex. Obviously, in the history of industrial development, increasing complexity is found almost without exception. On the other hand, this kind of evolution is not found in the varieties of human activity not dependent on logical arguments. This may, perhaps, be elucidated most easily with language as an example... Similar observations can also be made about the art of primitive man." M. Herskovits cites many concrete objections to the idea of the simplicity of primitive societies (3).

Spencer does not identify those concrete aspects of the environment, including the supra-organic environment, the presumed complication of which would have required development of thinking. Neither does he indicate the criteria of complexity that would have allowed deducing a hypothesis concerning the character of thinking in one society or another on the basis of what is known about its environment.

As we have seen, in Spencer's conception, experience is the mediating link between the development of the environment and the development of thinking. Here the same difficulties arise: there are no criteria for determining the complexity of experience in various cultures; it is not clear which specifically concrete experience or which aspects of the experience promote the evolution of thinking.

Let us turn to the adaptive function of human thinking. This assumption brings Spencer to a certain contradiction. He takes as a "point of departure the assumption of the postulate that primitive ideas are natural, and, under the conditions in which they occur, logical" (Spencer, 1876-1877, p. 110). If we understand this thought, expressed by Spencer in such an extremely general form moreover, including the assumption that ideas of "primitive" people correspond to actuality, then it is simply not always true. Indeed, what must we consider natural and logical in a phenomenon so widespread in primitive cultures (studied by Spencer) as animism? And actually, analyzing animistic beliefs somewhat later in the same work (p. 145), Spencer finds them less logical than the "ideas" of animals. He writes that before the emergence of human language and thinking, "primitive man has as little tendency to confuse animate and inanimate objects as the lower, dumb animals do." It develops that such an important event in the course of evolution as the creation of man is accompanied in this case not by the development of rationality, but by the rise of errors from which even the "lower, dumb animals" are free. Today it is easy to see that the function of such beliefs consisted not in adaptation to the environment—at least not in the sense that adaptation occurs in animals. The functions of human thinking differ from the functions of the thinking of animals.

Spencer did not succeed in connecting the development of thinking with the development of society in such a way that knowledge about a society could be used to formulate solidly based hypotheses concerning the nature of the thinking of that society. Characteristically, Spencer did not create a "ladder of development" for thinking that could be made to correspond to his evolutionary classification of societies (Spencer, 1876-1877, Chapter 10).

Let us return to the Spencer's concept on what it is specifically that changes in thinking in the course of its historical development. First, as we have already seen, conceptual systems do not always become more complicated as the environment becomes complicated. Durkheim (1914, p. 45 ff.) demonstrated that, on the contrary, in certain cases in the course of the development of a society, conceptual systems become simpler. Second, the change in units of thinking, which undoubtedly takes place, cannot be reduced to only an increase in the volume of concepts. For example, we can scarcely say that the rise of philosophical thinking in ancient Greece consisted in the emergence of concepts of broad scope in comparison with those that prevailed in mythological thinking. Philosophical and other scientific concepts differ qualitatively from those in mythology. Finally, third, as we shall see, there are bases for assuming that the course of the historical development of thinking includes not only units, but also operations.

As far as Spencer's idea of the heredity of acquired traits as a mechanism of evolution of human thinking, it has long been subjected to such bitter criticism that it is pertinent to remember the words of M. Harris: "...no major figure in the social sciences between 1860 and 1890 escaped the influence of evolutionary racism" (Harris, 1969, p. 130; see also pp. 121-122, 137, and others). In the study of the historical development of thinking, this idea of Spencer's was simply not needed after the works of Durkheim and his school, and in practice, it was refuted by the mass assimilation of scientific knowledge and other components of different cultures by people from traditional societies.

Spencer's views of the causes, content and mechanisms of the development of human thinking in the course of the historical development of society are now unsupportable. Incorrect is his concept of the "primitive" solitarily recognizing and explaining the world to the extent of his innate abilities, preoccupied with the "struggle for survival," and not with various concrete kinds of activity, widespread in traditional cultures. Most of Spencer's many followers tracked down in the literature evidence for the backwardness of the thinking of "savages" and unconditionally accepted the thesis on their inherited inferiority, discrediting the evolutionary approach to human thinking (see examples cited in Chase and von Sturmer, 1973). Among later investigators of the historical development of thinking, a productive analysis of Spencer's ideas was developed by H. Werner (1948) whose views merit separate consideration. Spencer's indisputable merit lies in the fact that he concretized ideas on the historical development of the human mind, which arose by the 18th century (see, for example, Harris, 1969; Tokarev, 1978, pp. 93-123), and initiated a comparative study of thinking in various societies existing at the time, pursuing the goal of tracing the path of the historical development of human thinking.

1.2. L. Levy–Bruhl and the Problems of the Historical Development of Thinking. The hypothesis developed in 1910 by the French philosopher and ethnologist, L. Levy–Bruhl on the existence of qualitative differences between primitive and "modern" thinking, on the pre-logical quality of primitive thinking and on the gradual development of logic in thinking in the course of the historical development of society remains thus far the most elegant and intriguing attempt to characterize "at one fell swoop" the differences in the thinking of people belonging to different cultures. This hypothesis was neither confirmed nor refuted and can hardly be verified in its original form both because of its inherent ambiguity and because of the inconsistent validity of the separate statements that comprise it.

From the very beginning, the ideas of Levy–Bruhl roused sharp arguments which continue to this day. As we know, in the later years of his life, Levy–Bruhl himself gave up his hypothesis in part. Nevertheless, it is referred to and evaluated in most modern works which discuss the problem of the specific changes in human thinking that have occurred in the course of humanity's historical development and the nature of the changes taking place: are the changes in thinking only quantitative or are there also qualitative transformations?

At the present time, among investigators of historical changes and cross-cultural differences in thinking, a critical attitude toward the ideas of Levy–Bruhl predominates. What follows is an attempt to show the value of some of these ideas; some, it seems to us, were not only revolutionary in their time, but even now deserve serious attention and require further definition, development and experimental confirmation. The purpose of the present work is not an exhaustive characterization of the views and work of Levy–Bruhl (for an excellent account, see Horton, 1973). Our immediate problem is to evaluate the views of Levy–Bruhl on two questions: in what do cross-cultural differences and historical changes in thinking consist (and what is their nature) and what causes these differences and changes. We will also consider the idea of Levy–Bruhl on the heterogeneity of thinking and those categories with which he described the types of thinking that he observed.

1.2.1. The Nature and Character of Cross-Cultural Differences in Thinking. Being close to the French sociological school of Durkheim, Levy–Bruhl shared its views relative to the origin of units (categories) and operations of human thinking. Durkheim, as is known, discovered a third, specifically human source of categories and laws of thinking (together with heredity and individual experience): culture. He demonstrated that concepts (as distinct from "general ideas" or notions) cannot, in principle, arise in each man separately on the basis of his individual sense experience, as empiricists assumed, but are assimilated by man from the culture. By the same token, the idea of the biological-hereditary transmission of thinking or the capacities for specific kinds of thinking became superfluous; this idea was unproven, but as we have seen in a preceding section, it was extremely popular in the second half of the last century. Sharing Durkheim's point of view on these problems, Levy–Bruhl rejected the basic errors of earlier investigators of the historical development of thinking (specifically Spencer's): the idea of the inheritance of acquired traits as a mechanism for the historical development of thinking (Levy–Bruhl, 1930, p. 25) and the concept of the individual solitarily comprehending the world and generalizing his sense experience to the extent of his innate ability. In Levy–Bruhl's view, an explanation of the patterns of thinking should be sought not in the individual psyche, but in the culture: "Collective representations are social facts...social facts have their own laws, laws that an analysis of the individual as such is not capable of producing. Consequently, to pretend to 'elucidate' collective representations exclusively on the basis of the mechanism of mental operations observed in the individual (from association of ideas, from a naive application of the principle of causality, etc.) would be to make an attempt doomed at the outset ... No matter how far into the past we might go, how "primitive" the societies that we observe might be, we always and everywhere come upon only the socialized consciousness, so to speak, already filled with a multiplicity of collective representations that were perceived by that consciousness according to tradition ..." (Levy–Bruhl, 1930, p. 12).

Durkheim in his analyses of "collective representations" stressed mainly what is the identical and the continuous in those methods of thinking that are dominant in various societies—specifically, in the beliefs of traditional societies and in scientific thinking characteristic of "modern" societies (see, for example, Durkheim, 1976, pp. 238-239, 429). Levy–Bruhl, on the other hand, isolated and studied specifically the <u>differences</u> in the thinking of people in various cultures corresponding to the differences between the cultures themselves. By the same token, Levy–Bruhl developed one of the most important results emanating from the position of Durkheim on the social origin and nature of thinking: if thinking is determined by society, then due to the diversity of existing human societies, thinking in them must certainly also be diverse. Levy–Bruhl (1930, p. 15) writes: "A number of social facts are closely connected with each other and mutually reinforce each other. Consequently, a specific type of society that has its own unique institutions and customs will inevitably also have its own unique thinking."

The basic difference between primitive and scientific thinking, according to Levy–Bruhl, is that the first is insensitive to logical contradiction while the second avoids it. This generalization is based on an analysis of rich empirical material gleaned by Levy–Bruhl from notes of travelers, missionaries, etc. Levy–Bruhl himself did no field studies, and his critics frequently cast doubt on the quality of the data he used. However, examples of "pre-logical" assertions similar to those on which Levy–Bruhl based his hypothesis are also easily found in ethnographic material collected in accordance with all the rules of field work.

The most notable of all the facts on which Levy–Bruhl depended for support was the identification of representatives of the Bororo tribe with red parrots. Levy–Bruhl (1930, p. 48-49) writes: "The Bororo ... boast that they are red arara (parrots). This does not at all mean that only after death are they converted into arara or that the arara are converted into Bororo and for that reason are entitled to appropriate treatment. No, the matter is something else completely. 'The Bororo,' says von den Steinen, who did not want to believe this absurdity, but who had to yield before their persistent assertions, 'the Bororo quite calmly say that they already now are actual arara just as if a caterpillar would announce that it is a butterfly.' This means that this is not a name that they call themselves, nor is it a proclamation of their affinity with the arara; no, what they insist on is that between them and the arara there is an essential identity. Von den Steinen finds it incomprehensible that they can consider themselves simultaneously to be human beings and birds with red feathers. However, for thinking subject to the 'law of participation,' this presents no difficulty" (4). According to Levy–Bruhl, "in the collective representations of primitive thinking, objects, beings, phenomena may be ... simultaneously both themselves and something else ... opposition between one and many, between one and the same and other, etc. does not dictate obligatory denial of one of the indicated terms when the opposite is confirmed and vice versa. For the primitive consciousness, this opposition is of only secondary interest. Sometimes primitive consciousness perceives this opposition, but very frequently, however, it does not. Often it is masked by the mystical unity of existence of these beings which cannot be considered as identities without falling into absurdity" (ibid.). "Simultaneous being in several places or omnipresent beings, identity of one being and several, one and another, individual and species—all of this which would shock and lead to despair if thinking were subjected to the principle of contradiction, all of this is allowed in pre-logical thinking" (Levy–Bruhl, 1930, p. 303).

Thus, the basic difference between thinking in "primitive" and "modern" societies consists in the fact that in the first, it is "pre-logical," and in the latter, logical. Here, Levy–Bruhl especially emphasizes that mental activity of primitive man does not represent a lower, less developed form of "our" mental activity (as Spencer and other evolutionists assumed), but differs from the latter qualitatively: "...We will reject reducing the mental activity of primitive man to a lower form of our activity" (Levy–Bruhl, 1930, p. 48)(5).

By the same token, Levy–Bruhl cast doubt on the universality of the laws of thinking which were described by Aristotle. He himself contrasted his thesis on the qualitative changes that thinking had undergone in the course of its historical development with the doctrine of the "psychic unity of humankind", the assumed similarity of the human spirit, which the English anthropologists-evolutionists used as a basis for explaining the likeness of beliefs and social institutions in different societies. However, the idea of the qualitative differences in thinking had a much broader and more general meaning. Piaget adopted this idea of Levy–Bruhl and, one might say without exaggeration, built modern child psychology on it. The significance of the work of Levy–Bruhl for the whole psychology of thinking was evaluated for its merits by A. N. Leont'ev (6). The discovery of qualitative transformations in thinking may be considered Levy–Bruhl's most important achievement. At the same time, it was specifically with this that he brought on himself unjust accusations of racism or cooperation with racism that continue to this day (for example, Shemyakin, 1950; Sharevskaya, 1953; Mukanov, 1980, 1981).

If we admit the presence of qualitative changes in the development of society and culture and simultaneously accept the thesis on the social determination of thinking, then we cannot but value the significance of Levy–Bruhl's discovery. From today's point of view, we cannot doubt, for example, that the philosophical thinking that appeared in ancient Greece is not a more developed form of mythological thinking, but differs from the latter qualitatively both in its units and in its operations.

While Spencer, being an associationist, assumed that in the course of historical development, societies change only the units of thinking (moreover purely quantitatively), but not its operations, Levy–Bruhl considered specifically the operations of thinking to be qualitatively variable. The historical development of thinking, according to Levy–Bruhl, consists of the fact that thinking is freed of the influence of pre-logical collective representations and begins to be subject to the laws of logic (Levy–Bruhl, 1930, p. 30-320). Levy–Bruhl was not engaged in the study of this process of development, limiting himself to comparing two extreme forms of thinking: primitive beliefs and modern scientific thinking.

Later we will consider the question of how successful Levy–Bruhl was in his attempt to describe the qualitatively different methods of thinking that he found as being "pre-logical" and logical. But first we will consider the views of Levy–Bruhl on the causes of cross-cultural differences and historical changes in thinking. Specifically what in a society determines the nature of the thinking operations that the society uses? Why do qualitative changes in thinking occur? Which factors determine the assumed movement of thinking from the "pre-logical" to the logical?

1.2.2. Causes of Cross-Cultural Differences and Historical Changes in Thinking. Levy–Bruhl paid relatively little attention to the problems of the determination of differences in the thinking of people in different cultures; for him, it seemed much more important to show the presence itself of qualitative differences and to describe these satisfactorily. Levy–Bruhl assumes the point of view of E. Durkheim and M. Mauss according to which thinking reflects the structure of the society (Durkheim and Mauss, 1963). For example, if a society is divided into four subgroups, then its members also divide the rest of the world respectively into four parts, and each of these four subgroups brings itself into conformity with different spheres of reality, with a certain part of the world, with certain animals, birds, plants, with a certain color, etc. Later it was demonstrated that the idea concerning the conformity of the structure of thinking to the structure of society which Levy–Bruhl shared (for example, 1930, pp. 16, 89, 314) was insupportable: societies were much more various in their structure than the classification systems that existed in them (Needham, 1963, p. 25-26).

Like those who hold his views, Levy–Bruhl stresses the role of different social institutions in the determination of the method of thinking (Levy–Bruhl, 1930, pp. 302-320 specifically). Thus, participation (implication), a characteristic of "pre-logical" thinking, corresponds to that unity which people sense between themselves and their totem animal. Levy–Bruhl considered the conditions for freeing thinking from the "law of participation" to be man's separating himself from society, that is, the development of self-consciousness (p. 305) and the development of division of labor (p. 311). The significance of these factors in the historical development of thinking evokes no doubt now, but Levy–Bruhl does not identify any clear causal connections here. Like other representatives of the French sociological school and investigators close to it, he operated with the concept of "collective representations (concepts)." These concepts Durkheim, Levy–Bruhl and others equated with society: "Different forms of thinking will correspond to different social types, all the more so because the institutions and customs basically are nothing other than a recognized aspect or form of collective representations, so to speak, objectively" (Levy–Bruhl, 1930, p. 15). Obviously, with such an approach, we cannot use the society to explain collective representations causally.

Neither did Levy–Bruhl discuss in detail the problem of the connections between collective representations and the thinking of the individual, this problem being within the competence of the psychology of thinking rather than the sociology of thinking. However, like Durkheim, he did not reduce the thinking of the individual to collective representations alone. Levy–Bruhl believes that in addition to these, the thinking of the individual also encompasses a certain "natural," "correct," thinking, individual in origin: common sense. He assumes that, as distinct from collective representations, common sense is logical and that the production of logical thinking in the course of the historical development of society consists in freeing the thinking of the individual from the influence of collective representations and in broadening the sphere of applying common sense, which, according to Levy–Bruhl, directly transforms into scientific thinking.

On this question the views of Durkheim and Levy–Bruhl sharply diverge (see a detailed discussion of this in Horton, 1973). Levy–Bruhl deduced science from individual common sense; Durkheim, from primitive religion in which nonempirical concepts appear for the first time which, like the scientific concepts arising on their basis, have "non-visual" (invisible) denotations. Durkheim considered the nonempirical concepts of primitive religion to be prototypes of scientific concepts, contrasting them with the empirical concepts (ideas) of common sense.

This problem has broad significance. According to Levy–Bruhl, "collective representations" interfere, on the whole, with adequately knowing the world through logical "individual thinking" (the origin and functioning of which remain uninvestigated in the work of Levy–Bruhl). In other words, according to Levy–Bruhl, culture, more than anything else, prevents logical thinking while, according to Durkheim, logical thinking can only appear due to culture. It is possible that this difference in views is partially due to the fact that Levy–Bruhl was completely engaged by the beliefs of primitive peoples while Durkheim also studied the cultural origin of concepts and categories connected with calculating time and, naturally, contributing to an adequate recognition of reality. Horton (1973) is completely correct in preferring the views of Durkheim on this question. However, while Durkheim one-sidedly stressed only what nonempirical concepts of primitive religion and modern science had in common and the continuity between them, Levy–Bruhl, also because of a similar one-sided comparison of the one and the other, found substantial, qualitative differences between them.

Seeing his task as the analysis only of collective representations, Levy–Bruhl did not consider specifically psychological problems such as the problem of man's mastering collective representations or the problem of interaction of the latter with the assumed "individual" common sense. The term "psychological" can be applied only to assertions that as historical development of society occurs, thinking becomes ever more free of emotional, affective components (Levy–Bruhl, 1930, pp. 73, 312 and others) and the role of thinking increases as compared to the role of memory (7).

It must be stated that Levy–Bruhl does not propose a successful solution to the problem of the features of thinking being determined by the features of the society and culture. From the point of view of adequacy and logic of thinking, according to Levy–Bruhl, culture plays a basically negative role. It does not create anything positive in this sense, but only interferes with reasonable "individual" thinking. Absolutely correctly considering the cause of the historical development of thinking to be the development of society, Levy–Bruhl at the same time could not indicate what aspect of the life of society is directly responsible for the change in thinking and what leads to a qualitative transformation in that thinking. Durkheim and Mauss's belief in the correspondence between the structure of society and the structure of thinking i not only factually incorrect, but is theoretically weak: there is no need for the structure of thinking to reflect the structure of society. It is also incomprehensible how changes in the structure of society can change thinking toward being logical. Levy–Bruhl clearly did not grasp the concept of th functions of human thinking and the change of these functions in keeping wit the historical development of society.

1.2.3. Historical Heterogeneity of Thinking. Between the two World Wars the ideas of Levy–Bruhl incited lively arguments, a review of which would require a special paper. Here we will discuss only two principal objections to his hypothesis, found also in one form or another in contemporary literature on ethnography and psychology. Both are directed primarily against the idea of qualitative differences in the thinking of people belonging to different cultures; this idea was identified above as the main discovery of Levy–Bruhl. At the same time, the views of the two groups of critics on the nature of human thinking are diametrically opposed.

On the basis that there cannot be thinking that does not correspond to the laws of logic, critics of the first group object to Levy–Bruhl's identifying qualitative differences in thinking. Such thinking would not only not help, but would directly interfere with man's orientation in the world and with solving problems. As an example, we will consider the argument against the existence of pre-logical thinking developed by the contemporary investigator, A. Wallace (1962). Let us imagine, writes Wallace, a hunter with pre-logical thinking who meets an unfamiliar animal. We assume that he reaches the following conclusion: a rabbit has four feet, this animal also has four feet, therefore it is a rabbit. If our forefathers had reasoned in this way, Wallace concludes, then unfamiliar animals would have eaten them long ago. (True, in this example, the reasoning is alogical rather than pre-logical, but that is not important here.) Wallace believes that all thinking without exception must correspond to the laws of logic, and that Levy–Bruhl's hypothesis on the existence of prelogical thinking is incorrect.

Such criticism is weak in that Levy–Bruhl (like Durkheim and his school) was not describing all thinking of "primitives" as a whole, but only their "collective representations." He noted: "Considered individually, to the extent that he thinks and acts independently of the collective representations, if that is possible, primitive man will feel, reason, and conduct himself most often as we expect him to. Conclusions and deductions that he will make will be the same as those that seem to us to be completely reasonable for the given situation" (Levy–Bruhl, 1930, p. 50; see also, p. 298 ff.). According to Levy–Bruhl, "primitives" are usually logical in their practical activity, which is more than can be said about the sphere of their "collective representations." Responding in 1934 to critical comments of Evans-Pritchard, Levy–Bruhl called attention to the fact that he never pretended to describe all thinking as a whole in people of traditional cultures. Moreover, he realized that he emphasized one-sidedly only the mystical in their thinking (Levy–Bruhl, 1952).

It is characteristic that critics of this group, rejecting the ideas of Levy–Bruhl on the existence of pre-logical thinking, consequently also rejected the very idea of qualitative changes in thinking during its historical development. They did not develop alternative hypotheses on what qualitative transformations in thinking might consist of. An exception among the critics of Levy–Bruhl in this respect was L. S. Vygotsky, who believed that Levy–Bruhl was unsuccessful only in describing the qualitative differences that he found in the thinking of people who belonged to different cultures (see the following section on this subject).

The other group of critics (compared to the first group) proceeded from the opposite view of the nature of human thinking, believing that pre-logical thinking exists, but that it is typical not only for traditional cultures, as Levy–Bruhl assumed, but also for highly developed western societies (for example: Goldenweiser, 1922, p. 386 ff.; Leroy, 1927). For this reason it is incorrect to speak of qualitative differences in thinking.

Evidently, in response to such objections, Levy–Bruhl developed the idea of heterogeneity of thinking in any culture, of any individual. Considering the transition from pre-logical to logical thinking in the course of the historical development of society, he wrote: "...Logical thought does not wholly exclude pre-logical thinking. Pre-logical thinking is based on several foundations so that it might be preserved. First of all, its traces continue to exist completely imperceptibly in a vast number of concepts. For these traces to disappear, all concepts that we use, for example, in everyday living, would have to express exclusively objective properties and relations of beings and phenomena. Actually, this occurs only with respect to a very small number of our concepts, specifically those that are used in scientific thinking" (Levy–Bruhl, 1930, p. 317) (8). Second, in thinking, emotionality is preserved as well as a connection with the motor system. "There will always be collective representations that express intensively experienced and felt participation ... in all known societies these are collective representations on which a multitude of institutions rest, specifically, many of the concepts which include in themselves our moral and religious rites and customs, our beliefs ... the need for participation even in our societies undoubtedly remains even stronger and more intensive than the need to know or to conform to the demands of the discipline of logic. The need for participation is deeper, it comes from greater depths ... the logical unity of the thinking subject, which is accepted as a given by most philosophers, is only a desideratum (something wished for), but not a fact ... our mental activity is simultaneously rational and irrational" (Ibid., pp. 318-320). Levy–Bruhl closes the preface to the Russian edition of Primitive Thought (1930, p. 4) with the words: "In human thinking, there are not two forms, one pre-logical, the other logical, separated from each other by a wall, but there are different mental structures that exist in one and the same society and often—perhaps, always—in one and the same consciousness."

The idea of heterogeneity in human thinking (together with the position that thinking undergoes qualitative changes in the course of its development should be considered as a second important discovery of Levy–Bruhl. As is apparent from the passages cited, the qualitative changes in the development of thinking consist not in that one kind of thinking is wholly replaced by another, but in that a new type of thinking is added to the existing types that is qualitatively different from them. In the case of heterogeneity too, a causal explanation is not the strong aspect of Levy–Bruhl's conception, but the description he presents of the general course of the historical development of thinking is substantive.

Many statements can be found in the works of Levy–Bruhl in which he does not take into account the position he deduced on the heterogeneity of thinking and contrasts all thinking of people in primitive (traditional) societies to all thinking of people in "modern" societies. Specifically, the thesis of Durkheim and Mauss, considered earlier, on the correspondence between the structure of a society and the structure of thinking pushed his ideas towards this contrast: obviously any society has one structure to which, according to these authors, some one kind of thinking must correspond. However, the actual material and - without a doubt—the field observations of ethnologists led Levy–Bruhl to the conclusion on the heterogeneity of thinking. This idea made it possible to admit the existence not only of what was different, but also of what was identical in thinking of people belonging to different cultures, while at the same time preserving the basic thesis of Levy Bruhl on the presence in thinking of qualitative cross-cultural differences. If prior to this, "our" and "their" thinking was compared, then after the appearance of the idea of heterogeneity of thinking in any culture and in any individual, various types of thinking were compared with each other.

1.2.4. The Categorical Apparatus of Levy–Bruhl. In his books Levy–Bruhl with rare skill "shows" to the European the inner world and method of thinking of a man from a primitive society in the way in which his thinking differs most from the scientific thinking of an educated European. Levy–Bruhl attains this mainly with the aid of rich factual material. He was significantly less successful in his analytical description of this thinking, using such concepts as the pre-logical state or participation. Factual material is clearly richer and more complex than the model created with the aid of these and other concepts used by Levy–Bruhl. In the work of Levy–Bruhl, differences in the thinking of people of different cultures remain without adequate analytical description. His posthumously published Notebooks (Levy–Bruhl, 1975) are dramatic protocols of ever newer and newer attempts to describe the given differences, whose existence he did not doubt, but which were beyond description. Here Levy–Bruhl rejected the position on the existence of logical differences between primitive and scientific thinking (Levy–Bruhl, 1975, pp. 7-9, 37-39, 49, 55, 61-62 and others) and considered other possibilities for describing the differences he found. He tried to reduce them to differences in general notions about the world proper for the various cultures; in the degree of emotionality of thinking; in units of thinking or concepts, to the study of which he gave little attention earlier (p. 127 and others); finally, to the differences in methods of using concepts in different spheres of life: in daily life, people in primitive and "modern" cultures use concepts in the same way, but people in "modern" cultures also have a specific method of using concepts that is applied in science, a method that is absent in primitive societies (pp. 173-176).

The last of the indicated descriptions is dated January, 1939 (Levy–Bruhl died in March of that year). It is easy to see that this description is close to one of the possible actual solutions of the problem of describing cross-cultural differences in verbal thinking. A decade earlier, Vygotsky developed the idea that the differences between the thinking of children of different ages and between the thinking of people belonging to different cultures consist specifically in the presence or absence in them of certain methods of using words in thinking.

The opposition used by Levy–Bruhl, "logical/pre-logical thinking" suffered from the following basic inadequacies.

1. The number of possible types of verbal thinking was arbitrarily limited in advance to two. There was neither a theoretical nor an empirical basis for this limitation. It was dictated by the character of the categories themselves with which Levy–Bruhl described various types of thinking. As a result, scientific thinking and common sense, "individual" in origin (as Levy–Bruhl assumed), as we have seen above, were actually deemed identical since, in comparison with "collective representations" of traditional cultures, both appeared to be "logical."

2. Thinking may be "logical" in at least three senses: a) in the sense of correspondence to reality; b) in the sense of factual correspondence of a conclusion to the laws of logic; c) in the sense of conscious application of the laws of logic in testing the correctness of a conclusion. Since Levy–Bruhl is speaking of logic "in general," his hypothesis is ambiguous and cannot be verified in this form (9).

In his Notebooks Levy–Bruhl begins to differentiate between physical and logical coherence of assertions (Levy–Bruhl, 1975, pp. 121, 126, 130, and others) and he reaches the conclusion that lack of physical coherence, but not of logical coherence is characteristic for primitive thinking, and he wrote mainly of logical coherence in his preceding works without distinguishing it from physical coherence. That the Bororo can be red parrots and that the missionary could find himself simultaneously in two different places is physically impossible.

However, Levy–Bruhl's Notebooks by no means form a basis for believing that at the end of his life, he came to reject the qualitative differences in the thinking of people belonging to different cultures that he discovered. On the contrary, to the last pages, he attempts to find new methods of describing these differences. We might say that he rejected the hypothesis of pre-logical thinking, but not the fact of the existence of qualitative differences he had discovered in human thinking. This was not noted by the critics of Levy–Bruhl who were trying not to describe or explain, but to reject qualitative changes occurring in the course of the historical development of thinking.

The difficulties that Levy–Bruhl experienced in his attempts to use existing terminology that already had specific meaning for describing "primitive" thinking qualitatively different from "ours" are specially analyzed by V. V. Petukhov (1977). He writes (pp. 20-21): "The method of building a language for the comparative description of primitive thinking consisted in compromise, in conventional use of available devices of interpretation (and of customary terminology) as a strictly serviceable means with a radical change in substantive meaning. Realizing the new content of the selected terms required constant additional amplification.... The descriptive language created by Levy–Bruhl is ... quite conventional ... the features of primitive thinking formulated in this language must be understood as neither its natural properties nor as a proper explanation of its structure and functioning ... if we consider the given description as a special phenomenology, then it may serve as material for constructing an objective theory of the historical development of cognitive processes."

The analysis and evaluation proposed by Petukhov appear to be correct. Similar difficulties ("waste of resources") were experienced by Piaget in his early efforts to use existing terms, specifically those related to philosophy and ethnology to describe the verbal thinking of the child that differs qualitatively from the thinking of the adult. (We should recall, for example, how many reservations, objections, elaborations the concept of child animism provoked and continues to provoke.) Subsequently, in describing the thinking of the child, Piaget began to use the language of logic, and in explaining its development, the language of biology. Now, as we know, in the study of the universals and cross-cultural differences in thinking the language of logic is used by C. Levi–Strauss. However, the application of logic does not appear to be the best method of resolving those difficulties which Levy–Bruhl and Piaget confronted in their attempts to describe the type of thinking that is qualitatively different from that to which we are accustomed. In our view, the typology of verbal thinking developed by Vygotsky would be more adequate; this takes into account the uniqueness not only of operations, but also of units used in various types of verbal thinking (see 2.3.3. below). In short, the difficulties which confronted Levy–Bruhl cannot even now be considered as overcome.

1.2.5. Conclusion. The principal service of Levy–Bruhl consists in the discovery of qualitative changes which thinking has undergone in the process of its historical development. He was the first to call attention to cross-cultural differences in thinking that could not be reduced to differences in the volume of concepts and in other quantitative indices. This discovery is significant not only for the study of the historical development of thinking, but also for the psychology and sociology of thinking as a whole. Up to this time it was realized to a great extent in the study of the ontogenesis of thinking, but in the study of cross-cultural development and historical changes, it still awaits successful concretization. The discovery of Levy–Bruhl retains its significance regardless of the fact that the scholar himself did not succeed in satisfactorily describing and explaining the facts he discovered.

Of great significance also is Levy–Bruhl's idea concerning the heterogeneity of thinking, the co-existence in any culture and in any individual of qualitatively different types of verbal thinking. This corresponds more precisely to reality than the notion, then widely accepted (and expressed sometimes by Levy–Bruhl himself), that "we" have one type of thinking, and "they", another.

Finally, being close to Durkheim's school, Levy–Bruhl freed the study of the historical development of thinking from biologism, at the same time preserving the idea of development. Levy–Bruhl was the first to show that in the course of the historical development of thinking there are changes not only in units (concepts), but also in operations that were previously considered to be universal. He did not succeed, however, in showing specifically what constituted the historical changes in the operations of thinking. The question of why thinking develops also remained open. The necessary connection between the development of society and the development of thinking was not disclosed.

1.3. L. S. Vygotsky and the Problems of the Cultural-Historical Development of Thinking. At the end of the 1920's and beginning of the 1930's, L. S. Vygotsky developed a cultural-historical conception of higher mental processes. According to this conception, the higher mental processes of man, mediated by signs, are determined not biologically, but by sociocultural factors. Consequently, for their explanation, we must turn not to nature, to biological evolution, physiological processes in the brain and so on, but to society, culture, history, to sociological, ethnographic, culturological data. By the same token, Vygotsky introduced into psychology a new explanatory principle not applied even today to any great extent in the psychological study of higher mental processes in man.

With Vygotsky, the problems of the historical development of the human psyche and data on cross-cultural differences in higher mental processes acquired a completely new status. If these problems and facts were formerly relegated to the periphery of actual investigative work in psychology, for Vygotsky, they were of primary importance both as evidence of the thesis on the sociocultural nature of higher mental processes and as material for the study of the patterns of their development which is not connected with biological maturation of the human organism. Enumerating those areas of psychology in which it would be rational to apply the so-called instrumental method, Vygotsky places first the "area of socio-historical and ethnic psychology studying the historical development of behavior, its various levels and forms" (Vygotsky, 1982a, p. 107).

We know that in his concrete studies, Vygotsky himself applied this explanatory principle primarily in the study of the ontogenesis of verbal thinking. However, in discussing the problems of ontogenesis, he frequently turned to data on cross-cultural differences in thinking, to the ideas of Levy–Bruhl, R. Thurnwald, and H. Werner on the historical development of thinking, and expressed his point of view on these problems. In this chapter, we will consider the views of Vygotsky on the historical development of thinking, paying principal attention to his ideas of what it is that changes in thinking in the course of its historical development and why.

1.3.1. The Significance of Studying the Historical Development of Thinking.

The study of the strictly historical development of human thinking attracted Vygotsky since here, as distinct from ontogenesis, organic development has no place. Because of this, we can observe "in a pure form" the development of thinking that is due only to sociocultural factors. This, obviously, makes it possible to "isolate" the role of cultural factors in the development of thinking, which is very important for a conception that maintains specifically that culture promotes the development of higher forms of thinking. In the child, "not only the use of tools is developing, but a system of movement and perception as well, the brain and the hands, the whole organism of the child. Both processes merge into one ... Consequently, the child's system of activity is determined at each level by both the level of his organic development and the level of his mastering his equipment" (Vygotsky, 1983, p. 34). The question arises: "In the process of investigation, how is it possible to separate the cultural and biological development of behavior and to identify cultural development which in fact is not found in a pure, isolated form?" (Ibid., p. 35). For a strictly historical development of thinking, typical is "the circumstance that development of higher mental functions occurs without a change in the biological type of the person" (Ibid. p. 26). "Primitive man does not display any kind of substantive differences in biological type, differences to which it might be possible to ascribe all major differences in behavior" (Ibid., p. 27). "Cultural-psychological development" appears here "in a pure, isolated form" (Ibid., p. 29). "For this reason, we must turn to phylogenesis which has not experienced uniting and merging of both lines" (Ibid., p. 25; that is, lines of biological and cultural development; phylogenesis actually means sociogenesis here).

Such is the principal reason that compelled Vygotsky to turn to data and ideas of various investigators of the historical development of thinking, of cross-cultural differences in thinking, when he discussed the problem of the development of thinking in children. For him, this area of study appeared to be the branch of psychology in which it would be possible to distinguish the role of biological and sociocultural factors in the determination of specifically human mental processes and their development.

1.3.2. Determination of Historical Development of Thinking. Vygotsky believed that signs and sign systems that are formed in the course of the historical development of a society play the same role in the psyche that instruments or tools play in work: both the former and the latter reinforce and transform natural processes (for example, movement of the hand or innate memory). "Psychological tools are synthetic formations; according to their nature, they are social, and not organic or individual adaptations; they are directed toward mastery of processes of one's own or another's behavior just as are techniques directed toward mastery of the processes of nature. Examples of psychological tools and their complex systems may be language, different forms of numeration and counting, mnemotechnical adaptations, algebraic symbols, productions of art, writing, plans, diagrams, maps, sketches, any possible arbitrary signs, etc." (Vygotsky, 1982a, p. 103). Both the signs themselves and the way they are used have a cultural, not a natural origin, and for this reason the higher mental processes, as distinct from the lower, are subject only to cultural-historical and not natural-scientific explanation. Vygotsky stresses many times that we must not look for an explanation of higher mental processes in the brain since they were generated not by the brain, but by the process of social-historical development of humanity (10). Signs and the way they are used are provided to the individual by society (and are not inherited and are not formed by each individual separately on the basis of his personal sense experience).

Vygotsky writes: "...Historical development of human practice and historical development of human thinking connected with it are a true source of logical forms of thinking, of the function of forming concepts and other higher mental functions. It is not the brain that of itself generated logical thinking, but the brain adopted to forms of logical thinking in the processes of the historical development of man. For this, it is not necessary to assume the existence of a special basic function of the brain. It is enough to assume that in the structure of the brain and in the system of its basic functions there are potentials, conditions for the rise and formation of higher syntheses" (Vygotsky, 1984, pp. 178-179). And in another place: "The brain contains conditions and possibilities for a combination of functions which would not have to be imprinted structurally ahead of time, and I think that all of modern neurology compels us to assume this. We see more and more the infinite variety and incompleteness of brain functions. It is much more proper to assume that the brain has enormous potentials for the development of new systems" (Vygotsky, 1982a, p. 128).

The historical development of human behavior and thinking appears to Vygotsky in the following form: "In the process of historical development, social man changes the methods and modes of his behavior, transforms natural instincts and functions, develops and creates new—specifically cultural—forms of behavior" (Vygotsky, 1983, pp. 29-30). The process of the historical development of human behavior "consisted not in acquiring new natural psychophysiological functions, but in a complex combination of elementary functions, in perfecting the forms and methods of thinking, in developing new methods of thinking based mainly on speech or on some other systems of signs" (Vygotsky, 1984, p. 221).

Thus, the historical development of thinking is determined by the development of society and culture. But specifically which aspect of society and culture? Vygotsky perceives "the development of technology and the development of a social structure corresponding to it as the principal factors in the psychological development of the primitive" (Vygotsky and Luria, 1930, p. 120). At one point, Vygotsky establishes the functional connection between thinking and activity: "...The higher intellect of man in comparison with animals would have no real significance in the life and history of man if it were not connected with completely new possibilities of activity, even human intellect itself could not have developed outside conditions of specific human activity" (Vygotsky, 1956, p. 474). Studying the ontogenesis of thinking, Vygotsky asserted that the highest type of verbal thinking—conceptual thinking or thinking in scientific concepts—arises in a child only in school in the course of his mastering scientific knowledge differing from everyday knowledge. By the same token, one of the types of thinking described by Vygotsky corresponds directly to certain types of activity and to a certain type of knowledge that appears to be its result. The terms for types of units of thinking that Vygotsky uses, "everyday concepts," "scientific concepts," suggest the idea of a connection between types of thinking and types of activity. Later, as we know, Vygotsky's idea concerning the cultural determination of higher mental processes was defined concretely in the approach from the standpoint of activity, which A. N. Leont'ev developed.

Vygotsky developed two different hypotheses about specifically which aspects of schooling have a transforming effect on thinking. According to the first, thinking becomes abstract as a result of the child's mastering the written language in school. According to the other hypothesis mentioned above, thinking in scientific concepts develops due to the child's mastering specific— scientific—knowledge. Let us note that in both cases, mastery of a new sign system appears as the moving force for development of thinking. In the 1970's both hypotheses were subjected to experimental testing in cross-cultural studies of thinking (see Chapter 3 below).

Vygotsky's general conception on the origin of categories and operations of thinking evidently goes back to the views of Durkheim and his school. At the same time, it differs substantially from these views (11). We will note only certain differences here, those that are important from the point of view of the problems being discussed:

1) as distinct from Durkheim, Vygotsky does not equate society with "collective representations," but perceives in social processes a determinant of "collective representations." For this reason, it becomes possible to explain these representations (culture) and their features through social (socioeconomic) processes. Such an explanation is the task not so much of psychology as of cultural science;

2) Vygotsky in his theoretical work stresses the significance of practical activity; Durkheim and his school did not consider and did not discuss the role of this in the formation of thinking;

3) being a psychologist, Vygotsky naturally assigns primary importance to problems of the child's assimilation of culture (through interiorization) and the transformation of the child's mind in the course of assimilating culture. As distinct from the psychologists, Janet and Piaget, who experienced the strong influence of Durkheim's ideas, Vygotsky considers, from the point of view of generation of certain forms and properties of thinking, the interiorization not so much of processes of <u>communication</u> (for example, arising from arguments among children through interiorizing of reasoning as an internal process) but actually of processes of culture in a narrower sense (for example, scientific knowledge);

4) if in the work of Levy–Bruhl, who was very influential at that time, it developed that "collective representations" added to "individual common sense" in primitive cultures and that they are more likely to interfere than to help man think correctly, then according to Vygotsky's conception, culture plays an exceptionally important constructive role in establishing and developing the thinking of the individual—without culture there can be neither verbal thinking nor its development.

1.3.3. What Is Changed in Thinking? As distinct from the great majority of investigators of the historical development of thinking, Vygotsky unconditionally accepts the thesis of Levy–Bruhl that in the course of its development, thinking undergoes not only quantitative, but also qualitative transformations. He is critical of representatives of the doctrine of psychic unity of mankind: "Natural sciences long ago assimilated the fact that all forms in nature are not synchronous, but may be understood only from the aspect of historical development. Only psychologists make an exception for their science assuming that psychology deals with eternal and immutable phenomena no matter whether these eternal and immutable properties are based on matter or on mind ... This antihistoric idea was expressed in its most absolute form in the well-known position of associative ethnic psychology which proclaims that the laws of the human mind are identical always and everywhere" (Vygotsky, 1982a, p. 152; cf. Vygotsky, 1983, p. 28). According to Vygotsky, "the development of primitive thinking consists not in the fact that this thinking accumulates an ever greater number of details, broadens its vocabulary ever more, reproduces details more finely. It changes its type in its very essence" (Vygotsky and Luria, 1930, p. 101).

Like many other critics of Levy–Bruhl, Vygotsky reproaches him for sometimes describing all thinking in primitive cultures as pre-logical (Vygotsky and Luria, 1930, pp. 117-119). But while other critics believed that Levy–Bruhl went "somewhat too far" in stressing differences between "primitive" and "modern" thinking, Vygotsky on the other hand believes that Levy–Bruhl's basic error was that he noted qualitative changes only in operations of thinking while in fact in the course of historical development of thinking, qualitative changes occur also in its units. "The inadequacy of Levy–Bruhl is that he assumes speech to be something constant. This leads him into paradoxes. One has only to assume that meanings and their combinations (syntax) are different from ours and all absurdities drop" (Vygotsky, 1982a, p. 161).

Here, according to Vygotsky, in the course of historical development, not only the words used in thinking change, but, and this is Vygotsky's main point, the methods of using words in thinking also change. Before Vygotsky and after, many investigators believed that the historical development of thinking was primarily connected with a change in the words used in thinking, dividing and categorizing the world differently in different epochs, beginning with the light spectrum and plants and ending with personality traits. As a rule, differences found in the cognitive processes corresponding to lexical differences between languages were not substantive from the point of view of psychology (see Chapter 4 below). Pertinent to this issue are the different variants of the hypothesis of linguistic relativity and evolutionist conceptions, beginning with Spencer who assumed that the development of thinking consists in quantitative growth in the volume of concepts. But according to Vygotsky, one and the same word may be used in different ways in thinking. The development of thinking consists primarily of the rise of qualitatively new methods of using words in thinking.

The approach developed by Vygotsky makes it possible to describe the development of thinking not from the linguistic, but from the psychological point of view. One and the same word with its specific denotation may represent qualitatively different structures of generalization that also determine operations possible for these or other units of verbal thinking. For more developed units of thinking more developed thinking operations are possible that cannot be realized with other units. Levy–Bruhl discovered qualitative differences in the operations of thinking without noting the same kind of difference in its units. Vygotsky takes into account both differences and insists on a connection between them: "Primitive man ... uses a word differently than we do. A word may assume a different functional usage. Depending on how it is used, that thinking operation will be in effect which is carried out by means of this word" (Vygotsky and Luria, 1930, p. 97). The methods of using a word in thinking are assigned not by the brain, but by culture: "... The human brain, having a ready stock, did not produce thinking in concepts itself at primitive stages of development of humanity and the child ... there was a time when thinking in concepts was a form unknown to humanity. Even now there are tribes that do not have this form of thinking ... the concept is a historical and not a biological category in the sense of the function that produces it. We know that in primitive man there are no concepts" (Vygotsky, 1984, p. 178). Vygotsky believed that "the key to understanding ... the thinking of primitive peoples must be seen in the fact that this primitive thinking is not accomplished in concepts, that it has a "complex" character, and that, consequently, in these languages, a word has a completely different functional use, is used in a different way, and is not a means for forming and conveying a concept, but acts as a family name for designating a group of concrete objects united according to a recognized factual relationship" (Vygotsky, 1982b, p. 161). "A primitive man thinks not in concepts, but in complexes. This is the most substantive difference that separates his thinking from ours" (Vygotsky and Luria, 1930, p. 99).

So Vygotsky described the most substantive differences in the thinking of "primitive" and "modern" man from the psychological point of view. Since modern man went to school and assimilated scientific knowledge, he acquired "true" concepts, scientific concepts that could not exist in "primitive" man who had not come into contact with scientific knowledge.

This difference is qualitative, but it by no means encompasses all of thinking as a whole. Vygotsky rejected the global contrast of "primitive" and "civilized" thinking: "It would be a mistake to think that a normal, cultured man would have made all his thinking completely logical" (Vygotsky, 1984, p. 191; see also 1956, pp. 169, 172, 196, 204; 1983, p. 63).

Thus, according to Vygotsky, the change in thinking in the course of its historical development consists in the appearance in thinking of qualitatively new methods of using words to which qualitatively new thinking operations also correspond.

1.3.4. Designs for Empirical Studies. Vygotsky assumed that the historical development of thinking may be directly and empirically studied in societies in which significant sociocultural transformations are occurring at a rapid rate. If investigators studying primitive thinking in one culture or another previously compared it with the thinking of Europeans, then Vygotsky believed that it would be possible and necessary to study the historic dynamics of thinking also. Such an idea came from Vygotsky's unique understanding of the historical approach to psychology: "Even now many are still inclined to present the idea of historical psychology in a false light. They equate history with the past. For them, to study anything historically means to study one fact or another from the past. This is naive understanding to see an impassable boundary between the study of the historical and the study of present forms. Moreover, historical study simply means applying the category of development to the study of phenomena. To study anything historically means to study it in motion" (Vygotsky, 1983, p. 62). As we know, in 1931-1932, A. R. Luria organized two psychological expeditions to Uzbekistan in order to test Vygotsky's ideas concerning the cultural-historical determination of higher mental processes and their changes in the course of the historical development of a society.

Less well known is the circumstance that at the end of the 1920's Vygotsky projected a plan for research on the pedology of national minorities (Vygotsky, 1929). The subject was the study of the mind of children living under various cultural conditions. But knowing about this plan is interesting also from the point of view of explaining Vygotsky's views on the historical development of thinking.

Vygotsky writes about three methods of studying the psychology of children in "backward" nationalities at that time in the Soviet Union: 1) European tests and experimental problems were used; 2) the same tests and problems were used, but their content was adapted to local conditions; 3) these tests and problems were rejected entirely and specific methods of study were created for each separate nationality. Vygotsky was not satisfied with any of these approaches. He rejected the first two because they made it possible to study basically what does not exist in the psychology of children in these cultures, leaving uninvestigated that which does exist in it. Vygotsky does not indicate what the inadequacy of the third approach is, but we may assume that his reason was that the results could not be compared.

Vygotsky's positive program consisted in studying the environment of the child's physical development. "... The study of the environment is placed at the center ... Pedological study of the national environment, its structures, its dynamics, its content is the primary problem; without the resolution of this, we cannot even approach solving all the other problems of our plan." "The formative effect of the social environment" was considered as the foremost object of study. The environment "basically determines he possibilities of practice and development which the child's innate potential confronts. If we take, for example, Moslem nationalities in which all decorative activity, all drawing was proscribed for centuries, it becomes completely clear that in children of these nationalities it would be impossible to expect any kind of full development of decorative activity (drawing) which is so characteristic for preschool children in all European countries." The environment "shapes and makes up all higher forms of behavior, everything that goes beyond the elementary functions in the development of the personality" (Vygotsky, 1929, pp. 375–377).

Particularly important for us here is Vygotsky's assertion that a necessary prerequisite for the study of ontogenesis of the mind in cultures different from the European is the study of the adult mind in the same cultures. The mind of the child must be studied not against a background of results of European children with the same tests and experiments, but against a background of the mental processes of adults in the given culture. "If we proceed from the point of view . . . of the specificity of children of national minorities is due primarily to. . . specificity of the environment, a natural conclusion from this will be the requirement to introduce into our psychological study a completely new plane: the study of the cultural historical development of the mind and behavior of man" (Ibid., p. 376). Vygotsky assumes that specifically the failure to take into account the adult "norm," the level of cultural-historical mental development in those cultures in which the mind of the child is studied "results in a situation where in the whole nation only one-sixth of normally talented [children] are identified according to the data of erroneously designed studies" (Ibid).

Thus, for Vygotsky, the study of cultural-historical mental development was not only of interest in itself and not only presented the possibility of studying "in a pure form" the role of sociocultural factors in the establishment and development of higher mental processes, but also represented a necessary prerequisite for the study of the ontogenesis of thinking in its dependence on the cultural environment.

To study the mind of the child and the adult of various nationalities, Vygotsky proposed to organize appropriate expeditions. "The organization of pedological expeditions must become as constant and necessary a means of scientific investigation as the 'field' method is in modern ethnography and ethnology" (Ibid., p. 378).

1.3.5. Conclusion. The role of Vygotsky in the study of the cultural-historical development of thinking may, in brief, be described as follows. First, he was the first among psychologists to develop a position on the cultural-historical origin of higher mental functions, including various types of verbal thinking, and he proposed a new explanatory principle applicable in their study. Second, he discovered the role of signs and sign systems in the formation and development of thinking and correspondingly, the role of these systems in explaining the historical development of thinking. Third, he developed a typology of verbal thinking that was expedient for the study of historical changes and cross-cultural differences in thinking (see 2.3 below). Fourth, Vygotsky proposed to study not simply cross-cultural differences in thinking, but historical changes in it, that is, to study, within the framework of a single culture, the thinking of people with different degrees of contact with the sociocultural transformations taking place.

What changes in thinking in the course of its development and why? Vygotsky believed that the method of using a word changes in thinking. These changes encompass both units and operations of verbal thinking. Vygotsky believed that the reason for the historical development of thinking is, first of all, the change in sign systems that mediate the processes of thinking.

Since the ideas of Vygotsky have been little used and little tested thus far in a real comparative study of the thinking of people in different cultures, their possible weak side may still remain undisclosed.

1.4. C. Levi–Strauss and the Problem of Archaic Thinking. After Levy–Bruhl, none of the investigators of so-called primitive, archaic, mythological thinking was as well-known or had as strong an influence on the conceptions of the general public about this thinking as the French ethnologist, Claude Levi–Strauss. He is known as the founder of the structural method in ethnology, as the investigator of myths and kinship systems, but the most important scientific achievement of Levi–Strauss is often believed to be "his deep understanding of the specifics of mythological thinking while at the same time admitting its cognitive and practical significance" (Meletinskii, 1976, p. 97). The conception of Levi–Strauss is frequently considered to be the opposite of the conception of Levy–Bruhl and a refutation of the latter. If Levy–Bruhl discovered qualitative differences between primitive and "modern" (scientific) thinking, considering the first pre-logical, and the second, logical, then Levi–Strauss insists mainly on the identity of the thinking of people belonging to different societies and different historical periods. At present the views of Levi–Strauss have many more supporters than those of Levy–Bruhl.

Two circumstances justify the attempt made below to consider the ideas of Levi–Strauss from the point of view of psychology. First, assertions related more closely to the competency of a psychologist than that of an ethnologist play an important role in them. With the exception of Jean Piaget (Piaget, 1971; Grinevald, 1983a), psychologists almost never subjected them to critical appraisal. The validity or lack of it of these assertions has a certain significance for evaluating the idea and method of Levi–Strauss as a whole. For example, Levi–Strauss explains the proposed universality of binary oppositions which he found in the culture of all societies by reference to assumed patterns of thinking which, in his opinion, depend in their turn on the principles of the working of the brain. Obviously, the reality of these patterns and principles, like their universality and the role they play in the respective processes, can be best evaluated by psychologists and physiologists.

Second, in the last two decades, various experimental methods have been used to study the thinking of people in so-called traditional societies whose culture Levi–Strauss studied. Both Levi–Strauss and many psychologists (but not all) assume that there is a correspondence between the features of thinking processes on the one hand, and features of texts generated, assimilated and understood by means of this thinking on the other hand. For this reason, it is possible and desirable to compare the data and conclusions of the ethnologist in his study of texts with the data and conclusions of psychologists arrived at by experimental study of the thinking processes in the same societies. In cross-cultural experimental-psychological studies, scant reference is made to the work of Levi–Strauss, and the influence of his ideas is obviously less here than anywhere else. Levi–Strauss in his turn does not refer to corresponding work of psychologists (except for certain notes concerning cross-cultural Piagetian studies, see Grinevald, 1983b).

The immediate goal of this section is to analyze the position of Levi–Strauss on the following questions which are of substantial interest in the study of the common (universal) and the different (cross-cultural differences, historical changes) in human thinking: 1) what is common and what is different in the thinking of people in different societies and epochs? 2) what are the causes of common traits, cultural differences and historical changes in thinking? In discussing the views of Levi–Strauss, we will naturally compare them with the views and data of other investigators, both psychologists and ethnologists. To begin, we will try to describe the views of Levi–Strauss briefly.

1.4.1. The Common and the Different in the Thinking of People in Different Societies. Levi–Strauss considers the functional aspect to be foremost in what is common and universal in human thinking. In all societies, thinking is directed toward a "disinterested" explanation of the world, that is, in thinking a cognitive interest always precedes the practical and is dominant over the latter (Levi–Strauss, 1966, p. 9). It is incorrect to think that in certain societies, in traditional or, conversely, in "civilized" societies, thinking fulfills only a narrowly practical purpose. The cognitive work of thinking, according to Levi–Strauss, consists in ordering and categorizing the world. If, since the times of the Wurzburg school, thinking has been treated in psychology mainly as problem solving, and classification and forming of concepts considered for the most part as "preparatory work" for thinking, then for Levi–Strauss, thinking is reduced basically to categorization.

Levi–Strauss also considers as universal the structures of thinking that classifies. This position is one of the central positions in his conceptions. Any cultural phenomenon may be reduced to these structures by appropriate analysis: "If, as we assume, unconscious mental activity consists in giving form to content and if these forms are basically the same for all types of thinking, ancient and modern, of the primitive and the civilized ... then it is necessary and sufficient to come to an unconscious structure lying at the base of each social institution or custom in order to find the principle of interpretation valid also for other institutions and customs, under conditions, of course, of adequately penetrating analysis" (Levi–Strauss, 1983, p. 28). Levi–Strauss considers the main problem of humanitarian sciences, anthropology in the broad sense as the general science of man, to be the establishment of unconscious structures in the human mind (Levi–Strauss, 1983, p. 75). Here it should be noted that Levi–Strauss distinguishes sharply the subconscious which represents an accumulation of memories and images and the unconscious which is always "blank." The unconscious in this sense (distinct from the psychoanalytic sense) is "alien" with respect to the mental content, like the stomach with respect to the food being digested. The function of the unconscious consists in its superimposing definite structures on any non-articulated elements coming "from outside"—urges, emotions, ideas, recollections; it gives them form. The structural principles of the unconscious are universal and few in number (a parallel from linguistics: there are many languages, but few phonological laws and they are true for any language [Levi–Strauss, 1983, pp. 181–182]). "One ... of the consequences of modern structuralism must be the freeing of associationistic psychology from that disfavor into which it fell. The great merit of associationistic psychology was that it noted the contours of elementary logic which is a common denominator of all thinking; its deficiency lay only in not understanding the fact that what was being spoken of here was primordial logic, the direct expression of the structure of the mind (behind which undoubtedly stands the structure of the brain), and not a passive generation of environmental influence on amorphous consciousness. But ... this logic of contrast and interdependence, exclusion and inclusion, combination and separation explains the laws of association, and not vice versa; a new associative theory must be based on a system of operations analogical in a certain sense to Boolean algebra" (Levi–Strauss, 1968, pp. 117-118).

Later we will consider the views of Levi Strauss on the origin of the assumed universal, unconscious structures with the aid of which man categorizes the world. Now we will consider their nature. According to Levi–Strauss, they are binary oppositions (dual contrasts). Levi–Strauss finds binary oppositions in all societies, in all spheres of life (for example: Levi–Strauss, 1966, p. 32, 131, 142). Applying the formal method of structural linguistics first in the study of kinship systems, Levi–Strauss then moved on to formal investigation of other components of social consciousness in traditional societies, showing that binary contrasts lie at the base of any texts of any cultures.

From the presence of binary structures in all natural languages and other human sign systems, Levi–Strauss draws the conclusion that they are common to the human mind in general. And he used his position on the universality of structures of thinking (in addition to analysis of myths) to show the principal sameness of thinking in people in all societies, in all epochs.

Levi–Strauss admits that science and magic represent different methods of ordering (categorization) of the world and obtaining knowledge, but he believes that they make use of identical thinking operations and do not differ from each other qualitatively. As evidence for this position, he specifically cites examples of agreement between results of scientific and results of archaic thinking (Levi–Strauss, 1966, pp. 12-13). Levi–Strauss rejects the idea that thinking in its operational aspect is subject to historical development: "The logic of mythical thinking is just as inexorable as logic can be, one day we will understand that the same logic works in mythical thinking as in scientific thinking and man always thinks equally 'well.' Progress, if this term still is to apply as before, occurred not in thinking, but in the world in which humanity lived, always endowed with thinking capabilities, and in which in the process of a long history, it met with ever new phenomena" (Levi–Strauss. 1983, pp. 206-207). Here the invariability of thinking is directly contrasted with historical development of humanity. If Levi–Strauss is right then we must find identical logic, identical operations in the thinking of people in any societies, in any historical epochs.

Now we will turn to those differences that Levi–Strauss finds among various types or methods of thinking. From what has been said, it is clear that the differences cannot pertain to operations of thinking which Levi–Strauss considers universal. He rejects the hypothesis of Levy–Bruhl on the pre-logical state of primitive thinking (Levi–Strauss, 1966, p. 228; 1968, pp. 104-105; 1983, pp. 206-207). According to Levi–Strauss, neither does the difference between primitive and scientific thinking consist in the assumed greater emotionality of the former, as English anthropologists of the last century wrote, and, as we have seen above, as did Levy–Bruhl and many other authors (Levi–Strauss, 1966, pp. 42, 268; 1983, pp. 183-184).

Levi–Strauss believes that the difference between mythical and scientific thinking consists in "not so much the quality of logical operations, as in the very nature of the phenomena subjected to logical analysis" (Levi–Strauss, 1983, p. 206). Specifically: primitive, mythical, "wild" thinking is oriented toward the concrete, the perceptible; scientific thinking, toward the abstract, "nonvisible" properties of things. Correspondingly, they classify the world on a different basis. This difference is fixed in the <u>units</u> of thinking.

Primitive thinking is a system of concepts confined to images (Levi–Strauss, 1966, p. 64). "The elements of mythical thought similarly lie halfway between percepts and concepts" (Ibid., p. 18). In linguistics, de Saussure applied the term, signs, to units intermediate between images and concepts. Levi–Strauss uses this term to designate elements of mythical thinking. Signs are concrete and this makes them similar to images, but according to potential of representation, they are similar to concepts. To elucidate, Levi–Strauss makes a comparison between an "a professional do-it-yourself man (*bricoleur*)" and an engineer. The first produces his creations from what he finds at hand, from ready parts, which preserve traces of their former purposes and applications. He has a limited number of tools and parts, and they are not specially created for solving the specific concrete problem, but were already in use. The engineer on the other hand, selects and produces materials and tools specially for each concrete task. The potentials for using any part that the *bricoleur* happens to have on hand are limited by its previous history. True, the possibilities of the engineer are also limited by the epoch in which he lives and by the material which he has. The difference between the engineer and the *bricoleur* is relative. Nevertheless, it is a matter of principle: the engineer always tries to go beyond the framework of the given while the *bricoleur* always remains within that framework. Signs carry in themselves traces of former applications and for this reason, the sphere of their application is limited while concepts create the possibility of going beyond the framework of the 'given' (Ibid., pp. 16-22). "Concepts thus appear like operators <u>opening up</u> the set being worked with and signs like the operator of its <u>reorganization,</u> which neither extends nor renews it and limits itself to obtaining a group of its transformations" (Ibid., p. 20). In the sign, the image coexists with the idea. Signs may enter into interrelation with a certain number of other signs, they make it possible to construct analogies and comparisons, but they always retain their own value; the connection with the image does not allow them to enter simultaneously as concepts into interrelation with a theoretically unlimited number of other elements" (Ibid.).

Thus, if Levi–Strauss does not find differences between the operations (logic) of mythical and scientific thinking, then the units used in these two types of thinking are different. In the first case, they are "signs" that carry an image load and for this reason do not allow going beyond the limits of visual experience. "Signs" represent a large number of concrete objects, but their imagery sets specific limits on their possible operations. Concepts act as units of scientific thinking, uniting objects on the basis of their abstract, "non-visible" traits. Concepts are not connected with images and for this reason the possibilities for their combination are infinite.

Visible traits of objects are the basis for so-called ethnosciences, popular botanical and zoological classifications, but such classification also brings order to chaos and sometimes its results coincide with modern scientific classifications. "Certainly the properties to which the savage mind has access are not the same as those which commanded the attention of scientists. The physical world is approached from opposite ends in the two cases: one is supremely concrete, the other supremely abstract; ... But ... these two courses...independently of each other in time and space, should have led to two distinct though equally positive sciences: one which flowered in the neolithic period, whose theory of the sensible order provided the basis of the arts of civilization (agriculture, animal husbandry, pottery, weaving, conservation and preparation of food, etc.) and which continues to provide for our basic needs by these means; and another which places itself from the start at the level of intelligibility, and of which contemporary science is the fruit" (Levi–Strauss, 1966, p. 69).

Correspondingly, in the history of thinking two periods of rapid development are identified: the neolithic (science based on visible, perceptible qualities of things) and modern (science far from the visible and based on abstraction) (Ibid., p. 15).

Among the distinctive traits of mythical thinking, Levi–Strauss also notes the drive to complete an all-embracing determinism while science establishes the causal explanations only on certain levels of knowledge, avoiding it on other levels (Ibid., p. 11).

To sum up: according to Levi–Strauss, the essence of human thinking lies in ordering and categorization of the world with the aid of universal, unconscious structures. These structures, binary oppositions, are the source of the universal logic of thinking. However, they may be applied to various properties of objects. If they are applied to sensibly perceived properties of objects, then the result is knowledge, the units of which are "signs." When these structures are applied to "abstract" qualities of objects, the results are modern scientific knowledge made up of concepts. According to Levi–Strauss, there is no functional difference between these two types of thinking: both one and the other order and explain the world.

Like the English anthropologists of the last century, Levi–Strauss persistently emphasizes not what is different, but what is common in human thinking in different societies and in different historical epochs. His new doctrine of the "psychic unity of mankind" differs from the ideas developed by A. Bastian, E. Tylor, J. Frazer and others in that, first, Levi–Strauss did not divide cultures into "primitive" and "civilized," "less" and "more" developed; second, he considered unity not in separate coinciding components of various cultures (such as social institutions, customs, myths, implements of trade, etc.), but in basic structures of thinking which, in his opinion, lie at the base of any components of any culture (cf. Leach, 1970, pp. 17, 26). As distinct from most of his predecessors in the matter of studying human thinking in traditional cultures, Levi–Strauss insists on the richness of the mind in these cultures, on the lively cognitive interest of their members that is satisfied with the aid of mythical thinking, on the complexity and logical quality of the thinking itself and the creations made with its help. Fully justified is the opinion that under the influence of the works of Levi–Strauss, "Our eighteenth century view of the 'noble savage' has recently been reconstituted in the Victorian picture of the "savage scientist," whose thought process is quite rational and orderly." (McDougall, 1976, p. 32).

1.4.2. Determination of Thinking. As we know, to the end of the last century, there were two opposed general ideas on the origin of units and operations of human thinking: nativistic and empiricist. Durkheim developed a third idea: cultural-historical. Accordingly, there are three different elucidating principles applied in the study of thinking. This very simplified scheme permits us, nevertheless, to determine the position of the ideas of Levi–Strauss among the conceptions of human thinking: it is a sufficiently "pure" variant of the first, the nativistic point of view; the other variants are represented in the works of such philosophers, psychologists and linguists as

Descartes, Kant, Jung, and Chomsky. And Levi–Strauss contrasts his point of view with the idea of Durkheim on the social, cultural-historical determination of thinking.

Levi–Strauss stresses more than once that the universal structures he found in the systems of kinship, myths etc. are unconscious structures of the human psyche that depend on the principles of the working of the brain (Levi–Strauss, 1968, pp. 117-118; 1983, pp. 28, 63). He supports the latter thesis both theoretically and by citing the physiology of the brain: "...the mind is only able to understand the world around us because the mind is itself part and product of this same world. Therefore the mind, when trying to understand it, only applies operations which do not differ in kind from those going on in the natural world itself ... the process of visual perception makes use of binary oppositions, and neurologists would probably agree that this is also true of the brain processes" (Levi–Strauss, 1973, p. 22).

Thus, the structures of thinking are universal and hereditarily set. The principles of the working of the brain determine the structures of thinking, which in their turn are the basis of culture. E. Leach describes the position of Levi–Strauss as follows: "Since all cultures are products of the human mind, then somewhere under the surface, there must exist traits common to all" (Leach, 1970, p. 26). "Collective consciousness" represents nothing more than a certain expression of the universal unconscious laws of individual thinking (Levi–Strauss, 1983, p. 63). This point of view is directly opposed to the Durkheim's idea on the social determination of the individual's thinking or, as Levi–Strauss expresses it, "on the primacy of the social over the intellect" (Levi–Strauss, 1968, p. 126). Levi–Strauss refers with empathy to the suggestion of Rousseau that the first logical operations grew out of man's understanding of the structure of the plant and animal kingdoms and only after the appearance of these operations did it become possible to establish certain social institutions (Levi–Strauss, 1968, p. 129). Here again his course of reasoning directly opposes Durkheim's.

To elucidate the universality of binary oppositions in culture and in thinking, Levi–Strauss refers to the probable principles of the working of the brain. But what of the differences in thinking—first of all, the differences between the "wild" and the "domesticated" thinking? Does Levi–Strauss correlate them with the features of culture and its historical development?

Levi–Strauss rejects the views according to which mythical and scientific thinking represent two stages or phases in the development of human knowledge (Levi–Strauss, 1966, pp. 22, 219). In his words, these two types of thinking coexist just as wild and domestic plants and animals coexist. "Wild" thinking in "modern" cultures continues to flower in art and in political ideology (Levi–Strauss, 1966, p. 219; 1983, p. 186). The problem of the functional connection between the indicated features of these two types of thinking and the spheres of cultures that Levi Strauss mentions is not discussed in his works.

Levi–Strauss assumes that the flowering of "wild" and "domesticated" thinking occurs at different times, the first during the neolithic epoch, and the second, in the epoch that came several thousand years later. Meanwhile, he says nothing about either the reasons for the appearance of these types of thinking or about the process of "domesticating" "wild" thinking (12). For him it is clearly more important to stress the equal worth of these types of thinking and the similarity of their operations.

In the book, Elementary Structures of Kinship, Levi–Strauss discusses the problem of parallels (he assumes imaginary) between children's thinking and adult thinking in traditional cultures. In this connection, he expresses the opinion that children's thinking represents a rich source of all possible thinking structures from which each culture and epoch selects, preserves and develops those that are appropriate to it (Levi–Strauss, 1969, pp. 93, and 85, 95). Thus, according to Levi–Strauss, the role of culture in the formation of thinking is essentially reduced to a selection among innate thinking structures (Levi–Strauss does not discuss the problem of the development of thinking in the individual or in the culture).

We may assert that on the problem of determination of thinking, Levi–Strauss limits himself to an attempt to deduce the probable universal structures of thinking from the probable principles of the working of the brain. He does not discuss the reasons for the appearance and coexistence of various types of thinking in any detail. He believes that thinking structures are innate and each culture selects a certain complement of structures that are appropriate to it.

1.4.3. Discussion of the Psychological Aspects of the Theory of Levi–Strauss. Certain critics of Levi–Strauss assert that binary oppositions and their combinations are completely inappropriate to the texts analyzed and to the thinking that engendered them, but are "inserted" into them by prejudiced investigators (for arguments for and against the reality of binary structures, see Ivanov, 1972, pp. 208-210, 212-214; 1983, p. 419). In response to reproaches for not differentiating the properties of the object and the subject of the investigation, Levi–Strauss responds that in view of the universality of binary structures, it is not important where they come from in each concrete case. We cite N. A. Butinov (1979, p. 119): "While E. Leach and Nur Yalman cannot decide in whose mind symmetrical structures of myths exist, in the mind of South American Indians or in the mind of Levi–Strauss ... Levi–Strauss perceives this as a confirmation of the correctness of his binary oppositions. The flow of thought in the Indian and in him are one and the same if both of them think through binary oppositions like a computer. 'In the last analysis, it makes no difference,' he responds to his critics, 'if my thought imparted a certain form to the thought of the South American Indians or their thought affected mine' (the last words are cited from Levi–Strauss).

Critics point to the fact that the persistent assertions of Levi–Strauss on the binary nature of thinking may have been inspired by the appearance of computers which work with a binary code (Leach, 1970, pp. 87- 88; Geertz, 1973, p. 354; Butinov, 1983, p. 437). N. A. Butinov (1979, pp. 117-118) writes: "It is specifically ... from the digital computer that the Levi–Strauss' attachment to binary oppositions proceeds ... For Levi–Strauss the digital computer is a visible image of the human mind. Having created this image, and together with it, his structuralist conception, Levi–Strauss attempts to support the separate conclusions that follow from this image by references to Kant, Hegel, Jean Jacques Rousseau, Freud, de Saussure and many other scholars as if he had taken specifically from them the hidden structure of the mind, its place in the subconscious and its binary nature. Actually, all of these references are only the result of the visible image, attempts to make a logical connection between the human mind and the digital computer."

As we have seen above, to confirm the reality and universality of binary oppositions, Levi–Strauss refers to probable principles of the working of the brain. It is not clear, however, specifically what kind of principles we are speaking of, what level of brain activity they pertain to, etc. In such a nonspecific form, this assertion is not verifiable. In this connection, S. Clarke (1981, p. 55) writes as follows: "...Since the practical and conceptual problems involved in identifying the neurological substratum of thought are, to say the least, immense, even reference to neurology cannot realistically be expected to provide the theory with any empirical content."

Evidently, Levi–Strauss actually "introduced" postulated binary structures into the texts, then "transferred" them also to the thinking and in the last analysis to the brain. This is a quite typical example of gravitation of psychologists and culturologists toward "grounding" psychical and cultural phenomena in the brain (in the 1940's and 1950's, on the patterns of higher nervous activity discovered by Pavlov, and now, on the functional differences between the hemispheres). The brain evidently appears to these investigators as if more "real" than culture and the mind and for this reason, "primary" with respect to these. Piaget, who in no way can be considered as supporting an explanation of the psyche through culture, nevertheless reproaches investigators who turn to unproven "innate schemes" (for example, Chomsky) in their lack of faith in history (Piaget, 1971, p. 88; see also Masing, 1973).

Levi–Strauss falls into a vicious circle when on the basis of studying the texts of various cultures, he postulates certain structures of thinking and principles of the working of the brain, then explains the principles of the construction of the texts through these postulated structures and principles (13). As a parallel from the history of psychology, we might here indicate the attempts to use instincts to explain human behavior. These attempts were unsuccessful specifically because instincts were postulated on the basis of studying behavior, then behavior was explained on the basis of instincts, the reality of which remained unproven (14). The result was *circulus vitiosus*.

Even if it were proven that the brain actually works in binary oppositions, we still cannot conclude from this that binary structures must also play the main role in thinking processes in the psychological sense. The direct transfer of the assumed innate principles of the working of the brain to thinking has neither a theoretical nor an empirical basis. The principles of the working of the brain undoubtedly place definite limits to the flow of psychical processes, but this does not at all mean that they determine their basic patterns.

To the objections concerning the lack of proof of Levi–Strauss' theory, it might be said that it will acquire the base that it now lacks when the reality, universality, and decisive significance of binary structures in thinking and in respective physiological processes are demonstrated with methods of physiology and psychology. However, the general ideas on the functions, structure and nature of thinking that are the basis of the theory are somewhat one-sided, vulnerable, and undeveloped to be relied on (specifically in explaining universals and cross-cultural differences in thinking). We will indicate what we consider to be certain weak points in the theory of Levi–Strauss.

First, the idea that "disinterested ordering of chaos" (see above) is a function of human thinking is of too general a character. It is justified as a retort to the assertion that thinking in any society fulfills only a narrowly practical purpose. But as soon as we move on to considering various types of thinking, whose presence within the framework of a culture Levi–Strauss admits, we have to specify the functions of the separate types and explain why these types of thinking developed, what caused the differences between them, and why one type of thinking and not another is applied in certain kinds of activity. Actually mythical and scientific thinking sometimes may yield identical results as Levi–Strauss stresses (see above). However, the reverse situation is more likely to be typical: mythical and scientific thinking solve different problems and they frequently solve the same problem in different ways. If this were not so, then the very need for the appearance of scientific thinking would be incomprehensible. Different types of thinking fulfill different functions.

Second, as we have seen above, Levi–Strauss's theory embraces only one of the aspects of thinking: categorization. Here we are not concerned with the differences between the psychological and ethnological approaches to thinking. R. Zimmerman, objecting to Levi–Strauss' reducing science to categorization of the world, writes: "... Modern science is not *classification*, but *explanation* ... the core of modern science is the construction of explanatory models and the testing of them through the verification of their implied, observable consequences" (Zimmerman, 1970, p. 225). Accordingly, scientific thinking (as well as other types of thinking) also cannot be reduced only to categorization. Thinking as problem solving is not included in the theory of Levi–Strauss. C. Hallpike (1979, p. 77) points out the fact that this theory does not even cover categorization fully: it "has little to say about the cognitive processes that generate ideas of causality, space, time, number." Generalizations based on such a narrow understanding of thinking must not be extended to cover thinking as a whole.

Third, binary oppositions are obviously a somewhat poor model for thinking even in the indicated narrow sense of the word. In linguistics, as Leach notes, binary oppositions do not adequately describe a process, for example, such as the acquisition by the child of rules for generating speech, for this a much more complex model is needed (Leach, 1970, pp. 112-113). We might also note that the theory of Levi–Strauss is as incapable as classical associative psychology of explaining such a trait of thinking as its goal-directedness.

Fourth, we cannot agree with the assertion of Levi–Strauss that the differences between types of thinking—in whatever way we define or describe them—can be reduced to what kinds of properties of objects the thinking includes, the concrete or the abstract. Obviously, any property of an object open to mythical thinking may be subjected to scientific thinking, and scientific thinking nevertheless remains scientific. Neither should we reduce the differences between types of thinking only to the differences between their units as Levi–Strauss does ("signs," that is, semi-images/semi-concepts and concepts). Operations are also different in mythical and scientific thinking. There is a basis for the belief that scientific concepts, for which (according to Vygotsky) awareness and system are characteristic, develop in both the child and in the history of a culture specifically because certain thinking operations applied in science, for example, ascertaining certain relations between concepts, can only be accomplished in units having the noted properties.

Fifth, Levi–Strauss speaks everywhere only of the unconscious structures of thinking, of unconscious operation of the binary oppositions. Consciousness plays no part in his ideas about thinking. U. Masing writes of the structuralists in general and of Levi–Strauss in particular: "Their ultimate and innermost goal is to reduce the number of elements that form the structure to a minimum and then nevertheless to 'generate' from the simplest complement anything they want and any texts. This simplest complement is either extremely elementary or consists of very general and vague abstract concepts. After such a complement is set, it is declared to be eternally and universally a fundamental, unconscious structure in the life of man, all of his reflections (mythology, philosophy, science). Speaking in the language of psychoanalysis, *the sophistries of the 'super-ego' are declared to be identical with the actions of the 'unconscious'!* All the phenomenal properties incompatible with those that can be deduced from this 'whole' are declared nonessential and incidental deviations .... Correspondingly, all historical processes are illusory; only the eternally synchronous biological processes really exist ..." (Masing, 1973, p. 7;

italics mine, P.T.). Data from the psychology of thinking indicate that reflection, i.e. awareness of units, operations and other aspects of thinking, plays an effective, constructive role in the thinking processes. A theory of thinking that does not take this role into account cannot be in any way complete.

Thus, we see that the general ideas about thinking on which Levi–Strauss depends in discussing problems of archaic thinking, the universal and the specific in thinking, are based on unproven assumptions on the exclusive role of binary oppositions both in the working of the brain and in thinking and on the possibility of direct transfer of patterns of the working of the brain to thinking. The theory considered includes only one of the aspects of thinking (classification or categorization of the world); the problem of the functions of various types of thinking remains undeveloped; no consideration is given to data from the psychology of thinking which are evidence of the difference between operations carried out in various types of thinking and of role of consciousness in the thinking processes.

In response to this, we might perhaps say that Levi–Strauss never really set himself the goal of creating any kind of a complete theory of thinking. However, we have seen above that he pronounces quite categorical judgments on the nature of archaic thinking, on the absence of differences between the logic of archaic and scientific thinking, on the similarity of thinking in any societies, etc. The features of Levi–Strauss's general ideas on the nature of human thinking, presented here, appear on his views on these problems. We will move on to discuss these views.

1.4.4. Discussion of the Views of Levi–Strauss on Archaic Thinking. The pathos of the conception of mythical, archaic, "wild" thinking developed by Levi–Strauss lies in the following: this thinking is not primitive and is not simple; it is just as logical as scientific thinking and does not differ qualitatively from the latter. The basic similarity of human thinking is provided for by the similarity of the brain, that is, by the oneness of humanity and it makes no sense to speak of the historical development of thinking (15).

It appears possible to agree only with the first of these assertions: archaic thinking is not primitive and is not simple. We know that for a long time not only thinking in traditional societies was considered primitive and simple, but these societies as a whole were also considered to be primitive and simple. In the last few decades, a reassessment of values occurred: both the traditional societies themselves and the people belonging to them are no longer considered primitive or simple. The indisputable merit of the work of Levi–Strauss lies in that it showed how rich and complex is the culture of traditional societies and, correspondingly, the thinking that provided for this culture.

But recognizing this ideological merit of Levi–Strauss by no means signifies an acceptance of his theses that reject qualitative differences and historical changes in human thinking. The assertion that primitive thinking is rich and complex is completely compatible with acknowledging the idea of cultural-historical determination of thinking and its historical development, which also includes qualitative transformations in thinking.

Levi–Strauss, as we have seen above, assumes that "in mythical thinking the same logic is operating as in scientific thinking, and man always thinks in the same way, that is, 'well'" (Levi–Strauss, 1983, p. 207). In other words, he rejects the idea of historical development of thinking in the course of the development of society. Piaget in his book, Structuralism, is perplexed by Levi–Strauss' ignoring the development of thinking: "we must admit that we do not really understand why the mind is more truly honored when turned into a collection of permanent schemata than when it is viewed as the as yet unfinished product of continual self-constitution" (Piaget, 1971, p. 114). With complete justification, Piaget asserts that postulating innate structures in no way frees the investigator from the need to explain their origin, only in this case in place of a psychological explanation, a biological explanation is now required (Ibid., pp. 12–13, 60, 88–89). Naturally Levi–Strauss does not give such an explanation. Neither does Piaget agree with the rejection of differences between archaic and scientific thinking. Here he expresses a preference not for Levi–Strauss, but for Levy–Bruhl, asserting that the type of thinking Levy–Bruhl describes coincides in a certain sense with the pre-operational and concrete operational intellect in the scheme of Piaget himself and that this type of thinking really exists in traditional societies (Ibid., pp. 116–118). Piaget believes that Levy–Bruhl at the end of his life somewhat too decisively rejected his conception of prelogical thinking. It is Piaget's opinion that the thinking of people in traditional cultures is not wholly pre-logical, but neither does it rise "higher" than the level of concrete operations. "I am convinced," writes Piaget, "that they are not capable of formal thinking" (see Grinevald, 1983a, p 74). (Naturally, Piaget is speaking of actual, and not potential inability.)

In its rejection of the historical development of thinking, the conception of Levi–Strauss is directly opposite the conceptions of such investigators as Levi–Bruhl, Piaget, and Vygotsky. It could not be used as a basis for predicting the existence of cross-cultural differences and historical changes in thinking disclosed in experimental-psychological studies nor could it explain them. It is evident that this (as well as the excessive simplicity of binary oppositions as a model for thinking) was responsible for the unpopularity of the theory of Levi–Strauss among psychologists studying cross-cultural differences and historical changes in thinking.

E. M. Meletinskii (1983, p. 510), like certain other authors, believes that it was especially Levi–Strauss who most convincingly refuted the theory of Levy–Bruhl. However, the results of experimental-psychological studies in which thinking of people who had attended school was compared with thinking of those who had not confirmed the conceptions of Levy–Bruhl and Vygotsky, and not the conception of Levi–Strauss (see Chapter 3 below). Substantial differences can be observed between archaic and scientific thinking, and some of these differences evidently are of a qualitative nature. These circumstances indicate that culture determines thinking to a much greater extent than Levi–Strauss assumes. Paradoxically, culturologist Levi–Strauss ascribes to culture a smaller role in the determination of thinking than Piaget, who is reproached by some psychologists specifically for failing adequately to take into account the significance of culture in the development of thinking. For example, as distinct from Piaget, Vygotsky assumed that so-called higher mental processes, including verbal thinking, are generated by culture, and for this reason they can also be explained only through culture and history.

V. V. Ivanov stresses similar positions in the theories of Vygotsky and Levi–Strauss. He writes: "Vygotsky, like Levi–Strauss, ... found in every-day behavior of modern man phenomena that date back to remote antiquity and may be considered as "fossils," as rudimentary functions" (Ivanov, 1983, p. 400). This is true, but it must be added that if Levi–Strauss discovered nothing other than "fossils" in thinking and does not discuss the differences between his own thinking and the thinking of the Indians leading a traditional form of life, then Vygotsky on the other hand stresses: "... Evidence of rudimentary functions that the behavior of modern man developed from more primitive systems does not in the least compel us to erase the boundaries between the primitive and the cultured man. No one would think to say that the fact that a chicken developed from an egg would lead us to equate the egg and the chicken" (Vygotsky, 1983, p. 61–62). Vygotsky believed that there are different types of thinking qualitatively distinct from each other. Some of them actually date back to remote antiquity, others arose relatively recently in the course of historical development of society and are thus far absent in traditional cultures. Such an approach differs essentially from the position of Levi–Strauss on the eternal coexistence of universal, biologically set types of thinking.

In another place, again uniting Levi–Strauss with Vygotsky, Ivanov writes (Ibid., p. 408) that "with a successive replacement of the 'age of biology' ... by the age of humane sciences, there must be an unbroken, successive connection between the sciences that replace each other. The possibility of a physiological basis for the conclusions of psychology and ethnology noted by Vygotsky may yet become nearly the central problem. Here, as in many other respects, Levi–Strauss turns to the science of the 21st century." Of course, Vygotsky, like many others, considered it necessary to correlate psychological data with data from physiology. But his solution to the problem brought up by Ivanov is directly opposed to what psychologists before him frequently suggested and what Levi–Strauss also proposed. Levi–Strauss believes that the brain predetermines the patterns of thinking. Accordingly, thinking must be explained with reference to the principles of the working of the brain.

Vygotsky, however, believed—and this is the main novelty in his solution to the old problem—that it is not the brain that determines thinking, but <u>culture</u> determines both thinking and the methods of using the <u>potentials</u> of the brain (see the preceding section).

Thus, the explanatory principles of Levi–Strauss and of Vygotsky are diametrically opposed and here Vygotsky's approach is original, but not the nativism of Levi–Strauss.

M. Cole and S. Scribner (1977, p. 10) write that the significance of Levi–Strauss's work "for the study of interrelations between culture and cognitive processes consists in a demonstration of the fact that ethnological data on the infinitely various products of different cultures are evidence, nevertheless, for the existence of universal operations of the human mind."

We have seen that the evidence Levi–Strauss presents is not very reliable. But the indisputable merit of Levi–Strauss is the fact that as distinct from many investigators who isolate and study only (or mainly) the differences in the thinking of people who belong to different cultures and cultural groups, he consistently also emphasizes the presence of universal traits in thinking. Naturally, the differences in thinking can only be studied against a background of assumed universals which Levi–Strauss attempts to describe, but which thus far have hardly been studied at all.

Criticizing the views of Piaget, described above, concerning the thinking of people in traditional cultures, Levi–Strauss asserts that "Piaget's problems" used in cross-cultural studies of thinking are artificial. Levi–Strauss believes that the people studied know very well how to answer not our questions, but their own (see Grinevald, 1983b, pp. 83–84). Levi–Strauss correctly notes that in cross-cultural studies of thinking—and not only in those in which the problems of Piaget were used (for example, on understanding the conservation of the amount of liquid)—problems are commonly used that were developed for the study of the thinking of European children. Only a few experimental works used problems that usually confront people in traditional cultures. Due to the one-sided character of the problems used, we now know more about what subjects in traditional cultures cannot do than about what they can do. The range of the problems used is sufficiently broad to confirm that the so-called thinking in scientific concepts does not exist in traditional cultures (and neither does thinking in formal operations according to Piaget). Levi–Strauss is correct, however, in believing that it is necessary also to use experimental problems which are drawn from theoretical and practical activity of people in traditional cultures in order for the conception of their thinking to be more complete, in order that the thinking might be described not only by the absence of some qualities, but also by the presence of others. In recent psychological studies, such an approach is decisively presented in the work of M. Cole (see the next section).

1.4.5. Conclusion. As distinct from most investigators, Levi–Strauss considers not the particular, but the general, the universal in the thinking of people in different societies. In speaking of thinking, Levi–Strauss has in mind basically only the categorization of the world. For this reason, it is not fair to apply his generalizations to thinking as a whole. The universality and exceptional role of the "common denominator of all thinking" identified by Levi–Strauss, the unconscious binary structures, have not been proven. Corresponding references to hypothetical psychological and physiological patterns are not convincing. The assumption that thinking operations are innate in nature also remains unfounded. Moreover, the hypothetical universality of innate binary structures scarcely excludes the possibility of historical changes and cross-cultural differences in thinking. The assertions of Levi–Strauss on the equal value of the logic of mythical and scientific thinking and on the identity of operations of these two types of thinking have not been supported. In the development of his conception, Levi–Strauss does not take into account data giving evidence on the constructive role of conscious awareness in thinking (for example, reflecting on its units and operations), on the differences in the functions and operations of various types of thinking, specifically, mythical and scientific thinking, on historical changes in thinking due to historical development of society, which have been established in experimental-psychological studies.

Therefore we cannot consider that Levi–Strauss demonstrated a hereditarily determined identity of thinking in all people based on the fact of biological unity of humanity regardless of what kind of society and what kind of historical epoch people belong to, in what kinds of theoretical and practical activity they are engaged, whether or not they were exposed to schooling, to scientific knowledge and similar problems. Levi–Strauss did not succeed in refuting the idea of the historical development of thinking, specifically the ideas of Levy–Bruhl. The conception of Levi–Strauss cannot elucidate experimentally established historical changes and cross-cultural differences in thinking.

The merits of Levi–Strauss in the study of so-called archaic thinking lie in his demonstration of the complexity of this thinking and in his stressing the presence of general, universal traits in human thinking.

1.5. Two Contemporary Psychological Interpretations of Connections between Culture and Thinking. The modern investigator working on theoretical problems of the historical development of thinking and cross-cultural differences in thinking can and must consider the results of appropriate experimental studies. But thus far answers to the main questions on the causes and character of changes and differences in thinking depend not so much on existing experimental data as on general ideas of investigators concerning the functions and structure of thinking, its determination and development, units and operations, methods of studying it, and many other aspects. Existing experimental data are still somewhat too sparse and contradictory to persuade investigators to change their general convictions and conceptions.

Our task does not include a review of all modern theoretical conceptions from which investigators of cross-cultural differences and historical changes in thinking proceed. We will not consider the theory of Piaget which (together with experimental methods pertaining to it) served as a basis for a powerful flow of comparative studies of thinking of both children and adults in various cultures and cultural groups. We are interested most of all in the conceptions which acknowledge the exceptional role of language in thinking. Currently there are two such conceptions: the conceptions of J. S. Bruner and M. Cole. Both not only consider data from cross-cultural studies, but also are a basis for many experimental works. We will consider these experimental data in Chapter 3. Here we are interested in the theoretical positions of the investigators.

1.5.1. J. S. Bruner on the Role of Cultural Factors in the Formation of Thinking.

Agreeing with much in the conceptions of Piaget on the course of development of thinking in the child, Jerome S. Bruner, as we know, at the same time ascribes much greater significance in the process to the cultural environment than does Piaget. He writes: "Like most investigators of cognitive development, we were deeply influenced by Piaget. But, although his works give the richest picture of these processes, they have one substantial gap since they are almost completely based on experiments in which the only variable is age. Piaget admits the important role of the environment only for conscience' sake ..." (Bruner, 1977, p. 324). Bruner wrote more than once about the fact that he felt the influence of the works of Vygotsky and Luria (Bruner, 1977, p. 9, 324; Bruner, 1985, p. 23). As they do, he assumes that "culture is a creator, preserver and conveyer of systems of augmenting natural possibilities" (Bruner, 1977, p. 382). He specifically mentions the following "means of augmenting" mental processes: "Methods of thinking which at first use everyday language, then reasoning shaped in some way, and subsequently, the languages of mathematics and logic" (Ibid.). According to Bruner, "the level of intellect reflects the degree of interiorization of actions using implements provided a person by the given culture" (Bruner, 1977, p. 322); accordingly, without culture the human intellect is impossible.

With such a general approach, it seems entirely natural to be interested in the differences between cognitive processes and the course of their development in children and adults in various cultures and cultural groups that provide their members with various "implements." Posing the question of "specifically what kind of differences in culture promote differences in the processes of thinking" (Ibid, p. 323), Bruner singles out two groups of cultural factors that affect thinking: value orientations and factors connected with various aspects of language and its use (Ibid., pp. 324–325). If the identification of the second group corresponds directly to both the spirit of the excerpts cited above and to the conception of Vygotsky, then identifying the differences in value orientations of various cultures as causes of differences in thinking is somewhat unusual.

As significant value orientations from the point of view of the source of differences in mental development, Bruner has in mind the orientation of culture either toward the collective or toward the individual. "Collectivist" orientation is characteristic for traditional cultures, and "individualistic," for "modern" cultures. According to Bruner, "the view is generally accepted that a collectivist value orientation accompanies an individual's lack of power over the outside world" (Ibid., p. 332). "Not having personal possibilities for affecting environmental conditions in any practical way," the individual "does not even understanding the meaning of personality. From the point of view of cognitive categories, because of this the individual must be less inclined to separate himself from other individuals and from the physical world; his consciousness of self is all the weaker, the less significance he ascribes to himself. Thus, in a culture, mastering the physical world and individualistic consciousness of self go hand in hand; on the other hand, collectivist orientation and a realistic world view occur where behavior and actions of man are not separated into categories separated from physical events" (pp. 332–332; the words, "collectivist" and "individualistic" should be in quotation marks and "realistic" has a very special meaning here: Bruner is speaking of not differentiating between the word and the denotation, that is, of nominal (or verbal) realism which is also called naive). To support this view, Bruner cites interesting data that in a Wolof tribe (Senegal) the movements of a small child are interpreted by the adults not so much as being directed toward achieving a specific effect in the physical world as being directed toward the adults. "... Interpretation by the adults of early actions of the child is, evidently, the factor that also determines the choice between individualistic and collectivist orientations. For the social interpretation of the act not only relates the one who acts to the group, but also relates the group, including the one acting, to the way they reflect external events" (p. 333). Bruner cites data that Wolof children have few manipulative experiences; that the Wolof adult frequently discusses relations among people with the child, but rarely, natural phenomena; that beginning at the age of two, adults more and more subordinate the wishes of the child to group goals while "western society recognizes the individual goals and desires as a positive function of age" (p. 334).

According to Bruner, "individualization" occurs in a child from a traditional culture only if he goes to school. In school, the child is freed of nominal realism, and "separating things and words, assumes an understanding that words are found in the head of man and not in the things they represent ...." The meaning of words is considered as changing from speaker to speaker: the conception of psychological relativity is born. Hidden in this concept is the distinction that man makes between himself and his point of view and the point of view of others. The individual is compelled to isolate himself from the group; willy–nilly he acquires self-consciousness, an understanding of the fact that he is the carrier of a singular view of things, a singular individuality" (pp. 352–353).

From the discussions of Bruner, it follows that it is not the "individualistic" orientation of the culture and corresponding development of self-consciousness that are cultural factors affecting the development of thinking—from which Bruner began his discussion—but on the contrary, the revolution in thinking that occurs in the process of schooling results in the development of full-blown self-consciousness in the child. True, Bruner is writing here of children from a traditional culture in whom "collectivistic" orientation prevents the development of self-consciousness and in whom, for this reason, it develops only in school as nominal realism recedes. Is it possible that an "individualistic" rearing in western cultures even before school engenders in children a developed self-consciousness that, according to the initial thesis of Bruner, in its turn results in substantial changes in thinking? Evidence against this is the fact that nominal realism is widely distributed in the thinking of modern schoolchildren, including pupils in the fifth grade (Brook, 1970; Williams, 1977; Ball and Simpson, 1977; T. Tulviste, 1985; Tulviste and Tulviste, 1985). If, like Bruner, we consider liberation from nominal realism a necessary condition or a basic part of certain qualitative changes in thinking, then we must admit that in these schoolchildren, the changes could not yet have taken place. Thus, the assumed development of self-consciousness as a result of "individualistic" preschool rearing does not in itself result in qualitative changes and, accordingly, in qualitative differences in thinking of children from traditional and from "modern" cultures.

The impression is that Bruner has not resolved the question of the decisive role of self-consciousness in the development of thinking. Meanwhile, we have not found any basis for thinking that the development of self-consciousness as an independent factor leads to substantial shifts in the development of thinking.

What has been said does not in any way mean that there is no connection between the development and nature of self-consciousness and thinking. Bruner is absolutely right in saying that in children growing up in traditional cultures, new traits in both self-consciousness and in thinking appear in school for the first time. (We will return to this problem in 3.3.4). But the concept Bruner presented that differences in value orientations of different cultures are responsible for differences in thinking processes of people who belong to those cultures appears to be inadequately developed.

We will turn to another group of factors enumerated by Bruner that supposedly promote differences in thinking, to the features of languages and their use. Bruner rejects the hypothesis of linguistic relativity of Sapir and

Whorf "in favor of instrumentalism characteristic of authors like Vygotsky and Luria" (Bruner, 1977, p. 324). He identifies three factors in language that may be significant from the point of view of determining differences in thinking: vocabulary, number of levels of generalizations, and syntactic properties of the language (Ibid., p. 336). Citing facts that are evidence that all three factors promote changes and differences in cognitive processes, Bruner ascribes a special significance to the third factor. He believes that schooling "extracts" words from situational, actual context and includes them in a linguistic, syntactic context which are a basis for opening up completely new possibilities for thinking. Citing Vygotsky, Bruner ascribes a decisive role in this process to exercises in written speech (p. 350). He writes that such semantic and syntactic properties of language as "richness and hierarchical organization of vocabulary, including verbal meaning in syntactic context, etc., are indispensable when man has to carry out the process of generalization apart from direct context of a situation. It is specifically in this that the written language differs from the oral. School in itself creates this possibility of using language, even spoken language, outside context since in the great majority of cases the things spoken about are not immediately present" (p. 351) (16) "... the inclusion of any kind of sign into the structure of a sentence indicates that it is more weakly bound to its situational context than to language context. A much greater freedom of action is derived from this: language context is much easier to change than actual context" (Ibid.).

Bruner believes that the main thing in the effect of schooling on thinking is that owing to "extraction" of words from situational context, the child begins to distinguish the word (concept) from the denotation, that is, the child is liberated from nominal realism. And "as soon as thought is distinguished from its object, a path is opened for symbolic processes leaving behind concrete facts to think in terms of the possible and not the actual. At this point of cognitive development, symbolic representation acquires the ability to go beyond the limits of possibilities provided by an iconic system ... a way is opened for the development of those stages of formal operations of which Piaget spoke" (p. 353).

Thus, from a consideration of the views of Bruner on the causes of development of thinking and cross-cultural differences in it, we moved on to the question of specifically which changes and developments the enumerated cultural factors promote in thinking itself. We might say that, differing from Piaget on the question of determination of development in thinking, Bruner not only applies the method Piaget used in describing the changes occurring in thinking, but also agrees with the fact that thinking everywhere, under any cultural conditions moves "forward" along a single, universal, predetermined path: "Depending on certain conditions of the environment, the development of cognitive processes may be quite high, early, and protracted. Completely excluded, evidently, is the possibility that different cultures generate completely different and non-comparable types of thinking. The probable reason for this are the limitations of our biological heritage" (pp. 354–355). We also note that Bruner pays more attention than Piaget to the methods of representation, that is, to the nature of the units of various types of thinking.

Ascribing more significance in the development of thinking to cultural factors than Piaget, Bruner pays substantial attention to the developmental effect of schooling on thinking. The decisive role is that of the circumstance that in school both written and oral speech of the teacher unfold outside the context of objects and operations with them. As a result of this, the child begins to use syntactic potentials of language more ably, and this goes hand in hand with the appearance and development of formal operations in thinking.

Separate links in the chain of Bruner's reasoning raise questions and observations. For example, even in traditional cultures when tales, myths, etc. are told, the objects spoken of are not nearby (or may not even exist). In the culture of traditional societies, there is a whole "invisible world" (for example, see Riftin, 1946). Consequently even here words are extracted from situational context and inserted into a syntactic context, that is, the phenomenon occurs that Bruner connects only with schooling. When Bruner writes that liberating the child's thinking from nominal realism in the process of schooling discloses "a path for symbolic processes, leaving behind concrete facts to think in terms of the possible and not the actual" (p. 353), it seems doubtful, nevertheless, that we are dealing with a phenomenon that appears for the first time only in school. We can scarcely believe that people in traditional cultures do not leave concrete facts behind in their thinking, that they think only of the actual, but not of the possible. In other words, those characteristics which Bruner suggests for the use of language specific to schooling and for the changes in thinking taking place in school are somewhat general and vague. Evidently it is not enough to say that in school words are extracted from a situational context and inserted into a syntactic context. It is also important to specify into what kind of syntactic context they are inserted. Also, it is not enough to say that being liberated from nominal realism permits thinking in terms of the possible; exactly which direction the assumed departure from immediate reality takes must be defined more precisely. If this is not done, then the assumed changes connected with schooling appear to be so substantial and all-encompassing that it is hard to imagine how people in cultures in which there is no schooling ever manage their life at all!

A characteristic feature of Bruner's conception is that, according to it, cultural factors as a whole and schooling especially (including the teaching of reading and writing) present thinking with the possibility of developing, but at the same time do not require this development, do not serve as the main cause of its development, and do not determine the direction of this process. Culture is seen more in the role of a midwife than a mother of thinking. Bruner seems to think that biological and not cultural factors are responsible for the fact that in the course of schooling, thinking develops specifically in this direction and not in another. It is here that we find the essential divergence between the conceptions of Bruner and those of Vygotsky.

In reading Bruner's work, one forms the impression that the thinking of people from traditional cultures and groups just waits for someone to "nudge" it, help it move "forward" along the path along which it "should" develop. It seems more reasonable to believe that the thinking of adults in traditional cultures, which (as distinct from thinking of children in any culture) provides for dealing with all types of practical and theoretical activity and the consequent problems that exist in that culture, changes only when problems arise whose solution requires a change in thinking. And in this case, it will develop not so much "forward" or "higher" as in the direction indicated by these new problems.

1.5.2. M. Cole on the Connections between Culture and Thinking. Michael Cole is known primarily as a consistent critic of the methodological aspect of cross-cultural studies of cognitive processes (Cole and Scribner, 1977; Cole and Means, 1981; Laboratory ... 1983, and others), as the author and initiator of extensive experimental studies of the connections between culture and thinking and culture and memory (Cole et al., 1971; Sharp et al., 1979; Scribner and Cole, 1981), and as a proponent of creating an interdisciplinary area of studies (ethnographic psychology or experimental anthropology of cognition) combining in itself the problems, ideas, and methods of psychology and cultural anthropology (in addition to the works cited, Laboratory ..., 1978, 1979; Cole, 1975, 1985). In this section, we will give principal attention to his general theoretical position and we will be interested primarily—somewhat one-sidedly—in problems concerning the causes of cross-cultural differences and historical changes in thinking and what sort of differences and changes these are. Since Cole, like the present author, experienced the substantial influence of the views of Vygotsky, Luria, and Leont'ev, and frequently depends on them and refers to them in discussing cross-cultural differences and changes in thinking, we will also consider the relation of his position to the views of representatives of the cultural-historical school. This will enable us to see the different possibilities of applying and developing ideas of Vygotsky's school in the study of the cultural-historical development of thinking.

We know that for various reasons, in solving experimental problems, people from traditional cultures and groups frequently do not exhibit the ability and skill that they exhibit in their usual activity in solving their usual problems in their usual situation. As early as 1937, F. Bartlett wrote about one study done in Africa in which traditional subjects could not continue a series of pegs set up by the experimenter: two blue, two red, two blue, etc. The conclusion suggested itself that subjects were incapable of creating a series of objects following a specific structural principle. Leaving the building, the experimenter saw how one of his subjects planted an avenue in which two trees of one species alternated in a strict order with two trees of another species, etc. (Bartlett, 1937). Cole makes far-reaching conclusions from such cases, which form the basis for his criticism of modern cross-cultural studies of cognitive processes. Thinking correctly that on the basis of particular experimental data one must not make judgments that people of one culture or cultural group or another lack one set of abilities or skills or processes or another—for example, abstract thinking, formal operations, nominal (semantic) classification, etc.—Cole believes that we must carefully study the real life, the real activity of people in a given culture and, on this basis, set up experimental conditions in which the people can exhibit their skills and capabilities.

There is no doubt about the soundness of this approach. As we shall see in Chapter 3, its subsequent application allowed Cole and his associates to discover in people from traditional cultures skills and capabilities, the "presence" of which was denied by other investigators on the basis of experimental data or inadequately based general notions on how people who had not attended school, illiterate people, must think, etc. Specifically, owing to the work of Cole and his associates, who carefully studied the real activity of adults in traditional cultures, we now know that they are capable not only of functional, but also of semantic classification of objects and words, and that the widespread notion that they are nominal realists, that they cannot distinguish an object from its name, does not reflect reality.

At the same time the subsequent implementation of this methodological demand made by Cole presents certain difficulties in the study of cross-cultural differences and historical changes in thinking. Let us suppose that having carefully studied the activity of people in a certain traditional group, we did not find that they use, let us say, Piaget's formal operations. Accordingly, we could not create experimental conditions in which the subjects would exhibit operations of this type. According to Cole, even in this case we still do not have the right to assert that there are no formal operations in the thinking of people in this culture or group. He believes that on the basis of experimental data judgments can be made only about what the subjects can do, but not about what they cannot do (Cole, 1975, p. 164).

It has been noted in the literature (Tulviste, 1978; Jahoda, 1980) that such an approach will lead an investigator into an endless search. With negative results, we can always say that we were simply not successful in setting experimental conditions in which the subjects would apply the abilities or processes they have, but which they were not able to exhibit. And substantial differences in thinking, if they do exist, remain undiscovered.

Cole believes that they do not exist. He assumes that all people in any cultures or groups have the same "basic," as he calls them, cognitive processes. Cole and Scribner write: "So long as we are only concerned with demonstrating that human cultural groups differ enormously in their beliefs and theories about the world and in their art products and technical accomplishment, there can be no question: there are marked and multitudinous cultural differences. But are these differences the result of differences in basic cognitive processes or are they merely the expressions of the many products that a universal human mind can manufacture given wide variations in conditions of living and culturally valued activities? (p. 172) ... We are unlikely to find cultural differences in basic component cognitive processes ... There is no evidence that any cultural group wholly lacks a basic process—such as abstraction, or inferential reasoning, or categorization. ... We might start with the hypothesis that sociocultural factors play an important role in influencing which of the possible alternative processes (visual or verbal representation, for example) are evoked in a given situation and what role they play in the total performance" (Cole and Scribner, 1974, p. 193).

What are these "basic" processes and what causes their assumed universality? Cole does not list these processes, but from the citation, it is apparent that he has in mind, for example, abstraction, deduction, categorization, visual and verbal representation. There is no basis for doubting universality of these processes. But at the same time, from general and child psychology we know very well that there are various forms of all these processes. There are classification on the basis of visible traits, functional and nominal (semantic); classification in which the criterion is perceived and in which it is not perceived, etc. Deduction can be made on the basis of the content of the premises or their form or on the basis of the one and the other; here it is possible to perceive the logical connection between premises and the conclusion or not to perceive it, etc. The visual image may be iconic, diagrammatic, symbolic, etc. And if we look at the "basic" processes from this point of view, then there are no *a priori* bases for asserting that all of their types are universal.

Cole, following Luria, uses the concept of "functional systems." The "basic" processes are formed into functional systems that, according to Cole, may be different in different cultures. Cole and Scribner write that according to Luria both functional systems and their separate components are formed in the course of the development of the individual and depend in great measure on the social experience of the child. But Cole does not consider the question of whether this experience is the same in various cultures or not, whether the possible differences in this experience might result in differences not only in functional systems, but also in separate components of these systems, that is, in "basic" processes.

What favors the proposed universality of these processes? Obviously, the following possibilities exist here: either these processes are generated by universal general biological and/or physiological processes or by universal features of all human cultures, or by both factors interacting with each other. As distinct from many other investigators, for example, Bruner, or the followers of Piaget, Cole does not cite biological factors including heredity. Neither does he assert that these proposed universals in the cognitive processes depend for their existence on cultural universals. The impression is formed that Cole's conviction of the universality of "basic" processes comprising functional systems flows not so much from some theoretical notions or even from experimental data (17) as from nobleness, from a desire, following the founder of cultural relativism, F. Boas, to consider all cultures and all mental types as "different, but equal" (these words Cole cites in Cole, 1975, p. 164). (Concerning differences between the positions of Cole and Boas on many problems, see Cole, 1983; Laboratory ..., 1983).

It seems to us that this general approach to the problem of universals, cross-cultural differences and historical changes in thinking, worthy of respect, which was first directed against considering the mentality of people from traditional cultures as "underdeveloped" and against its being identified with child mentality, can also be fully retained even if theoretical arguments or experimental data compel us to reject the idea of the identity of "basic" processes in all people regardless of their cultural identity (activity, education, etc.). Why is the idea of equality compatible with differences in functional systems, but, let us say, not with differences in the method of classification or in the way deductions are made? It seems justifiable to admit that people in all cultures have identical physiological possibilities for the formation of any type of thinking. Such an assumption can hardly be doubted. Of course, it is tempting to postulate universal mental processes as Vygotsky did, for example ("lower" or natural processes), but in this case their universality has to be established and they cannot include processes in which variations as substantial as those in the processes listed above were observed.

Thus, in Cole's conception, functional systems appear as the variable values. As distinct from Piaget's formal operations, for example, they are connected with concrete forms of cultural practice, with certain types of activity (Laboratory ..., 1983; Cole, 1985). In this connection, Cole cites the work of A. N. Leont'ev and recommends goal-directed activity carried out under specific cultural conditions as a basic "unit" in the study of the connections between culture and thinking. We know that for Leont'ev, activity is both the unit of analysis and the source that generates the psyche and, correspondingly, the elucidating principle. Cole assumes activity only as a unit of analysis, believing it impossible to consider culture and cognitive processes as two separate realities, one of which could be explained by the other.

The functional systems are formed in the child in the course of his joint activity with adults. Here Cole looks for support to Vygotsky's idea of interiorization as a mechanism for the development of higher mental processes. According to Cole, the development of thinking consists in extending existing functional systems to new objects, situations, or conditions, and this process frequently occurs with the participation of an adult.

Cole prefers not to speak of the historical development of thinking, evidently understanding that in the eyes of the general public "developed" means "better." But at the same time, Cole naturally must speak of those changes that occur, for example, in the thinking of a child or an adult from a traditional culture when he goes to school. As we have seen, Cole assumes that these changes are moderate and do not pertain to the "basic" processes. Cole et al. (1971, p. 233) write: "... cultural differences in cognition reside more in the situations to which particular cognitive processes are applied than in the existence of a process in one cultural group and its absence in another." Here we are speaking of groups that differ from each other according to such sociocultural indices, for example, as the presence or absence of schooling, participation in traditional or "modern" types of economic activities, etc.

Thus, according to Cole, the role of culture in determining thinking consists in that it determines which "basic" processes participate in solving one set of problems or another under one set of conditions or another, and which do not. This is more than the role assigned to culture by Piaget, but less than the role assigned it by Vygotsky.

The number of functional systems appears to be infinite as does the number of situations to which they correspond. G. Jahoda writes: "... the functional systems view does not hold out the prospect of a more effective solution of cross-cultural problems. ... It appears to require exhaustive, and in practice almost endless explorations of quite specific pieces of behavior with no guarantee of a decisive outcome ... what is lacking in Cole's approach are global theoretical concepts relating cognitive processes of the kind Piaget provides, and which save the researcher from becoming submerged in a mass of unmanageable material" (Jahoda, 1980, p. 126). Cole and his followers admit that the criticism is justified (Minick, 1980; Cole, 1983; Laboratory ..., 1983), but in response they propose to study those same situations and functional systems as well as the transfer of the systems from some situations to others. They assume that such general categories as, for example, formal operations, abstract thinking etc. are unproductive in the sense that they are used in attempts to characterize all human thinking activity (Cole, 1983), while experimental results are evidence of the fact that they are used by people who have "mastered" them in some types of practice, experiments or conditions of an experiment, but not in others. However, the existence of unsuccessful generalizations does not mean that we must completely reject attempts to generalize types of thinking or functional systems.

We will briefly consider the relations of the views of Cole to those of Vygotsky, Luria, and Leont'ev. In Vygotsky he is especially attracted by the idea of the development in the child of intramental functions from intermental functions through interiorization. After Leont'ev, he accepts activity as an initial unit in the study of the relation between culture and thinking. The expeditions of A. R. Luria at the beginning of the 1930s in a certain sense served as a prototype of Cole's experimental studies, but he always regarded the theoretical and methodological aspects of Luria's studies critically; over time his criticism became sharper (for example, Cole, 1985). In 1976, in a foreword to an English edition of Luria's book, <u>On the Historical Development of Cognitive Processes,</u> Cole wrote: "My own interpretation of such data is somewhat different, since I am skeptical of the usefulness of applying developmental theories cross-culturally. Thus, what Luria interprets as the acquisition of new modes of thought, I am more inclined to interpret as changes in the application of previously available modes to the particular problems and contexts of discourse represented by the experimental setting" (Cole, 1976, p. XV).

In the segment quoted, we are concerned with the most essential divergence between the views of Cole and those of representatives of the cultural-historical school. Of course, the transfer of skills is an important mechanism for the development of thinking and, correspondingly, an appropriate object for study. But, according to Vygotsky and his followers, the development of thinking cannot be reduced only to the transfer of existing skills to new material. These investigators proceeded from the notion that culture develops and the development of culture (appearance of new types of activity, according to Leont'ev) results in more substantial changes in mentality than transfer of skills. Specifically, new types of verbal thinking appear, sometimes qualitatively different from those that existed earlier. If we are interested in the origin of one type of thinking or another, we must turn to the history of culture. Cole, however, leaves open the question of the origin of "basic" processes of thinking and rejects the idea of historical development of thinking. He turns to culture to find in it those unchanging basic processes and their combinations (functional systems). If representatives of the cultural-historical school believe that culture is a factor that generates and develops thinking and its separate types, and for that reason human thinking cannot but be explained through culture and history, then according to Cole, the role of culture consists of making combinations, linking "basic" processes, the origin of which is not discussed.

1.6. Conclusions. In the work of authors concerned with theoretical problems of the historical development of thinking and the connections between culture and thinking, we attempted to find answers to two questions: what promotes historical changes and cross-cultural differences in thinking? Of what do these consist?

The answer to the first question may be considered satisfactory if it lets us deduce a sound hypothesis on the nature of thinking in a given culture on the basis of some knowledge of the culture. In Berry and Dasen (1973) we find: "... we believe that there have been enough anecdotal or merely descriptive studies. It is no longer of great interest that two cultural groups produce different means or patterns of scores on a set of tests or tasks. What would be of interest is the prediction of such differences based upon prior analysis of crucial cultural variables" (Berry and Dasen, 1973, p. 426).

Not one of the conceptions considered can be acknowledged as satisfactory from this point of view.

On the basis of Spencer's views, we will have to make a judgment on the nature of thinking in a certain culture on the basis of how complex the environment is—both natural and supra-organic—in which its members live. Spencer, however, has not presented us with a measure which we might use to evaluate the degree of complexity of the environment. Also, there are no rules on conformity between complexity of the environment and the volume of concepts. Moreover, Spencer's concept allows us to make assumptions only on the nature of the units of thinking, but not on the nature of operations that are carried out with these units.

On the basis of the views of Levy–Bruhl, we must be interested primarily in the kind of structure a given society has, that is, how it is divided into groups. But in no way can we judge the logical or "pre-logical" quality of the thinking in this culture on this basis.

On the basis of Vygotsky's views, we would have to ask whether a given culture has schooling and/or reading and writing. If it has, then—and only then—will we be able to assume that that type of thinking exists in it that Vygotsky called thinking in scientific concepts with all of its particulars.

On the basis of the views of Levi–Strauss, we can boldly assume that differences between the thinking in the cultures we are interested in and our own thinking are so insignificant that they present no problem.

On the basis of Bruner's views, we will be able to explain in what spirit people in this culture rear their children—"collectivist" or "individualistic," whether or not they teach them to read and write. Then we will find out whether or not they use concrete or formal operations in their thinking. True, we will not be completely convinced that the presence of these factors necessarily indicates the presence of those operations.

On the basis of Cole's views, we can immediately predict that the "basic" processes in people in this culture are the same as ours, but then to the end of time we will have to study the types of activity that exist there and the variety of conditions under which the activity takes place.

Now let us look at existing answers to the second question: in what do cross-cultural differences and historical changes in thinking consist?

According to Spencer, in the volume of concepts. But other investigators justifiably assert that this is not enough.

According to Levy–Bruhl, in the logical quality of thinking. But it is not altogether clear what he has in mind here.

According to Vygotsky, in the method of using words in thinking, which includes both units and operations of thinking. But how can we justify applying to adults the typology of thinking developed with material on the development of thinking in the child?

According to Levi–Strauss, in units of thinking. But Levi–Strauss says nothing about how we can verify this assertion. Moreover, the same problem arises here as in Spencer: are there differences only in the units? Why are various types of units needed if all operations of thinking can be done with the same units?

According to Bruner, in logical structures of thinking. But it is not enough to tell us about units and operations of verbal thinking.

According to Cole, in functional systems, the number of which is infinite. Some of these are evidently universal, others not.

In the next chapter, on the basis of ideas of the cultural-historical school, we will try to present our answers to these two questions. In doing so, we will also rely on many of the positions discussed in this chapter.

CHAPTER 2

What Changes in Thinking During Its Historical Development and Why

In the preceding chapter we found no satisfactory answer to these two questions. In the sections of this chapter we will discuss certain problems, the resolution of which may facilitate the formation of a theory of the historical development of thinking in which both questions will be answered satisfactorily.

We will start with two basic considerations.

First. In psychology, thinking is defined as problem solving. Why do people in different cultures and cultural groups sometimes solve problems in different ways? Obviously because frequently the problems are different. We solve problems in algebra or physics differently from the way we solve the problem of what to give a child for his birthday. In many cultures people never have the need to solve a type of problem that is typical for algebra and physics. In other words, thinking in different cultures and groups performs partly different functions.

Second. If, following Vygotsky and his successors, we propose that methods of solving problems are learned by children from the culture in the course of interaction with an adult, then it seems obvious that thinking in different cultures and groups must be different. It is obvious that any culture prepares the child for solving problems that are typical of it. In other words, the functions of thinking determine its character.

2.1. The Activity Approach to the Problems of Historical Development of Verbal Thinking. The results of comparative experimental-psychological studies of thinking of people belonging to different cultures are frequently regarded with distrust by both psychologists working in other areas of psychology and by those involved in other sciences. Comparatively "weak" results of the subjects from traditional cultures and groups in solving many experimental problems arouse suspicion regarding the adequacy of the problems, the strangeness of the experimental situation itself for the subjects, the incomprehensibility of the instructions for them, and the subjects' lack of appropriate motivation, etc. Such criticism does not change with a growing flood of ever more precise and reliable data on cross-cultural differences in thinking. In general and on the whole, it is based on three conceptions that are usually not explicitly stated which affect also the experimenters themselves who are working in the field of cross-cultural studies to a certain degree.

First, many assume that thinking of all people, regardless of the culture to which they belong, "must" be identical on the whole. Second, it is believed that if the reality of cross-cultural differences and historical changes in thinking are admitted, then by the same token, the ability of the subjects from traditional groups must be recognized as being lesser or poorer. Third, if any kind of differences in thinking of people in different cultures are admitted, then they are represented as being nonessential and without a qualitative character.

Actually if we proceed from widespread conceptions on the biological (including directly physiological) determination of the human mind and its development, then on the basis of the biological unity of mankind, we must consider the thinking of people in different cultures to be identical on the whole. However, if we admit the existence of significant cross-cultural differences in thinking, then we must also admit their fated character since they must indicate differences in the structure or in the hereditarily determined principles of functioning of the brain systems. Thus, we are left either to dispute or ignore cross-cultural differences in thinking, or to admit irremediable inequality in mental capacities of people belonging to traditional cultures and those belonging to "modern" societies. Neither the authors of cross-cultural studies nor their critics want to agree with the latter position. It is common knowledge that people from traditional cultures frequently exhibit high capabilities in solving various kinds of problems, and children from these cultures are successful in school and acquire a university education, for example.

The authors of studies of cross-cultural differences and historical changes in thinking do not have a general conception according to which differences and changes in thinking would appear as something natural and normal. Because they have no satisfactory conception of the causal connections between culture and thinking, the differences in the latter are frequently presented as random and exotic.

Since the time of the French sociological school it has been quite clear that the causes of cross-cultural differences in thinking must be sought in society (and not in the structure of the brain, not in "innate abilities," etc.). Accordingly, various sociological correlates of differences in thinking are now established in cross-cultural studies: the kind of occupations and educational level of the subjects, their being literate or illiterate, the degree of contact with European civilization, features of material and intellectual culture, etc. However, as a rule, in these studies, it is assumed only that cultural factors may have an influence on thinking, but thus far there is no general conception according to which changes and differences in culture would, without fail, have to bring about changes and differences in thinking. The existing approaches do not allow deducing theoretically sound hypotheses on the basis of a study of a culture as to what features the thinking in that culture must have.

As a result of this, the differences and changes in thinking discovered in experimental studies are usually explained by "back dating" or lef unexplained. For example, most unexpected for investigators was the undoubted circumstance that in adults in many traditional cultures, not only formal, but also concrete operations according to Piaget are "absent." Thus far, this fact has not been explained (more likely, why these operations appear in children in "modern" societies has not been explained). No less surprise and disbelief is engendered by the fact that adults from traditional groups solve the simplest (from the point of view of an educated person) verbal-syllogistic problems the content of which is familiar to them only by chance and simply do not solve similar problems the content of which is not within their personal experience.

On the whole, the status of cross-cultural differences and historical changes in verbal thinking remains indefinite thus far. What is needed is an approach in which these differences and changes would appear as necessary, regular and natural, and not random, exotic, and lacking the "need to exist."

2.1.1. The Status of Cross-cultural Differences and Historical Changes in Thinking. Cross-cultural differences and historical changes in thinking acquire an essentially different status if they are considered from the point of view of the activity approach developed by S. L. Rubinshtein (1973, 1959) and A. N. Leont'ev (1975). This approach considers man's activity as causing the appearance and development of his mental processes. The principal merit of the activity approach is that it establishes the functional connection between culture and the psyche and permits a causal explanation of mental processes through activity. According to Leont'ev, the psyche is generated by activity while the brain, capable of creating a physiological basis for various mental processes and their combinations, acts only as a necessary condition for the existence and development of the psyche. In other words, the psyche arises and develops in the process of activity and due to the carrying out of activity, and is functionally appropriate to it. Precisely on the basis of information on activity can a hypothesis be constructed concerning mental processes, their development and characteristics. We will not discuss here the general theoretical problems of the activity approach and its being original with Rubinshtein or Leont'ev; we will limit ourselves to an attempt to apply it to certain essential theoretical problems of the historical development of thinking, observing in it a successful concretization of an elucidating principle deduced by L. S. Vygotsky for the study of higher mental processes. This principle, as was mentioned in Chapter 1, can be reduced to the following: since higher mental processes are generated not by nature, but by culture, then they must be explained not through nature, but through culture and history.

It is obvious that both the activity of people in various societies that now exist and the methods of preparing a child for carrying out types of activity common in one culture or another differ in many ways from each other. From this point of view, the thinking of people, generated by mastering and accomplishing various kinds of activity and functionally appropriate to it, must of necessity also be different, and common kinds of activity must generate common, universal traits of thinking. The activity approach provides a basis for assuming the existence in any culture, for example, of formal or concrete operations (according to Piaget) or thinking in scientific concepts (according to Vygotsky) only if there are types of activity in the culture which can be done only with this kind of thinking.

The activity approach differs in this from Cole's approach, considered above (1.5.2), to the problem of connections between culture and thinking. Cole believes that all the "basic" thought processes must exist in people. From the point of view of the activity approach, if a culture lacks one or another type of activity (which exists in other cultures or groups) with problems typical for it, then there is no basis for assuming that people in that culture must practice thinking that is functionally appropriate to this activity and applicable to solving problems of this kind.

If thinking appropriate to certain types of human activity were hereditary, we would undoubtedly have to expect a basic similarity in the thinking of peoples of any cultures and epochs. Then human thinking would have to be shaped definitively in the course of the formation of man as a biological species. But there is no basis for assuming that such specific types of thinking as, for example, formal operations (according to Piaget) or thinking in scientific concepts (according to Vygotsky) would have to arise during phylogenesis or anthropogenesis, and then be transmitted hereditarily. It is difficult to understand why these types of thinking would have to be formed in anthropogenesis if most of humanity that has nothing to do with schooling and scientific information even today gets along very well without them. It seems more sensible to think that they arose within the cultural history of mankind to the extent that those types of activity and those problems that specifically require such thinking arose.

From the point of view of the activity approach, the presence in thinking of cross-cultural differences, regardless of how substantial these are, does not at all mean that people from traditional cultures and groups have lesser abilities for thinking. If we proceed from the idea of thinking being engendered by activity, then the results of cross-cultural studies must be considered as evidence not for innate capabilities of people in one culture or another, but for the idea that one or another culture engenders or does not engender a certain type of thinking in man, that the adults (whether in the course of practical activity or in the course of special training at home or in school) do or do not teach the children to solve certain types of problems. Here we may speak of capability in the following sense: do the people of different cultures have the same physiological potentials and prerequisites for mastering various types of practical and theoretical activity and the types of thinking appropriate to these? In other words, is the brain of any healthy person, regardless of which culture he belongs to by birth, capable of assimilating any culture? In this sense, there are neither theoretical nor empirical bases for doubting the similarity of the capabilities of people of different cultural origins. Thus, groundless are the apprehensions that the inevitable conclusion drawn from admitting the reality of substantial cross-cultural differences in thinking must be that innate abilities of people belonging to different cultures are unequal.

In essence, investigators trying to deduce psychic unity of mankind from biological unity (for example, Levi–Strauss) share the general position of those in the past century oriented toward evolution (for example, Spencer) who attempted to deduce fated differences in mental capabilities of peoples of different ethnic origins from assumed differences in the structure of the brain. Both similarly assume that the mind is determined by the brain and for this reason must in the end be explained by deducing its patterns from the structure or principles of functioning of the systems of the brain. From the point of view of the activity approach, the similarity of the brain as a physiological basis for the mind only presents similar potentials for mastering any types of activity and the types of thinking appropriate to these. At the same time, the brain does not at all determine or engender the types of thinking. Thus, if we accept the point of view that activity determines mental processes, then the presence of cross-cultural differences and historical changes in verbal thinking will appear as a natural and normal phenomenon. The advantages of the activity approach in determining the status of cross-cultural differences and historical changes in thinking lead us to expect advantages also in explaining the <u>causes</u> and <u>nature</u> of these phenomena. Why does verbal thinking change in the process of the historical development of a society? Why in comparative studies of thinking in different cultures and cultural groups do we find specifically these and not other differences and correspondences? What kind of transformations in thinking should we expect with these or other changes in social life? Here we will consider only the general, principal solutions to these problems that follow from applying the activity approach to them.

2.1.2. The Development of Activity as the Cause of the Historical Development of Thinking. In Chapter 1 we saw that the existing theoretical approaches do not yield a satisfactory answer to the question of the causes of historical development of verbal thinking. Some of these indicate the possibility of historical changes in thinking without, however, disclosing a need. As a concrete example we cite the hypothesis on the important role of literacy in the development of verbal thinking found in both the studies of the ontogenesis of thinking and in cross-cultural studies. Vygotsky (1956), Bruner and Greenfield (Bruner, 1977, p. 350 et al.; Greenfield and Bruner, 1966; Greenfield, 1972), and Goody (Goody and Watt, 1963; Goody, 1977) are among the investigators who assume that literacy is the powerful factor that engenders abstract, formal, or scientific thinking in people. They cite convincing arguments in favor of the idea that literacy <u>can</u> cooperate in the development of thinking. At the same time the need for change in thinking with acquisition of literacy is not demonstrated in their work. In the last analysis, changes in thinking that occur in school appear as a nonobligatory, additional product of becoming literate as if they were "free of charge supplements" to it. Exactly as in Levy–Bruhl, historical development of thinking appears as a phenomenon that accompanies historical changes in the structure of society, and according to the conceptions of linguistic relativity, features of verbal thinking accompany certain lexical and grammatical features of languages with no particular necessity.

From the point of view of the activity approach, thinking must necessarily change through history because of and to the extent that problems appear in connection with the development of new types of activity which cannot be solved with existing types of thinking. Activity determines which methods of thinking exist in one culture or another and which of these methods is applied in any given case.

Beginning with the Wurzburg school, psychologists have treated and studied thinking mainly as problem solving. The advantage of the activity approach over others is specifically that in analyzing the formation, development and functioning of mental processes, it proceeds from their real functions without being limited by the common references to adaptation to the environment.

A. N. Leont'ev (1975, pp. 75, 81) writes that the unsatisfactory quality of the classical S-R scheme "is that it excludes from the field of research the cogent process in which real connections of the subject with the object world are made, his objective activity (in German, *Tatigkeit*, as distinct from *Aktivitat*) ... in psychology the following alternative was devised: either to keep the basic binomial formula: action of the object—changes in ongoing condition of the subject (or which is essentially the same thing, the formula S-R), or to devise a trinomial formula including a middle link ("middle term")—the activity of the subject and, correspondingly, conditions, goals, and means of that activity— a link that mediates the ties between them. From the point of view of determination of the psyche, this alternative may be formulated thus: we will take either the position that consciousness is determined by the surrounding objects and phenomena or the position that consciousness is determined by the social existence of people, which ... is nothing more than the real process of their life. But ... human life ... is a complex, more precisely, a system of activities replacing one another."

Here it is important to emphasize two points. First, if we proceed from the words of Leont'ev that we quoted, then we must assume that the historical development of thinking is promoted not simply by adaptation to the environment, to the surrounding objects, but by what people do with respect to them. For example, the character of the concepts used depends not only on their referents and physiological processes in the brain, but also on the fact that referents are recognized and concepts are formed in doing some types of activity. Second, the activity approach directly compels the assumption that different people (including those of different cultures) must think of identical parts of the environment differently in many situations, and that one and the same person must think of them using different methods, and, depending on the activity, applying to them sometimes one and sometimes another method of thinking with units and operations typical of these methods. It is perfectly obvious that in societies with astronomy and in those without it, people must think differently about the moon. It is just as obvious that one and the same person must think about the moon differently when occupied with astronomical observations than when writing poetry. It is not the moon that determines how it is thought of in one culture or another, in one situation or another. The method of thinking is determined by the type of activity and the problems characteristic for it.

Among current approaches to the development of thinking, the activity approach seems to be the only one that permits us to deduce, on the basis of certain information about a culture (society), hypotheses on the nature of the thinking it uses that would be based not only on already known empirical connections, but also on methodologically convincing conceptions on the causal connections between culture and thinking. To the extent that people's activity develops, the development of their thinking is a phenomenon that is not only natural, but necessary. Like the very fact itself of the development of thinking, the character of the changes taking place in it may be predicted on the basis of information on the development and character of types of practical and theoretical activity and the appearance of new types of problems corresponding to them that could not be solved by methods of thinking that existed earlier.

2.1.3. Relation of Cultural and Biological Factors in the Determination of Verbal Thinking. Obviously, the advantages of the activity approach in determining the status and causes of historical changes and cross-cultural differences in thinking are due in part to the circumstance that this approach, following Vygotsky, ascribes to culture a much greater role in the formation of higher mental processes than existing biological approaches (for example, the conceptions of Piaget). On this question, the activity approach differs essentially also from the conceptions of the French sociological school which, as we saw in Chapter 1, postulated natural, individual thinking to which collective conceptions were as if added (for example, Durkheim, 1914, p. 39) (1). The activity approach does not postulate primordially provided thinking; only external activity of people and a normally functioning brain are postulated. From this point of view, verbal thinking can only arise in the course of a person's activity, in the course of his assimilating culture. Verbal thinking is formed by interiorization, and the "process of interiorization consists not in that external activity is transferred to a pre-existing internal 'plan of consciousness'; it is a process in which this internal plan is formed" (Leont'ev, 1975, p. 98).

Naturally physiological laws place certain restrictions on the processes of thinking. At the same time, thinking is not determined by physiological factors. On the contrary, functional physiological systems, corresponding to the higher mental processes, are themselves determined by activity, by culture: "...Higher forms of conscious human activity did not arise through evolution from biological laws of brain development, but are the product of more complex social-historical processes—the result of social labor, using tools and socializing with one another through language codes formed in social history. Specifically under the influence of social-historical practice, new "knots" are formed in the brain systems, new functional systems are formed, new "functional organs," owing to which ever newer and newer functional constellations arise in the human brain which itself remains essentially anatomically unchanged" (Luria, 1977, p. 25). Such an approach was formulated for the first time, as we have seen in Chapter 1, by Vygotsky.

Now, as a rule, in cross-cultural studies of thinking, what is different in the thinking of people of different cultures is explained through culture while what is common is deduced from the fact of biological unity of humanity. In other words, the studies most often proceed from the idea that thinking develops according to its own universal laws prescribed by biological factors and culture adds some kind of nuances to this process. For this reason, we speak of the influence or effect of culture on the cognitive processes and their development. From the point of view of the activity approach, we must speak of culture's engendering verbal thinking and its various types. Obviously if the nature of the units and operations of verbal thinking can be deduced from culture, as follows from the activity approach, then it is no longer necessary to use two different explanations to explain what is common and what is different in thinking. The universals of thought (you see, many types of activity are common to all human societies) and the cultural-historical differences in thinking seem to be on the same plane of elucidation.

2.1.4. The Evolutionary and Activity-Theoretic Approaches to Cross-Cultural Differences in Thinking. Let us turn to the problem which confronts all authors of cross-cultural studies of thinking, but about which we usually do not write. In the past century, European scholars had no doubt that "European" thinking, which they identified with scientific thinking as a rule, represents a higher degree in the development of thinking. The thinking of people from traditional cultures was considered underdeveloped and was equated (or at least compared) with the thinking of European children. Some followers of Piaget, particularly Hallpike (1979), even now maintain a similar point of view. On the whole, however, confidence in the superior development of "European" thinking was severely shaken or, in any case, is not touted. Under the influence of cultural relativism and other ideological trends, the methods of thinking in different cultures are considered different but equal; their identity is stressed, and not the differences between them. Sometimes persistently emphasized is the circumstance, which provokes no doubt, that in some experiments the results of the subjects from traditional cultures and groups are "no worse," or are even "better" than the results of subjects attending school (for example, Ember, 1977). However, attempts to "establish equality" are not very convincing since in most experiments the results of subjects from traditional cultures are nevertheless significantly "poorer" and frequently specifically these studies elicit the most interest since it is here that the determining role of a factor of culture such as schooling appears especially clearly.

If we proceed from the activity approach, then the results mentioned are evidence not so much of the "low" or "high" level of mental development as of the presence of certain methods of thinking (primarily scientific) in some cultures and their absence in others in which there are no corresponding types of activity. It is scarcely sensible to place responses pertaining to different methods of thinking on one and the same scale of development/underdevelopment. Let me give an example: during an expedition of Tartu University to isolated mountain regions of Kirghizia in 1977, one of our "traditional" subjects when asked whether grass was alive or not (the Russell–Dennis scale for studying animism in thinking) responded: "No. If it were alive, it would scream when a cow eats it." This response differs from those that we get in educated subjects, but it differs not as much in the level of development as in type. In a paradoxical way, it is specifically not wishing to admit qualitative differences in the thinking of people from traditional and "modern" cultures that leads to the conclusion on the underdevelopment of thinking in traditional cultures. Evidently, development/underdevelopment may be spoken of more expediently within the framework of a single type of thinking.

The activity approach not only allows us to reject comparing the incomparable, but also to explain the qualitative differences found. It differs in this from conceptions that are satisfied with establishing a "low" or "high" level of the development of thinking. As an example, we will cite the eminent follower of Spencer, H. Werner. He writes that genetic psychology "does not deal with any actual or speculative history of mankind; it deals with developmental levels. We ask, e.g., not whether a pattern of functions is relatively early or late in the historical scale, but whether it represents a low or a high level of mentality." (Werner, 1948, p. 17). Werner rejects the explanations of historical changes in thinking. Cole and Scribner (1977, pp. 34–36) justifiably note that Werner only describes separate levels of development without disclosing the reasons and mechanisms of transition from one level to another. The activity approach is directly opposite to that of Werner: the development of thinking is not postulated, but is explained by the development of activity. Moreover, the need to give subjects marks for their results vanishes.

It is understood that what has been said does not mean that in principle we must not place one type of thinking above another, consider one of them more and the other less developed, etc. It is important for us to emphasize the circumstance that methods of thinking in a culture or cultural group can reasonably be evaluated primarily from the point of view of what kind of problems they were meant to solve.

2.1.5. The Possibility of Reconstructing Thinking of Past Epochs. The activity approach permits a reconsideration of a problem that has been discussed in the literature for a long time: is it possible to use data on thinking in presently existing traditional cultures to reconstruct thinking that occurred in previous historical epochs and to what extent? In rejecting this possibility, references were usually made to the fact that traditional societies had passed through as long a path of development as "modern," "civilized" societies. More precisely, the point is not the "path" itself, but the circumstance that "much time has passed."

Let us turn to child psychology. Although achievements in mental development of the child are connected with the age of the child, obviously no one assumes that age acts as the cause of ontogenesis. It must be included in its conditions. It follows that not time, but activity of people must be considered as the cause of the historical development of the psyche during the historical development of societies. In a comparative study of the historical development of the psyche, it is expedient to depend not on the chronological, but on the stage typology of the cultures. Stages can be identified not on the basis of age of the culture, but on the basis of its character. With respect to folkloristics, V. Ya. Propp wrote: "In the West thus far, the principle not of stage, but of simple chronological study predominates. There ancient material will always be considered as older than material recorded in our time. At the same time, from the point of view of development by stages, ancient material may reflect a comparatively late stage of an agricultural system, but a modern text may reflect a much earlier totemic relation" (Propp, 1976, p. 30). Propp believed that "ancient materials can be understood only in light of primitive materials" (Ibid., p. 189; as "primitive" he has in mind ethnographic data on presently existing traditional societies).

Evidently, in studying the historical development of thinking, we must first proceed from the stage characteristics of a culture. Thinking of people in presently existing traditional cultures is comparable to thinking of our ancestors to the extent to which their activity is comparable. If in any culture no substantial changes occurred over a certain period of time and no new problems developed requiring a change in thinking, then from the point of view of the activity approach, there is no basis for assuming that changes in the thinking processes occurred although there would have been enough time for this. On the other hand, with ancient Greece as an example, it is clearly apparent that in the case of substantial changes in activity, transformations in thinking may occur at a surprisingly rapid rate.

As has been known for a long time, there is yet another major difficulty along the path of historical reconstruction of thinking. Is it possible on the basis of the extant results of one activity or another to make judgments on the processes of thinking used in the given activity? As early as the middle of the last century the Russian historian, K. D. Kavelin, and the physiologist, I. M. Sechenov argued about this. Kavelin believed that the human psyche must be studied according to the products of its mental activity while "Sechenov, admitting the psychic to be a process, believed it impossible to study the psyche according to the products of the intellectual culture of peoples, according to their beliefs, language, art, etc." (Budilova, 1983, p. 124. cf. also pp. 115, 123–125, 131). An idea similar to that of Kavelin later formed the basis of Wundt's "psychology of peoples" (Volkerpsychologie) which is now almost forgotten (possibly undeservedly). The possibility of reconstructing thinking according to products of activity was rejected more than once. F. Boas (1926) believed that we must not use the texts of one culture or another as a basis for judging the thinking of individuals belonging to it. A similar point of view is common now as well. M. Crick (1982, p. 291) writes: "Many felt ... that the actual thinking of individuals must not be judged on the basis of analyzing collective representations." Without discussing here this whole problematic, we will note that from the perspective of the activity approach, reconstructing thinking according to products of activity is possible in principle since there is a functional correspondence between one type of activity or another and the thinking that is applied to it. The methods of verbal thinking appear, function, and are transmitted together with corresponding types of texts as a means of generating, understanding and using the latter. This is the source of the principal possibility of using preserved texts to reconstruct the features of the thinking corresponding to them (2).

The significance of cross-cultural studies for historical psychology in the narrow sense of the word, that is for reconstructing the psyche of people of past epochs, lies in the fact that the variety of presently existing societies permits empirical studies of both the products of various types of activity and the process itself of the activity and the psyche of people participating (and not participating) in certain types of activity. We can establish empirically the correspondences between products of activity, the character of the activity itself and the mental processes applied to it and study the patterns of these correspondences. As soon as the patterns of correspondences are established, it will be possible to reconstruct on a solid basis the psyche of the people who produced the preserved cultural artifacts. Sometimes types of activity common in traditional cultures and mental processes corresponding to them are clearly analogous to those that were characteristic of the past of "civilized" societies.

2.1.6. The Activity Approach and the Method of Cross-Cultural Comparison. It seems that the method of cross-cultural comparison opens great possibilities for confirmation, further development and amplification of the activity approach itself. The variety of the human societies presently existing in the world allows us to study the various types of mental processes engendered by the various types of activity that have a place—sometimes foremost—in some cultures but are absent in others. If a hypothesis were developed on what kind of activity probably engenders a certain type of thinking, then such a hypothesis could be directly verified by comparative studies in the different cultures in which this type of activity is present or absent (for example, science). Obviously, the possibility is opened here for the study of the results of such "natural experiments" as could not have been created in Europe or America. It becomes possible to study also what effect the appearance in a culture of a new type of thinking has on earlier existing types of thinking, etc.

The application of the activity approach promotes a closer connection between the psychological study of thinking and the study of culture and society, and overcomes the existing break between history, sociology and ethnography on the one hand and psychology on the other. It not only considers the activity of people as a factor that has an effect on thinking, but also considers it as a system within which the appearance and development of human thinking is both possible and necessary. Specific application of the activity approach in the study of historical changes and cross-cultural differences in thinking requires ethnographic study of the types of practical and theoretical activity as well as development of methods that would make it possible to establish what types of thinking are applied to what types of activity. The advantage of cross-cultural studies over the usual "intracultural" studies from this point of view is that in cross-cultural studies, thinking is compared in societies and groups in which the most varied types of activity exist, are absent or are developing.

2.2. The Historical Heterogeneity of Verbal Thinking. In the section on Levy–Bruhl we mentioned the phenomenon of the heterogeneity of verbal thinking (or "cognitive pluralism") consisting of the fact that in any culture, in any individual, there is not one, single and homogeneous thinking, but different types of verbal thinking. In the literature on the psychology of thinking, this phenomenon has thus far almost never been given a satisfactory explanation. The idea of heterogeneity of verbal thinking rarely is considered in discussing either the theoretical problems of the historical development of thinking or the results of experimental studies of historical changes and cross-cultural differences in thinking. In this section, we will first cite certain data from the history of the idea of heterogeneity of thinking, then we will propose a possible explanation for the phenomenon of heterogeneity of thinking from the position of the activity approach, and finally, we will consider certain consequences for the study of the historical development of verbal thinking flowing from recognizing the fact itself of heterogeneity and from the proposed explanation.

2.2.1. The History of the Problem. In the works done at the end of the last century and beginning of the present century, which experienced the strong influence of evolutionism, the phenomenon of heterogeneity of thinking is most often noted in the following form: having achieved the higher stages in the development of thinking, man sometimes nevertheless drops to a lower level, to stages of the development of thinking already passed in onto- or sociogenesis. This was described in studies on the history of culture, ethnology, historical development of thinking, child psychology, and psychopathology. It was believed that the stages passed in the development of thinking are not lost without a trace, but are preserved in the form of survivals. A return to them was considered as a disappointing phenomenon, a regression. In studies of the ontogenesis of thinking, its various "preliterate" types were treated—and still are most often treated—as not having an independent significance on the rungs of the ladder leading to scientific thinking. It is difficult to understand why they must be preserved when a savage or a child has attained a higher stage in the development of thinking.

In ethnology, the notions of the rudimentary nature of "lower" types of thinking were replaced by admitting the circumstance that various types of thinking may fulfill various functions, specifically, "lower" types have functions different from scientific thinking which usually was (and is) considered as higher. In discussing the views of Levy–Bruhl in Chapter 1, we have already cited his words that "the need of participation even in our societies undoubtedly remains even stronger and more intensive than the need to know or to conform to the demands of the discipline of logic" (Levy–Bruhl, 1930, p. 319). Levy–Bruhl also writes that "logical thinking that strives for its expression in pure concepts and in rational organization of its concepts is not coextensive, that is, corresponding in its extent and content to that thinking that found its expression in collective representations. This thinking, as we know, consists not in only its intellectual function ... The traits proper to logical thinking are so clearly different from the properties of pre-logical thinking that ... we have been tempted to conclude that ... when logical thinking thrusts its law on all operations of consciousness, pre-logical thinking must disappear completely. Such a conclusion is too hasty and is not legitimate ... There will always be collective representations that will express intensively experienced and perceived participation ... The living inner feeling of participation may be enough or even more than enough to outweigh the force of the discipline of logic" (pp. 317–318). In other words, "pre-logical" thinking must certainly be preserved for the reason that it fulfills functions which scientific thinking does not.

In modern cultural sciences, the idea of heterogeneity of culture, heterogeneity of texts is widely accepted, even trivial, and investigators often refer to a corresponding heterogeneity of the processes of verbal thinking in the individual.

We will limit ourselves to a few examples. I. G. Frank-Kamenetskii wrote that "the possibility of transmitting identical phenomena in two ways in speech reflects the duality of modern consciousness, combining with a scientific world view the whole aggregate of conceptions related to the ordinary world view" (Frank-Kamenetskii, 1929, p. 107). This author identifies mythological, scientific-logical, ordinary, and poetic consciousness to which specific types of texts and "layers of language" correspond. F. Kh. Kessidi (1972, p. 46), discussing the problem of the origin of philosophy in ancient Greece, notes that "man ... has not only common sense, but together with it also the capacity for speculative thought which may take various forms in the process of its development: mythological, religious, artistic, philosophical, and scientific thinking. Each of these does not disappear, but retains its significance even after the appearance of higher forms." Let us also remember the position of Levi–Strauss, mentioned in the section dealing with his work, that in the so-called modern cultures, "savage" thinking continues to flourish in art and political ideology just as it does in various forms of practical activity (Levi–Strauss, 1966, p. 219 and 269; 1983, p. 186).

Yu. M. Lotman and B. A. Uspenskii (1973, p. 292) expressed the idea that "heterogeneity is a primordial property of human consciousness for the mechanism of which the presence of two not completely interchangeable systems is essentially necessary." Later this idea was developed in detail by Lotman. He assumes that creativity, the production of something new both in culture and in the individual, is possible only because there is a translation of knowledge from one language of representation to another. Due to existing differences between languages, the translation cannot in principle be completely adequate, and due to this, in the process of translation, new knowledge is generated. In other words, the heterogeneity of thinking is an indispensable condition for generating new texts. "No thinking apparatus can have only a single structure and be monolingual: it must necessarily include in itself semiotic formations which make use of different languages and are mutually not translatable. A necessary condition of any intellectual structure is its inner semiotic nonhomogeneity. A monolingual structure may explain the system of communicative connections, the process of circulation of some already formed information, but it cannot explain the formation of new information. For the development of that, patterned and expedient anomaly, which is the essence of new information or a new reading of the old ... as a minimum, a two-language structure, is required. In other respects, this explains the puzzling fact of heterogeneity and polyglotism of human culture ... At all levels of the thinking mechanism, from the two hemisphere structure of the human brain to culture at any of its levels of organization, we can find bipolarity as the minimum structure of semiotic organization" (Lotman, 1978, pp. 5–6).

According to Lotman, both in processes of thinking and in texts generated by these processes, an interaction of different languages of representation can be found. "Not one of the texts actually given us is a product of some kind of single generating mechanism. Such texts would be useless as generators of new meanings. Even scientific texts which would have to be created within the limits of the 'pure' metalanguages, are 'contaminated' with analogies, images and other borrowings from different semiotic spheres foreign to them. As far as other texts are concerned, their heterogeneity is obvious. They all represent creolization of discrete, nondiscrete, and metalanguages with only a certain domination toward one side or the other" (Lotman, 1981a, p. 15). In the process of interaction of two languages of representation, a trope appears as a device for changing the basic meaning of the word (tropes include metaphor, metonymy, synecdoche, irony). According to Lotman: "a trope is not an adornment that belongs only to the sphere of expression ..., but is a mechanism for constructing a certain content that cannot be constructed within a single language. A trope is a figure generated at the interface of two languages, and in this respect it is isostructural with the mechanism of creative consciousness as such" (Lotman, 1981b, pp. 17–18). Lotman emphasizes that metaphor, metonymy and other devices of analogical thinking are applied not only in artistic, but also in scientific thinking: "Rhetoric is proper to scientific consciousness to the same extent as to the artistic. In the area of scientific consciousness, two spheres can be identified. The first, the rhetorical, is the area of approximation, analogy and simulation. This is the sphere of promoting new ideas, establishing unexpected postulates and hypotheses that formerly seemed absurd. The second is the logical. Here the new ideas are subjected to confirmation, the conclusions flowing from them are analyzed, and internal contradictions in evidence and arguments are eliminated. The first, the 'Faustian' sphere of scientific thinking comprises an integral part of investigation" (Ibid., pp. 18–19). Specifically, Yu. M. Lotman and Z. G. Mints believe that it is exactly through the nondiscrete-continual thinking that "conceptions of iso- and other morphisms that played a decisive role in the development of mathematics, philosophy and other spheres of theoretical knowledge were developed" (Lotman and Mints, 1981, p. 41).

On the whole, according to Lotman "the mutual influence of the continual cyclical and discrete-linear consciousness occurs over the whole extent of human culture and comprises a distinctive feature of human thinking as such. This makes the impact of mythological thinking on logical thinking, and vice versa, and their convergence in the sphere of art a constant factor in human culture.

This process occurs in different ways at different historical stages since the weight of each of the types of consciousness varies in different cultural epochs" (Ibid. pp. 41–42).

As we can see, the heterogeneity of thinking, including the heterogeneity of verbal thinking, appears in Lotman's conception not only as a natural and normal phenomenon, but also as a necessary prerequisite for any forms of creativity both in culture and in the mental activity of the individual. This idea has been echoed in the investigations of functional asymmetry of the brain (Lotman, 1983; Chernigovskaya and Deglin, 1984 et al.), but it has not been considered thus far in the psychology of thinking.

Thus, in cultural sciences, the coexistence of various types of texts and types of thinking corresponding to them is considered a natural and normal phenomenon. The heterogeneity of texts and types of thinking within any culture is considered to be an essential characteristic of culture.

At the same time, in psychology one-sided evolutionism was much more persistent in the discussion of the problem that interests us, and its influence persists to this day. Thus far, different types of verbal thinking are treated first as stages of its development and are evaluated primarily from the point of view of which level of development they represent and not from the point of view of the function they fulfill.

The works of William James (1910) and John Dewey (1922) are an important exception here. Three stages or types of thinking, common sense, scientific and philosophic thinking, "each of which superlatively suits the specific goals," appear as equally valuable and functionally related to the different "spheres of life." Specifically, James recognizes the value of the stage of common sense, at which "all humanity stopped, as being outside the circle of European civilization. It is completely adequate for all practical goals of life" (p. 113). In history, this stage appeared earlier than the latter two, but it still retains its significance: "... Our basic methods of thinking about things were discovered by our very remote ancestors and were somehow preserved over the course of the experience of all subsequent time. They form one great period, one great stage of equilibrium in the development of the human spirit, the stage of common sense. All other stages developed on the basis of this initial stage, but they could never completely eliminate it" (p. 106). James does not provide a psychological analysis of different types of thinking or their differences from each other.

Another eminent representative of pragmatism, John Dewey, although he insists on "recognizing as the end goal of such an organization of the mind, such habit of thought which we call 'scientific'" (Dewey, 1922, p. 7), at the same time believes that education must not allow the ability to think concretely to be replaced by "abstract reflection." "Neither is theoretical thinking a higher type of thinking than practical thinking. The person who is able to use both types of thinking at will is higher than one who can use only one" (p. 126).

Thus, in psychology it was specifically the pragmatists who knew how to regard the different types of thinking not only from the point of view of an evolutionary criterion—which type is higher and which lower—but also from the point of view of the functions the types of thinking fulfilled.

Among the psychologists for whom the idea of development was central, the phenomenon of heterogeneity of thinking was noted by H. Werner. He poses the question of how people whose thinking belongs to different stages of development can understand each other. Werner writes: "The developmental method of approach ... shows that the European mentality is ... highly variable; that man possesses more than one level of behavior; and that at different moments one and the same man may belong to different genetic levels. In this demonstrable fact that there is a plurality of mental levels lies the solution to the mystery of how a European mind can understand primitive types of mentality" (Werner, 1948, p. 39; cf. p. 4). As distinct from James, however, Werner does not consider the functions of "less developed" types of thinking in the behavior of the European. From the point of view of the evolutionist, it would be entirely natural to expect that an educated man would always think scientifically.

The conception of the historical heterogeneity of thinking was shared by L. S. Vygotsky who referred in this connection to the works of H. Werner and P. P. Blonskii: "In his behavior an individual displays in a set form the various completed phases of development. The genetic multilevel nature of the personality, containing in itself layers of diverse antiquity, communicates to the personality unusually complex structure and simultaneously serves as a genetic ladder connecting through a whole series of transitional forms the higher functions of the personality with primitive behavior in onto- and phylogenesis" (Vygotsky, 1983, p. 63, 140–141; cf. 1960, pp. 89–90). With respect to thinking, Vygotsky wrote: "... We must not imagine the process of replacement of separate forms of thinking and separate phases in its development to be a purely mechanical process in which each new phase appears when the preceding one is completely finished and concluded. The picture of development is much more complex. Different genetic forms coexist just as layers of the most varied geological epochs coexist in the earth's crust. This situation is not the exception, but more likely the rule for the development of all behavior as a whole. We know that human behavior is not constantly at one and the same upper or lower plane of its development. The newest and youngest forms that have arisen quite recently in human history are used in human behavior side by side with the oldest ... far from always does an adult think in concepts. Very often his thinking is done at the level of complex thinking, sometimes dropping to still more elementary, more primitive forms" (Vygotsky, 1956, p. 204). "...Although the thinking of an adult may include the formation of concepts and operating with them, nevertheless it is scarcely possible that all of his thinking is filled with these operations. ... In our everyday life, thinking in pseudoconcepts occurs very frequently" (Ibid., p. 196).

We find the functional approach to heterogeneity of units of verbal thinking in Luria (1959, p. 536): "A characteristic trait of the structure of verbal meaning in an adult is the fact that the word preserves for him all the systems of connections it has beginning with the most elementary and obvious and ending with the most complex and abstract, and that, depending on different tasks, one system of connections or another may dominate. Without this, no flexible thinking would be possible, and man applying the system of most abstract connections for solving the most concrete life problems would always risk finding himself in the position in which a schizophrenic finds himself when the second signal systems separates from the first and his behavior loses its sensible and expedient character." These words contain the idea of functional correspondence between the nature of problems resolved in one case or another and the nature of the units of thinking used. As a whole, however, in the psychology of thinking (and all the more in child psychology and pedagogical psychology) developed thinking is simply equated with scientific thinking while the "prescientific" types of verbal thinking are denied independent significance. This is equally true with respect to the conception of Piaget (3) and other approaches to the development of thinking (on this point, see: Tulviste, 1981c).

2.2.2. Heterogeneity of Verbal Thinking and the Activity Approach. The activity approach considers human activity primarily as having objects and results, and in this way makes it possible to unite in one system a certain type of activity, a type of thinking, and the results of activity—specifically, verbal texts. From the point of view of this approach, the connection between variety—both cross-cultural and intracultural—of types of activity and heterogeneity of thinking seems obvious. The reason for heterogeneity of verbal thinking must therefore be perceived not in a random preservation in society and in the individual of "old," "lower," stages in thinking "passed" in socio- and ontogenesis, but in the variety of activities present in the society and carried out by the individual. Historically, heterogeneity arises as new types of activity, which require and generate new types of thinking, appear during development of material and intellectual production; at the same time, to the extent that former types of activity that fulfill some role in the culture are preserved, the "old" types of thinking that correspond functionally to these are preserved.

No one type of verbal thinking is applicable to all types of activity, to solving any problems, and for this reason it cannot replace other types of thinking. It is quite obvious, for example, that scientific thinking which is directed toward elucidating phenomena according to certain laws and, correspondingly, to solving certain types of problems, cannot replace artistic thinking which has different functions and is applied in solving problems of a different type. The same can be said of everyday thinking (common sense). From the point of view of the activity approach, it makes sense to speak not so much of lower or higher stages in the development of thinking as to speak of types of thinking functionally corresponding to certain types of activity. Since no culture consists only of science, there is no basis for assuming that people must consistently apply only scientific thinking. In psychological literature, the widespread notion of equating developed thinking with scientific thinking and over-estimating the value of scientific thinking (at the expense of other types) is connected with the fact that the common underestimation of the role of culture in the formation of verbal thinking has thus far allowed psychology to get along without any conception of culture. Accordingly, culture has been naively equated with science as its most prestigious element. As we have seen above, in culturology, such an approach to culture has been surmounted. In this connection, V. V. Ivanov et al. (1973, pp. 18–19) write that "traditional history of culture considers for each chronological period only the 'new' texts, texts created by that epoch. In the actual existence of a culture, texts transmitted by the given cultural tradition or imported from outside the culture always function together with the new texts. This gives each synchronic state of a culture traits of cultural polyglotism." It is reasonable to propose that similar polyglotism can be observed in the thinking of an individual involved in various types of activity and required to solve various problems. It is quite obvious that if we consider the ontogenesis of verbal thinking primarily as the mastery of the types of verbal thinking present in the culture, then in view of the heterogeneity of the assimilated culture and the presence in it of various types of thinking, the thinking being developed in the child will necessarily have to be heterogeneous.

2.2.3. Heterogeneity of Verbal Thinking and the Explanation of Cross-Cultural Differences in Thinking. Certain inadequacies of modern studies of cross-cultural differences and historical changes in verbal thinking appear to be surmountable if we take into account the idea of heterogeneity of thinking and the idea of its depending on the variety of types of human activity.

Sometimes the implicit assumption of intracultural homogeneity of thinking results in a situation where all thinking of the people in a culture is characterized on the basis of sparse experimental data—for example, it is declared to be concrete or abstract. Ignoring the heterogeneity of thinking leads to overestimating the role in it either of universals or of cross-cultural differences; historical changes are either considered to be absolute or are rejected. On the basis of one set of specific data or another, in the best case we can make judgments on the presence and nature of one or another particular type of thinking in a given individual or in a given society, but not on the general character of their thinking "as a whole."

If we proceed from the idea of the historical heterogeneity of thinking, then those arguments that frequently were used to dispute the possibility of qualitative change in thinking in the course of its historical development appear to be less convincing. Thus, M. Cole et al. (1971, pp. 222–225; Cole et al., 1976) are inclined to reject the idea that the current spread of schooling in developing countries results in a qualitative transformation in thinking because, first, traditional subjects and those with schooling understand one another, which would be impossible if their methods of thinking differed from each other qualitatively; second, the results of these two groups of subjects differed from each other in some but not in all experiments. Both situations can be explained by the presence in both groups of common types of thinking, which does not contradict the presence in them also of qualitatively different types of thinking (4).

We can easily resolve the apparent contradiction that people from traditional groups in complete mastery of ethnosciences, common sense, artistic thinking, etc., cannot at the same time solve certain problems that seem extremely simple, to an educated individual (for example, simple verbal syllogistic problems). Failure to solve these problems may be explained by the circumstance that in traditional cultures the type of activity for which these problems are characteristic, that is, science, is absent, and it is entirely natural for this reason that the type of thinking corresponding to it is absent.

D. Cooper in his work on the logic of primitive thinking (Cooper, 1975, p. 147) writes that the assertion of "childishness" of primitive thinking is incompatible with another assertion according to which "primitives" think completely logically and rationally outside the magic-religious sphere: "In order that whole ethnic groups capable in general of consistent thinking would suddenly become 'like children' when they think about a certain sphere, pre-supposes a schizoid intellect, and we cannot agree with this." Without considering here the special problem of "childishness" of thinking in traditional cultures, we note that far from all types of activity presuppose consistent logical thinking; in some types it is simply not applicable. It is easy to name such types of activity even in European cultures.

J. Goody properly writes that in current literature on the problems of relations between culture and thinking, there are two extreme points of view and both are one-sided and for this reason not acceptable. According to one of these, thinking in all cultures is the same in its essential traits. According to the second, "our" thinking differs in a radical way from "their" thinking (Goody, 1977). From what has been said above, it follows that both these points of view should be rejected since they are based on a false assumption that a single kind of thinking corresponds to each culture. Types of thinking correspond not to separate cultures, but to separate types of activity. It makes sense to speak not of primitive and civilized thinking, but of common sense (everyday, practical thinking), scientific thinking, artistic thinking, etc. The basis for this division is the functional correspondence of certain types of thinking to separate types of activity and to those problems that must be solved in the course of one activity or another.

On a methodological plane, it is necessary to consider that any experiment may provide data not on thinking as a whole, but on one type of thinking and on which types of thinking specifically a given individual is applying in solving the experimental problem presented. A general notion of types of thinking that exist (or do not exist) in one culture or another may be provided by an analysis of types of activities that exist in the given culture and the nature of the problems that must be solved in the course of carrying out the activities.

Thus, coexistence in any culture of different types of verbal thinking appears to be a natural and necessary phenomenon. It is evidence not at all of a disappointing regression to an earlier stage in the development of thinking, but of the variety of the problems that people must solve in doing various types of activity. This does not at all mean that different types of thinking function apart from each other—more likely, their interaction and simultaneous flow are characteristic in the actual solution of problems.

2.3. The Problems of Typology of Verbal Thinking. In psychology, ethnology, culturology, the humanities and other scientific studies, it becomes necessary to describe the features of verbal thinking applied in one form of activity or another, in solving one set of problems or another, in producing certain kinds of texts typical of people in one culture or another, in children of a certain age, in the left or the right hemisphere, etc. In the preceding section, we saw that many investigators considered it expedient to speak about a phenomenon called heterogeneity or polymorphism of thinking, that is, about the presence of various types of thinking in one and the same individual. A basis was also presented for the point of view according to which heterogeneity of thinking is due to heterogeneity of human activity. In this section, we will discuss the problem of ways of describing the identified types of verbal thinking. Such a discussion seems to be a necessary prerequisite to considering cross-cultural differences and historical changes in verbal thinking established in the respective experimental studies.

2.3.1. Critical Notes on Existing Typologies. For many decades, in studies of so-called primitive thinking, or, to use the current term, the thinking of people in traditional cultures, various opinions concerning its nature have been expressed in ethnological and psychological literature. Among them, it is easy to find direct opposites: some investigators consider this thinking as prelogical, others, as logical; some, as concrete, others, as abstract; some, as magical or mystical, others, as realistic; some, as exclusively practical, others, as indifferent to experience, etc. If we proceed from the point of view cited according to which thinking in any society is heterogeneous in view of the existence in it of various types of activity, then all attempts to describe thinking in one culture or another with any kind of single term will have to be recognized as inadequate. It would be expedient to apply a typology that would allow discriminating and describing various types of thinking existing in a given culture. For this reason, it is counterproductive to contrast all thinking in traditional cultures (as primitive, traditional, archaic, "underdeveloped", etc.) with all thinking in "modern" societies: various types of thinking exist in both.

Binary contrasts of types of thinking are widely used in both psychology and ethnology. U. Neisser (1967, p. 297) writes: "Historically, psychology has long recognized the existence of two different forms of mental organization. The distinction has been given many names: 'rational' vs. 'intuitive,' 'constrained' vs. 'creative,' 'logical' vs. 'prelogical,' 'realistic' vs. 'autistic,' 'secondary process' vs. 'primary process.' To list them together so casually may be misleading; the 'autistic' thinking of schizophrenics, as described by Bleuler (1912) is surely not 'creative.' Nevertheless, a common thread runs through all the dichotomies."

For us, it is important that in all the cases listed by Neisser, we are dealing specifically with dichotomies, with dividing thinking into two types on the basis of some kind of single trait. A similar approach is also characteristic in discussing cross-cultural differences and historical changes in thinking. Sometimes one of the types is ascribed to certain societies, and another to others (for example, thinking in traditional cultures appears to be concrete, and thinking in "modern" cultures, abstract). Sometimes, however, within any one culture, two types of thinking are identified (for example, people in the given culture think sometimes concretely, sometimes abstractly depending on the circumstances). In both cases, attempts to describe verbal thinking with one pair of terms suffer, it seems to us, from at least some of the following shortcomings:

a) They arbitrarily, without theoretical basis or empirical confirmation, limit the number of possible types of verbal thinking to only two types. As a result of this, essentially different methods of thinking appear to be identical or combined. Thus, Levy–Bruhl differentiated logical and prelogical thinking, which resulted in his illegitimately combining common sense and scientific thinking since both of these were, in a certain sense, logical in comparison with prelogical and "mystical" collective representations. F. Klix (1983, p. 146) differentiates magical and rational thinking, which again leads to uniting into one type such methods of thinking as common sense (everyday, practical thinking) and scientific thinking which differ in their units and operations.

b) In these oppositions only one half is described as a rule, and the other is characterized only negatively as being devoid of the traits present in the first half.

c) The characteristics of thinking used in these oppositions are relative and not absolute and for this reason we cannot say specifically what kind of thinking we are dealing with in each individual case. For example, all thinking is to some degree abstract and for this reason we can speak of the abstractness of the given thinking only relative to some other kind of thinking (5);

d) As a rule, methods of thinking identified in these oppositions are established a *priori*, or are derived directly from empirical data. In both cases, they have no necessary theoretical basis and consequently no elucidating significance.

e) The categories used for describing thinking usually are not in a one-to-one correspondence with the parameters of the processes and results of thinking. For example, the pair of categories, "abstract thinking/concrete thinking," widely used in psychology including cross-cultural studies of thinking, does not have one definite meaning. On the one hand, a concept that has a large number of subordinate concepts (for example, Brown, 1968, p. 266) is considered abstract. From this point of view the concept, "tree," is abstract, and "oak" or "fir" are concrete concepts. On the other hand, a concept whose denotation is difficult to sensibly imagine (for example, Paivio, Yuille, and Madigan, 1968) is termed abstract. In this case, the concept, "abstraction," is abstract, and the concept, "tree," is concrete. By means of special experiments, it was demonstrated that these two characteristics are not interrelated—a concept abstract in the first sense is not necessarily abstract in the second, and vice versa (Kammann and Streeter, 1971). (There are also other meanings of the terms, "abstract" and "concrete.")

As we have seen in the section on Levy–Bruhl (1.2), the situation with the categories, "logical/nonlogical (prelogical)," is no better. Thinking may be logical in at least three different senses: it may correspond to reality; it may be internally consistent; it may be subject to confirmation from the point of view of explicit laws of logic known to the thinker. Usually the investigators do not indicate specifically which kind of logic they are talking about.

The listed inadequacies become apparent not only in cross-cultural psychological studies and ethnological work on thinking, but also in the psychology of thinking in general, including studies of children's thinking. Widespread typologies of verbal thinking do not have an adequate theoretical basis and do not make it possible to describe and explain without ambiguities the empirical, including experimental, data.

2.3.2. J. Piaget's Typology by Stages. The experiments of Piaget are widely used in both child psychology and in experimental comparative study of thinking in different cultures; these experiments make it possible to establish the stage of intellectual development of the thinking of children of different ages or of adults belonging to one cultural group or another: the preoperational stage or the stage of concrete or formal operations. This typology is free of certain of the inadequacies listed above. Specifically, a positive description of each stage is given; the stages are unambiguously established by means of appropriate experiments; identifiable characteristics of thinking are absolute and not relative. At the same time, there are inadequacies in this typology that make it impossible to recommend it as optimal for use in cross-cultural studies of thinking as well as in the study of the development of thinking in the child.

The stage typology of Piaget is based on the subjects' solving experimental problems not related in any direct way to the types of practical or theoretical activity in any society. As we now realize, the well-known problems concerning understanding the conservation of amount of liquid are not solved by many adults in traditional societies. Not long ago, P. Ya. Gal'perin and D. B. El'konin (1967, p. 606) wrote about the probable reasons for a child's solving these problems correctly: "... We assume that in the interval between these various responses, the first, when the child takes into account only the difference in levels [of water in the two vessels of different shape, P.T.] and the second, when he considers not just this difference—the child is confronted by problems of determining the amount of a substance, milk, "sand grains," modelling clay, etc.—and one way or another, he becomes familiar with the fact that this amount is expressed by volume, but the volume is characterized by three linked, mutually interconnected measurements. The child ... finds himself in an environment that is more or less organized to teach him that which will constantly confront him in this environment." In light of today's cross-cultural data, it is clear that such an experience does not generate ability in people to correctly solve problems on conservation of amount in an experimental situation, although there can be no doubt at the same time that in practical life all adults consider conservation of amount. On this point, M. Cole writes: "... I cannot at all understand the cognitive status of the people who do not solve the problem of conservation of amount. Imagine such a study among people living in a semidesert habitat where from time to time there is a severe shortage of water and where legends tell of the ability of the local inhabitants to find scant sources of water (for example, among the Australian aborigines). Are we supposed to believe that the local adults pour water into tall, narrow jars so that 'there would be more water?' Do they think that they lose some of the water when they pour it from a bucket into a barrel? It seems to me that they would have perished long ago. I also find it difficult to imagine that they would not be able to figure out an action and the reverse action. But if we must transfer an explanation of negative results of children in Geneva to adults in traditional societies (please note that I am not arguing against the fact that many traditional adult subjects show negative results in understanding conservation of amount in an experimental situation), then what other conclusion can we reach?" (Cole, 1975, p. 170, also compare Cole and Scribner, 1977, pp. 186–191).

The artificiality of experimental problems which we use to determine a subject's placement at one of Piaget's stages or another does not permit relating the experimental results obtained to any traits of the culture to which the subject belongs. Because of this, the results of cross-cultural studies of the Piagetian studies are interpreted, as a rule, at the level of correlation and not of causal connections with sociological indicators. In other words, the reasons for the "presence" of one stage of intellectual development or another in a cultural group and its "absence" in another remain undisclosed. The functional connections between types of thinking and the nature of the problems which the subject usually is required to solve in real life remain undisclosed.

We know that in people from traditional cultures, schooling results in the development of ability to solve Piaget's problems on conservation of quantity. Nevertheless, it is still not clear which are the specific components of schooling result in the emergence of this ability. It seems expedient to work with problems more similar to those that people must solve in their real life.

We will also note that Piaget's typology is not a typology of <u>verbal</u> thinking and for this reason neither does it correspond directly to verbal texts of different cultures.

2.3.3. L. S. Vygotsky's Typology and Its Applicability to the Study of the Historical Development of Thinking.

Relatively free of the shortcomings listed in the preceding sections is the typology of units of verbal thinking developed by L. S. Vygotsky (1956) on the basis of data on the development of verbal thinking in the child. It is based on the following assumptions: 1) the unit of verbal thinking is the meaning of the word; 2) the meanings of words develop; 3) the development consists in a transition to qualitatively new methods of using words in thinking, which also results in qualitative changes in thinking. Vygotsky considered this typology to be applicable also to the social historical development of thinking: "The principal progress in the development of thinking is noted in the transition from the first method of using a word as a proper name to a second method when the word is a symbol of a complex, and finally, to a third method, when the word is an instrument or means for developing a concept" (Vygotsky and Luria, 1930, p. 101). According to Vygotsky, complex thinking is used not only by children and "primitives," but also, as he writes, "extremely frequently" by adults in "modern" cultures (compare also 2.2).

Without analyzing Vygotsky's typology in detail (for a more detailed discussion, see, for example, Davydov, 1972, pp. 187–202), we will concentrate on only some of its essential points—primarily on the differences between the everyday, or pseudoconcept as a higher form of the complex and the scientific concept. At the base of the complex lie "connections disclosed in direct experience" (Vygotsky, 1956, p. 169). "While connections of a single type, logically equivalent to each other form the base of a concept, the most various factual connections which often have nothing in common with each other form the base of a complex. In a concept, the objects are generalized according to one trait, in a complex, according to the most varied factual bases ... The diversity of connections that form the base of a complex is the principal trait that differentiates it from a concept characterized by uniformity of connections forming its base" (Ibid., 170). Here the complex and the scientific concept differ according to denotation. However, in some cases the denotation in a complex and in a scientific concept is identical. In this case, in differentiating them, other traits described by Vygotsky can be used that are of a purely psychological nature.

Scientific concepts are systemic: together with referring to the object (denotation), they include reference to other concepts (Vygotsky, 1956, pp. 247–249). "Outside the system, concepts stand in a different relation to the object than when they enter into a specific system ... Outside the system, only connections are possible in concepts that are established between the objects themselves, that is, empirical connections. From this we have the supremacy of the logic of the action ... Together with the system, there appear relations of concepts to concepts, a mediated relation of concepts to objects through their relation to other concepts: a generally different relation of concepts to the object arises; in concepts supra-empirical connections become possible" (Ibid., p. 309). Correspondingly, scientific concepts are also mastered systematically in the course of schooling. At the same time that everyday (or pseudo-) concepts move from familiarity with real things (and, on the other hand, with the word), "up" to generalizations, the development of scientific concepts descends from primary verbal definition to the concrete, to reality (Ibid., p. 215).

The systemic quality of scientific concepts is connected with their conscious realization. "The realizability and systemic quality are completely synonymous with respect to concepts . . . " (Ibid., p. 248). " . . . Concepts are realized through the formation of a system of concepts based on certain relations of community between concepts ... conscious realization of concepts results in their arbitrariness ... Scientific concepts are gates through which conscious realization enters into the kingdom of children's concepts ... specifically in that sphere first of all, thinking makes a transition through the boundary separating the preconcept from true concepts" (Ibid., pp. 250–251). In preconceptual thinking objects represented in a concept are consiously realized, but with scientific conceptual thinking, the concept itself is consiously realized (owing to establishing its relation to other concepts), and the decisive condition here is the circumstance that the development of the scientific concept begins "with the verbal determination of the concept, with operations that presuppose a nonspontaneous development of the concept" (Ibid., p. 286). "Abstraction and generalization of one's thinking are essentially different from abstraction and generalization of things" (Ibid., p. 304). This ability to reflect can then be applied also in relation to everyday concepts (Ibid., p. 285). ". . . The general basis for all higher psychological functions, the development of which comprises the basic neoformation at the school-age level, is conscious realization and mastery" (Ibid., p. 272).

Of special interest is the fact established by Vygotsky that "various relations of community also determine different types of operations possible for the given thinking. Depending on what is functioning and how that which is functioning is constructed, the methods and nature of the functioning itself are determined" (Ibid., p. 325). ". . . Establishing logical relations between concepts in judgments and inferences requires movement ... along ... lines of relation of community, along horizontals and verticals of the whole system of concepts" (Ibid., p. 308). Thus, according to Vygotsky, there is a "unity of structure and function of thinking, a unity of concept and operations possible for it" (Ibid., p. 309). This hypothesis of Vygotsky received its initial experimental confirmation in the work of T. Tulviste (1985).

We know that these ideas and Vygotsky's method of differentiating between everyday and scientific concepts were subjected to detailed methodological criticism, primarily in the works of A. V. Brushlinskii (1968) and V. V. Davydov (1972). Specifically, it was pointed out that "the determining difference between everyday and scientific concepts was found not in their objective content, but in the method and ways of assimilation" (Davydov, 1972, p. 201). Without discussing in the present work all of the typological problems that Vygotsky left unsolved, at this time in the spirit of the activity approach, we will try to correlate the specific traits of thinking in scientific concepts, described by Vygotsky, with the functions carried out by this type of thinking.

Is it right to transfer the typology developed on data of ontogenesis to the historical development of thinking? Does this not mean that we equate the thinking of adults in traditional cultures with the thinking of Moscow children with whom Vygotsky and his colleagues worked? We have seen that Vygotsky applied this typology with respect to people from traditional cultures, believing that they think in complexes, but do not have scientific concepts. On the other hand, Vygotsky believed that "it is completely inadmissable ... to apply the ontogenetic scale to a phylogenetic area" (Vygotsky, 1929, p. 374; phylogenesis in this case means cultural-historical development).

These questions are very critical in current discussions of cross-cultural differences and historical changes in thinking. M. Cole and other investigators reproach the followers of Piaget especially for actually equating the thinking of adults from traditional cultures with the thinking of preschoolers. J. Bruner writes: "Reading Luria's account of the expedition ... to Uzbekistan and Kirghizia ... which was written (so Luria assured me in conversation) in the spirit of Vygotsky's ideas of the earlier period, I was struck by the degree to which the 'modernization' of peasant thought by collectivism was framed in the same language and the same theoretical mode as Vygotsky's discussion of the growth of the child from prescientific to scientific thinking. ... When I had occasion to review Luria's book (Bruner, 1977), I commented on that parallel and made some critical remarks about the simplistic assumption that cultural change was like the growth of the child." When they met, Luria said to Bruner that he liked the review, but at the same time, as Bruner writes, he did "not give up the Vygotskian idea of the parallel between the modernization of the peasant and the growth of the child" (Bruner, 1984, p. 94).

A consideration of the parallels between ontogenesis and the cultural-historical development of verbal thinking would lead us along a tangent, for this reason, I will refer the reader to a detailed discussion of these problems in my other works (Tulviste, 1977, 1981c; Tulviste, 1982). At the same time, I will have to justify applying Vygotsky's typology to the directions of investigation that interest us here and say why I believe it is possible to share the position of Vygotsky and Luria on this point.

First, for the cultural-historical psychology of Vygotsky, Luria, and Leont'ev, specifically children's thinking, strictly speaking, does not exist. Since the development of verbal thinking in the child is considered by this school as assimilation of types of thinking that exist in the given society, the various types of "children's" thinking, from this point of view, are nothing other than the historically formed types of "adult" thinking characteristic not only of children, but also of adults. In other works (Tulviste and Lapp, 1978; Tulviste, 1981c), we attempted to show that even a seemingly specifically juvenile phenomenon in thinking such as animism is assimilated by the child from the culture and cannot in any way be lost after the child begins to think in scientific concepts since it fulfills important functions in certain types of completely "adult" thinking (for example, that used in poetry). In adults, we "do not notice" such thinking because we are inclined to consider primarily scientific thinking and common sense as thinking and not to consider, for example, poetic or religious thinking as thinking. In the child, however, the various types of complex thinking come to our attention because the child does not think in scientific concepts and, correspondingly, he uses various forms of complex thinking in situations in which an adult will not use such forms and in solving problems which an adult will solve by means of scientific thinking. For this reason the different preconceptual types of thinking were described as types of childlike thinking. Actually, according to the words of Vygotsky (see above), they are also used "extremely frequently" by adults "in everyday life." If this opinion is correct, then we are right in applying Vygotsky's typology in the study of the historical development of verbal thinking since it describes not so much the thinking of European children as those types of thinking that are, for the stated reasons, usually considered as childlike, although in reality they are used everywhere by adults in carrying out many types of activity to which they correspond functionally.

Such reasoning cannot be applied with respect to those conceptions of the development of thinking that, like the conception of Piaget, postulate the presence of a verbal thinking specific to children. In studying the thinking of adults in traditional cultures, when C. Hallpike (1979) uses Piaget's categorical apparatus which describes thinking that Piaget assumes only children use in Europe and America, he is actually equating (although with reservations) the thinking of these people with the thinking of European and American children.

However, in light of Vygotsky's conception, the assertion that adults in traditional cultures think in complexes means that they apply the same type of thinking that European adults use in "everyday life," that is, outside school, science and those spheres of activity in which scientific knowledge and methods of solving problems typical of science are used. It is understood that children who are not yet able to think in scientific concepts also use this thinking.

Second, as far as the parallel that Bruner complains of is concerned, it seems to us that it is very real. Neither the European child nor the adult from a traditional culture think in scientific concepts: the first, because he has not yet mastered it; the second, because in his culture (according to definition) there is neither science of the modern type, nor corresponding problems, nor school. When a person from a traditional culture enters school, he begins to form a new type of thinking, thinking in scientific concepts. That is, the same process begins in him as in the child who is in school.

It is understood that this parallel requires certain reservations. It is, however, very real.

Thus, it seems possible to apply the separation of everyday and scientific concepts proposed by Vygotsky, as well as certain other aspects of his typology, to the cultural-historical development of thinking. But here we need to keep in mind that in the thinking that Vygotsky termed everyday thinking, substantial differences can probably be found between the adult from a traditional culture and the European child—in view of the obvious differences in the types of activity in which they are engaged and the problems that they must solve.

Ethnology and culturology disclose parallels between the types of thinking used in different spheres of a culture and the features of juvenile thinking described by Vygotsky. Yu. M. Lotman and B. A. Uspenskii (1973) match the mythological type of text with mythological type of thinking in which the word functions as a proper name (cf. quotation from Vygotsky and Luria, 1930, p. 101, cited above). P. Worsley refers to Vygotsky, believing that in traditional societies, together with texts generated by thinking in complexes (for example, by totemic classifications), texts exist which are constructed on the basis of thinking in scientific concepts (ethnobotanical and ethnozoological classifications) (Worsley, 1967, p. 154). (Incidentally, the examples of classification of the latter type given by Worsley do not confirm this position— totemic and ethnoscientific classification are most likely generated by different types of thinking, but even the latter do not presuppose thinking in scientific concepts in Vygotsky's sense.)

We know that one of the important factors that influences the development of thinking of third-world people is the spread of schooling. It is specifically in school that many of the people in traditional cultures meet with scientific information for the first time, with the necessity of solving "scientific" (school) problems differing substantially from the problems they are used to. Since Vygotsky connected the appearance of thinking in scientific concepts specifically with schooling, it is reasonable to propose that one of the substantial historical changes in thinking may be described as the appearance of thinking in scientific concepts in people from traditional cultures. It is understood that this thinking does not replace previously existing types of thinking, but is added to them. The change in thinking induced by schooling in this case must consist primarily in the appearance of a new method of using the word in thinking—using it as a "scientific concept."

It must be said that if scientific thinking, among various types of verbal thinking, was most often the object of study in psychology, then in ethnology and semiotics, conversely, investigators tried to describe and explain the features specifically of "primitive," archaic, mythological thinking, with comparatively little concern for scientific thinking, which, especially in early literature, was seemingly assumed to be the norm and little studied for this reason. As a consequence of this, the results of psychological and ethnological studies can relatively rarely be compared with each other.

We are inclined to see the advantages of the typology of verbal thinking developed by Vygotsky in the following:

a) the number of possible methods of using a word in thinking (that is, types of verbal thinking) are not limited here "in advance" as is the case in dichotomous typologies;

b) the descriptions of thinking that are used are not relative, but "absolute," and may be unequivocally established;

c) the typology considered is a typology specifically of verbal thinking and the described types can be matched relatively easily with verbal texts functioning in various cultures, which opens up the possibility of considering in psychological studies of thinking data from cultural sciences in which one aspect or another of verbal culture and verbal texts is studied. Many representatives of humanitarian sciences justifiably believe that there is a correspondence between the type of thinking used in one form of activity or another and the results of this activity, that is, in the given case, between types of verbal thinking and types of verbal texts.

The main advantage of Vygotsky's typology is that the types of verbal thinking described in it may be matched with various kinds of activity. This gives the typology a theoretical basis and an elucidating character. In other words, it permits not only a description, but also an explanation of cross-cultural differences and historical changes in verbal thinking. We noted above that Vygotsky functionally connected thinking in scientific concepts with scientific knowledge as a specific type of knowledge, and thinking in complexes, with "everyday life." The latter concept is, of course, somewhat general. There are bases for assuming that other types of practical and theoretical activity besides science are matched by methods of using the word in thinking that are fixed, typical and characteristic specifically of them. The construction of such typology is a separate problem. We will only note that for poetry, for example, exploitation of the sound aspect of the word and its ambiguity is characteristic. As one of the traits of religious thinking, E. Leach (1976, pp. 69–70) identifies the perception of the metaphor as metonymy, etc. (6).

Thus, the specific methods of using the word in various types of activity may be established by appropriate analysis. In this case, the typology under consideration here, developed by Vygotsky on the basis of limited experimental material, acquires a more complete and theoretically sound character. In its initial form, it had a weakness typical of many typologies of thinking: while one type (thinking in scientific concepts) is described by means of definite positive qualities, the other (thinking in complexes, which according to Vygotsky, has several subtypes) is characterized by their absence.

In comparison with Piaget's stage typology, Vygotsky's typology is in an uncomfortable position because it is based on an incomparably smaller amount of experimental material. Also, there are no standard methods for establishing the presence, absence or degrees of development of one type of thinking or another.

2.3.4. Verbal and Nonverbal Features of Types of Verbal Thinking. In descriptions of "primitive" thinking, as "prescientific" types of verbal thinking widespread in European culture, principal attention is frequently given to the nonverbal aspects. The emotionality of this thinking, its imagery, its closeness to perception and action, etc. are stressed. Actually, the differences between types of verbal thinking applied in various forms of activity clearly cannot be reduced only to differences in methods of using the word in thinking. However, since we are speaking of thinking, the units of which are specifically the meanings of words, then it seems to us that their "verbal" aspects, on which Vygotsky's typology is based, will be of special importance in the descriptions of types of verbal thinking. If we consider that human activity is productive and that those types of activity which use predominantly verbal thinking, frequently produce a verbal text, in the last analysis, the nonverbal aspects of verbal thinking are also embodied in words.

Identifying specifically "verbal" aspects of various types of verbal thinking is also more promising than identifying their logical characteristics. Mainly the logical structure of thinking operations is described in the works of C. Levi–Strauss and the late Piaget. P. Ya. Gal'perin and D. B. El'konin (1967, p. 619) see in the one-sided, logical consideration of thinking characteristic of Piaget, a form of "reducing the psychic to the non-psychic." They "do not agree with either the statement that logic is the only or even the main criterion of thinking or that the level of formal-logical operations is the highest level of the development of thinking ... Logical relations of objects and logical operations with them are one of the means of thinking. It is a powerful means ... but by far not the only means; it is not always indispensable in the first place, and never forms the thinking process itself" (Ibid., p. 600, 621). This problem, as we know, is debatable. In any case, we are justified, however, in describing the processes and results of thinking in the first place not by some kind of external characteristics, but by those units and operations that are actually used in the processes. This method of description has still another advantage: the traits described will be recognized as immanent to the processes and results of the thinking being studied. That is, the problem cited by critics of Levi–Strauss that has not been given a satisfactory answer will be eliminated: are the binary oppositions and their combinations which Levi–Strauss discloses in analyzed texts part of the texts themselves and the thinking which generated them or does the investigator add to the analyzed material those means of analysis that he uses (cf. 1.4). The problem of how logical patterns are represented in thinking is open (although this problem, naturally, can be resolved in principle), whereas a person's realizing or not realizing that a word is separate from its referent, or thoughts are separate from their object can be relatively easily established just as his awareness, nonawareness or degree of awareness of one set of thinking operations or another can be established.

2.3.5. Qualitative Differences Between Types of Verbal Thinking. H. Spencer, introducing the idea of evolution into psychology, considered all development of the mind, including the historical development of thinking, as a series of gradual quantitative changes taking place over a long period of time. The idea that there are no universal, once and for all prescribed "laws of the mind" and that thinking is subject in the course of its historical development to qualitative transformations appeared for the first time in the works of Levy–Bruhl. This idea, given a productive development in the works of Piaget on child psychology, is by no means popular in the studies of cross-cultural differences in thinking. This can be explained partly by the unpopularity of the genetic approach in this branch of psychology and partly by other reasons of an ideological order. Representatives of cultural-historical psychology, on the other hand, assume that in the historical development of the mind, there are not only quantitative, but also qualitative changes (for example, Vygotsky and

Luria, 1930, p. 101; Leont'ev, 1931, p. 55; Vygotsky, 1956, p. 165; Leont'ev, 1973, p. 294). Luria (1971, pp. 48–49) writes: "... Various forms of practice that correspond to various periods or structures of social-economic development determine the formation of structurally different psychological processes ... significant social-historical shifts connected with a change in social-historical structures and radical cultural changes result in radical changes in the structure of mental processes, and primarily, in radical transformation of cognitive activity." Qualitative transformations in cognitive processes in this case are derived from qualitative changes occurring in the life of the society, practice and culture. We may assume that admission or rejection by an investigator of qualitative changes in thinking in the course of its historical development depends to a certain degree on what his views are on the history of society and on the connection between society and the mind. The example of Piaget, however, is evidence that the biological approach to development of the mind may also be connected with admitting and emphasizing qualitative changes.

Proceeding from the selected activity typology of verbal thinking, it would be reasonable in the first place to pose a question not on the qualitative differences between thinking of people in different epochs and in different cultures, but on whether there are qualitative differences between the types of verbal thinking that are used in different activities. It is quite obvious that the differences described by Vygotsky between everyday thinking (common sense) and scientific thinking are of a qualitative nature, and that both the units and the operations of these two types of verbal thinking differ qualitatively. An everyday concept (pseudoconcept) may be more or less developed, that is, it may correspond to its potential circle of referents with a varying degree of precision, but even at the highest level of its development, it will be poor in realization or definition. As fine and precise as the use of an everyday concept may be, it will not in itself lead to its conscious realization and definition—and it is in this that it differs from even the least developed scientific concept no matter how poorly the latter is mastered in the course of schooling. Obviously, no development of common sense or thinking in scientific concepts will lead to the emergence of artistic thinking. One and the same word in a physics textbook and in a poem will be used with meanings certainly different qualitatively from each other.

If a specific type of thinking exists in one culture and is absent in another, then obviously there is a qualitative difference between the thinking of people in the two cultures. On the whole, the only type of thinking which can be subjected to "pure" cross-cultural comparison is scientific thinking since science (and schooling) exist in some cultures and are absent in others. "Pure" comparisons are not possible with respect, for example, to artistic or ideological thinking since there is no society without art or ideology.

2.3.6. Interconnections between Types of Verbal Thinking. Naturally, different types of verbal (and nonverbal) thinking interact and influence each other. This pertains to the development of thinking in a culture and in an individual as well as to the real functioning of thinking in solving any problems. The emergence of science and scientific thinking in a culture leads to changes in art, practical activity, religion, etc., and in those types of thinking that are applied in these forms of activity. When a person from a traditional society masters scientific thinking in school with the realization of units and operations characteristic of scientific thinking, in principle this permits the realization of units and operations used in other types of thinking, etc.

In the section on heterogeneity of verbal thinking, we mentioned that the different types of thinking function not separately, but together. In scientific or artistic activity, other types of thinking—for example, common sense—are used, not just units and operations of verbal thinking specific to these types of activity. Regardless of the long tradition of contrasting scientific thinking and common sense, characteristic of European cultures, and of the contrasting evaluation ascribed to these two types of thinking (see, for example, Olson, 1975), common sense is indispensable also in scientific activity. In other words, in any kind of activity, the method of thinking specific to it interacts with other methods that are in essence typical for other types of activity.

Finally, there are cases in which there is a recognized inconsistency between units and operations of verbal thinking: complexes function in operations typical for scientific thinking or, conversely, scientific concepts are applied in operations typical for other types of thinking. Yu. M. Lotman and B. A. Uspenskii (1973, pp. 294–295) give this example: "If in texts appearing recently [the authors refer to texts of Russian symbolists, P.T.], mythological elements may be rationally, that is nonmythologically, organized, then the directly opposite situation may be found in baroque texts where, on the contrary, abstract constructions are organized according to the mythological principle: elements and attributes may behave like heroes of the mythological world. This may be explained by the fact that the baroque appeared against a background of religious culture; meanwhile, modern symbolism was engendered against a background of rational consciousness and its customary associations."

Just as the basic types of human thinking—sensory-motor, image, verbal— function together under normal conditions, so do various types of verbal thinking interact. However, they differ from each other in function, units and operations, and for this reason it is expedient to differentiate them. Such a differentiation is supported by cases where one type is absent in some cultures.

Finally, we will consider one more problem. We know that so-called primitive thinking was frequently directly identified with, or at least placed in the same order with either the artistic or the religious. We have seen that it is scarcely proper to speak of primitive thinking as a special type of thinking. As in "modern" cultures, thinking in traditional cultures is a heterogeneous phenomenon inasmuch as various types of practical and theoretical activity exist in them. The indicated identifications and parallels are evidently the result of two circumstances. First, the attention of ethnologists investigating thinking in traditional cultures is most often directed not toward common sense, but toward the religious thinking of people of these cultures. This is the source of equating "primitive" with religious thinking. Second, in culturology, the notion is widely accepted that in traditional cultures various spheres of culture and, consequently, types of thinking are less differentiated than in "modern" cultures. For this reason, there is reference to mythopoetic thinking from which artistic, religious and scientific thinking developed in the course of the history of culture. It is understandable that each of these three types of thinking is marked by some traits that are also proper to nondifferentiated mythological thinking, but instead of a rough analogies, it would be of interest to analyze in detail these common and different traits against the background of the actual historic process of differentiation of cultural spheres. Thus far, attempts of this kind were undertaken basically only with respect to scientific thinking, and this leaves room for superficial identification of artistic and religious thinking with the "primitive."

2.3.7. Conclusion. Among the existing typologies of verbal thinking the most suitable for application in psychological studies of development of verbal thinking in a culture and in an individual is the typology developed by L. S. Vygotsky, which is based on various uses of the word in solving problems specific to various types of activity. Structural features of types of thinking identified in this typology are explained by their functions which are in turn determined by the types of activity in which these types of thinking are used. Vygotsky describes types of thinking not according to their external traits, as is done in typologies prevalent today, but according to <u>units</u> and <u>operations</u> of thinking unequivocally established by appropriate experiments (for example, according to their realizability).

For Vygotsky, the method of using the word in thinking is a variable quantity in the historical development of verbal thinking. Cross-cultural differences in verbal thinking consist of the presence of certain methods of using the word in thinking in some cultures and their absence in others. At the same time, qualitative changes in the development of thinking consist in the appearance of new types of thinking; within separate types quantitative changes may, and undoubtedly do occur.

Obviously, other typologies of verbal thinking that are appropriate to the purposes of one study or another in one area or another of psychology may also be proper. For example, the described typology would scarcely be adequate in pathopsychology. However, if we consider the reason for the development of verbal thinking to be the appearance of new types of activity and, correspondingly, new types of problems, then in constructing a typology, it seems expedient to proceed from methods of using the word in thinking that are specific to various types of activity.

2.4. The Emergence of Reflection and Control of the Course of Thought during the Historical Development of Thinking. Various authors studying the ontogenesis of thinking have noted that at a certain stage of development, reflection appears in the thinking of the child. For the child, thinking begins to appear as an independent reality different from that external reality that is reflected in thoughts. The child begins to realize the course of his thoughts, his thinking operations. Thinking itself becomes the object of thinking; according to Piaget, in thinking there appear "operations on operations." According to widespread opinion, this occurs at the age of 11–12.

Together with reflection appears the possibility of consciously verifying the course of thought, both one's own and another's. This permits, first, pointing to logical contradictions and inconsistencies in thoughts. Second, some problems can now be solved more confidently and with fewer errors than when reflection and the possibility of checking the course of thought were absent. Third, some authors (for example, Vygotsky) believe that with the appearance of reflection, the thinking operations themselves change: new operations emerge that are not available to nonreflective thinking. Owing to the latter circumstance, it becomes possible to solve problems that, according to these authors, could not be solved without reflection. For example, R. Skemp (1961) believes that solving algebra problems (as distinct from arithmetic problems) absolutely requires awareness of the operations being done.

Since some investigators connect the appearance of reflection in the thinking of the child with mastery in school of scientific information and with the need to solve certain school (learning) problems, it is expedient to pose the question: do people consciously reflect on their thinking in cultures in which there is no schooling, scientific knowledge or problems? Does reflection exist in all cultures, is it the same everywhere, and did the people always consciously reflect on their thinking operations? In order to get a preliminary, hypothetical response to these questions, it would seem reasonable first to see in what the authors who study the origin of reflection in the thinking of modern European or American children perceive the reasons for its emergence and its functions, then to ask in which historical and presently existing societies these hypothetical reasons and functions exist.

2.4.1. J. Piaget and L. S. Vygotsky on the Emergence of Reflection in the Thinking of Children. Piaget took up the problem of the origin of reflection in the thinking of the child many times (1924, 1932, 1969, 1973). He writes: "More than anything, the child's growing awareness of his own thinking ... depends on social factors. ... Contact with others and the experience of discussion make him notice his own subjectivity and realize in this way the very process of thinking"

(Piaget, 1973, p. 109). During the period of egocentrism, the child does not realize his thoughts: "Since the child thinks only for himself, he has no need to realize the mechanism of his own reasoning ... His attention is directed wholly toward the external world, to action and not at all to his own thought placed between him and the external world. On the other hand, since the child will try to adapt himself to others, he will create a new reality between them and himself, the plane of thought expressed and discussed where operations and relations directed thus far by action begin from this point to be directed by imagination and words. It is specifically to this extent that the child will feel the need to realize both those relations and those operations that were until then unconscious specifically because they sufficed in practice" (Piaget, 1932, pp. 379–380)."... Only with the pressure of arguments and contradictions will he try to justify his thoughts in the eyes of others and in this way he will develop in himself the habit of observing his thoughts ..." (Ibid. p. 325).

According to Piaget, reflection is necessary primarily so that man might logically substantiate his thoughts, his point of view: "... the subconscious thought of the child ... is much farther removed than ours from the need for logical substantiation and from deducing ideas from other ideas ... for thought that is not conscious of itself, logical substantiation is not possible. Logical substantiation of ideas occurs on an altogether different plane than invention of an idea; while the latter is unconscious and is the result of a new combination of preceding experiences, logical substantiation, on the other hand, requires deliberation and the use of language, or more briefly, introspection constructing over spontaneous thought 'the thought of the thought,' which alone is capable of being logically necessary ... among children, those incapable of introspection are ready at the same time to substantiate any idea in the strangest and most illogical way ... while those who know how to use introspection with greater adroitness are at the same time most capable of producing evidence ..." (Ibid., pp. 331–332).

Thus, according to Piaget, the general reason for the emergence of reflection in the thinking of the child lies in contact, in arguments with other children, in the necessity of proving that his own point of view is justifiable and that of others is not. There can be no doubt that in any currently existing (and, obviously, previously existing) societies, children cannot remain egocentric, but must, as Piaget puts it, "adapt to others." They are forced to argue and prove their case. Thus, the reasons for emergence of reflection in thinking cited by Piaget exist everywhere and always. Maintaining the position of Piaget, we must assume that reflection and logical substantiation of ideas are universals of human thought.

The point of view on the origin of reflection in the thinking of the child adopted by Vygotsky leads to a different assumption regarding the incidence of reflection. At the outset Vygotsky shares the opinion of Piaget: reflection arises owing to arguments requiring the child to prove the soundness of his thought. Vygotsky even uses this example to illustrate his well-known law of the development of higher mental functions: "in the development of the child, all higher mental functions appear on the scene twice: first as activity of the collective or social activity, that is intermental function and a second time as individual activity, as the child's internal method of thinking, as an intramental function" (Vygotsky, 1956, p. 449). Vygotsky writes: "The studies of Baldwin, Rignano and Piaget showed that argument appears first in the children's collective and with it the need to justify one's idea, and only later does deliberation develop in the child as a unique background of internal activity, the peculiarity of which consists in that the child learns to realize and confirm the basis of his ideas. Piaget writes: *'per se, we are willing to trust the word and only in the process of interaction does the need to verify and confirm ideas arise' "* (Ibid., p. 449, and p. 87).

We can understand why Vygotsky in this case accepts the point of view of Piaget without reservation. The latter connects a certain transformation in thinking directly with the effect of a certain social factor, an argument among children. It is curious that in his later works, Piaget, who explains ontogenesis of the intellect through biologically understood interactions of the organism with the environment, in this case remains loyal to a social explanation: "In the plan of the intellect, cooperation is ... a discussion conducted objectively ... From it and on its basis arises subsequently interiorized discussion, i.e. deliberation or reflection ..." (Piaget, 1969, p. 217). While we frequently observe a divergence in elucidating principles in Piaget and Vygotsky, they both use social factors to explain the appearance of reflection.

However, discussing the problem of the appearance in the child of "scientific concepts" in his book, Thinking and Speech, Vygotsky comes to a different idea about the concrete social factors that engender reflection in the thinking of the child. Here these are factors not so much social (in the narrow sense of the word) as cultural (again in the narrow sense of the word).

We will specify first that Vygotsky defines reflection or conscious realization of thoughts the same way that Piaget does: "to consciously realize any operation means to move it from the plane of action to the plane of language, that is, to reconstruct it in the imagination in order to express it in words" (Vygotsky, 1956, p. 236). "Conscious realization is the act of consciousness, the object of which is the activity itself of consciousness" (Ibid., p. 246). According to Vygotsky, the ability to consciously realize one's own thoughts arises in the child not simply in the course of interaction, but in the course of his mastering scientific concepts in school with the help of the teacher: "... At the base of generalization lies generalization of one's own mental processes which leads to mastery of the processes. In this process, the decisive role of instruction is most prominent. Scientific concepts with their completely different relation to the object, mediated through other concepts with their internal hierarchic system of interrelations among themselves, are the area in which conscious realization of concepts, that is, their generalization and mastery, evidently appear first ... Thus, conscious realization arrives through the gate of scientific concepts" (Ibid., p. 247). Vygotsky assumes that in the child "the reason for his not consciously realizing concepts lies not in egocentrism, but in the unsystematized state of spontaneous concepts which due to this lack of conscious realization, must necessarily be unrealized and involuntary ... conscious realization of concepts is accomplished through the formation of a system of concepts based on certain relations of community among concepts ... by their very nature, scientific concepts assume a system" (Ibid., p. 250). Vygotsky also explains here that scientific concepts form a system and are given to the child in a system where the concept is in certain relations with concepts of a higher and lower order, etc., through which it is defined, and such verbal definition through other concepts is conscious realization. Thus, for the emergence of reflection, mastery of scientific knowledge and schooling is required.

The function of reflection, according to Vygotsky, consists in a person's "being sensitive to inconsistency, being able to synthesize logically, not just to range judgments, being able to make deductions" (Ibid., p. 249). Vygotsky believes that reflection is characteristic for thinking in scientific concepts which alone have the potential for such operations as "defining concepts, comparing and differentiating concepts ... establishing logical relations between concepts in opinions and conclusions" (Ibid., pp. 307–308). In the absence of systematized information and, correspondingly, reflection in thinking, "only those relations between concepts are possible that are possible between the objects themselves ... judgments have a purely empirical, verifying character" (Ibid., pp. 310–311). "Together with a system, relations of concept to concept appear ... in concepts, supra-empirical connections become possible" (Ibid. p. 309).

Thus, both Piaget and Vygotsky explain the appearance of reflection in the thinking of the child by social factors, and do not consider it as a "natural" feature of human thinking. However, while Piaget considers interaction a deciding factor, Vygotsky believes that the deciding factor is assimilation of a certain component of the culture in the narrow sense of the word—of scientific knowledge—in the process of schooling.

If we adopt Vygotsky's point of view, then we would be justified in assuming the presence of conscious reflection only in those societies in which there is scientific information and schooling. Only there would we be able to find thinking for which features indispensably requiring reflection are characteristic, sensitivity to logical inconsistency, possibility of logical analysis and deduction, defining concepts, etc. If Vygotsky is right, then the spread of schooling must be followed by the spread of conscious reflection and correspondingly, of new thinking operations.

2.4.2. The Connection between Conscious Reflection and the Solving of Science Problems. We have seen that both Piaget and Vygotsky believe that one of the functions of reflection is to enable a person to verify logically, the course of his thought. It is appropriate to ask the question: in what kind of activity is specifically logical verification of ideas indispensable? It is exactly here that the opinions of Piaget and Vygotsky diverge: Piaget assumes that a logical basis for opinions is necessary even in the arguments of children among themselves, but Vygotsky believes that this necessity arises for the first time in operations with scientific information, scientific concepts.

It is quite evident that besides logical verification and logical basis for ideas, there are other devices for verifying, refuting or demonstrating ideas and conclusions. Obviously, Piaget did not study concretely the arguments that children of various ages use in disputes among themselves and which by interiorization become disputes in "an internal dispute," in the deliberations of the child. Even without having at one's disposal appropriate empirical data, one may assert that children, just like adults, most often demonstrate their being right by references not to logic or lack of logic of various arguments that arise in disputes, but to their correspondence or lack of correspondence to reality or generally accepted opinion, to their inconsistency, by applying *argumentum ad hominem*, etc. In the absence of convincing empirical data, it is scarcely possible to agree with the opinion that for the emergence of the ability to provide a logical basis for his thoughts, it is sufficient for the child to participate in arguments with his peers that arise in (any) cooperative activity.

On the other hand, in scientific activity, it is clearly indispensable to argue logically, to examine the course of thought, and to demonstrate the logical rightness of a conclusion. On this point, A. N. Leont'ev (1964, pp. 92–93) writes: "... A loss by the internal theoretical activity of direct and continuous contact with material objects makes it necessary that experience actually be taken into account in the very process of thinking ... theoretical thinking cannot get along without the direction of some kind of prescriptions or rules that would serve it as an Ariadne's thread. Without this, wrote Leibnitz, our mind would not be able to travel the long road without losing the way. In conjunction with this road, which the process of cognition travels in the internal, strictly mental plane, becoming more complex and 'longer,' there arises the need to consciously check and regulate this process: in other words, the task arises of making thinking itself the subject of cognition. The science of thinking, logic, serves this task."

Apparently there is no doubt that reflection and logical confirmation of ideas are primarily characteristic specifically for scientific activity. In experimental studies of children solving mathematical problems, R. Skemp (1961) and L. L. Gurova (1976) showed what the functions of reflection specifically are in this case. According to Skemp, arithmetic (with certain exceptions) does not require reflection. (This was demonstrated earlier by Piaget's experimental results which indicated that 7- to 10-year-old children can solve arithmetic problems correctly without being at all able at the same time to explain how they got the answer or incorrectly reproducing the thinking that led to the solution. For example (Piaget, 1924, p. 193): "This board is 4 meters long. And this board is three times longer. How many meters long is it?— 12 meters.—How did you get this?—I added 2 and 2 and 2 and 2 and 2 and 2, every time, 2. —Why 2?—Because then you get 12.—Why did you take 2?—So as not to take a different number.") According to Skemp, algebra, on the other hand, always requires reflection: one must realize the concept, operation, methods of solving, one must know how to select or realize the methods of solving that are appropriate to one concrete problem or another. (On this difference between arithmetic and algebra, see also Vygotsky, 1982, p. 203). Gurova (1976) generalizes the results of the study she did of pupils solving geometry problems in the following way: "... necessary for effective solution is realization of the operations ... that govern the course of solving the problem and its result ... The process of solving the problem is, on the whole, a realized and effective process if the operations that regulate and direct the course of the solution and check the correctness of its result are consciously realized."

Of course, from what has been said, it does not follow that other types of activity besides science do not assume conscious regulation and conscious checking of the course of thought. Neither is there any doubt that a person who has the ability to consciously realize his thoughts can to some extent do this with any activity. However, the circumstance can scarcely be considered accidental that precisely in the course of learning to solve scientific (but not practical, artistic, etc.) problems, children begin consciously to regulate and check the course of the solution. It was demonstrated specifically with scientific problems that success in reaching a solution depends directly on a person's ability to reflect. Finally, specifically in science, as distinct from other types of activity, certain concepts must without fail be defined (realized), and this, as Vygotsky believed, is the prerequisite for realizing the connections between concepts established by thinking, that is, thinking operations.

Thus, there are certain bases for assuming that the need for reflection, for the conscious regulation of thinking and for logical verification of conclusions is inherent primarily in science, and not in just any kind of human activity. This circumstance compels doubt that the features mentioned are found in the thinking of people not exposed to schooling and to scientific information.

We must note that our discussion has somewhat simplified the matter. First, there are various types of arguments, including those among children. Probably the arguments of children in different cultures are not always identical. Thus, Bruner (1977, pp. 334–335) gives an example from the work of J. Gay and M. Cole: "Among Kpelle children, in an argument, the one who has the last word wins. ... This criterion is of a social character—the opponent was unable to find a retort—and not an objective character connected with the things in the surrounding world. The object of discussion is secondary to the personality of the discussant." Arguments of this kind are not uncommon in our culture also, but perhaps among Kpelle children they are more frequent (although it is unlikely that all their arguments are of this type). Evidently, various types of arguments may have various consequences for the development of thinking and, specifically, of reflection in children. Second, we can imagine that in those cultures in which there is science and schooling, the child even before going to school meets with scientific methods of arguing for a point of view—for example, parents call his attention to logical inconsistencies of his ideas. Third, psychological literature even now contains references to reflection in general while it is quite clear that there are actually various materials for reflection and various levels of reflection.

2.4.3. What We Know about Thinking as a Precursor of the Emergence of Reflection and Control over the Course of Thought. Leont'ev has been quoted above as saying that he connects the appearance of logic as a science of the laws of thinking with the historical development of theoretical thinking: verifying the course of thoughts, which is necessary for developed theoretical thinking, requires knowledge of the rules of thinking. In this connection, a number of questions arise related to problems of historical changes and cross-cultural differences in thinking: does knowledge of thinking exist in all cultures? is it identical everywhere? does thinking itself in its units and operations depend on what kind of knowledge about thinking the thinking person has? what role can knowledge of thinking play in the processes of thinking?

The development of knowledge about thinking has been studied in child psychology to a certain extent. In the 1920s, Piaget established that a child's knowledge of thinking develops and that it is qualitatively different from the knowledge of thinking that adults have. Piaget studied the concept of thinking in children of various ages (Piaget, 1973, pp. 49–76). Recently, the question of the development of children's knowledge of thinking and the possible effective role of this knowledge in the thinking processes has again been studied in child psychology within the framework of studies of so-called metacognition (for example, Flavell, 1976, 1981). The research work, however, is thus far limited basically to explaining how concepts of cognitive processes emerge, develop and are differentiated in children: "to think," "to know," "to guess" etc. (for example, Johnson and Maratsos, 1977; Johnson and Wellman, 1980). On the theoretical level, J. Flavell (1981) asserts that knowledge of cognitive processes is drawn upon mostly in those cases when: a) complex problems are being solved; b) when the situation is unusual or new to the person solving the problem; c) when the result is very significant; d) when the problem is difficult to solve. In works on metacognition with which we are familiar, no question was raised on specifically what kind of knowledge of cognitive processes the solving of one kind of problem or another requires and whether all of these types of problems require applying knowledge of thinking to the same degree. In child psychology thus far there are no data on what the connection is between the presence (or absence) and nature of general knowledge of thinking on the one hand, and the features of the thinking processes themselves on the other.

Meanwhile it is quite evident that people in contact with logical knowledge of thinking, familiar with the rules of drawing conclusions, having some concept that there are not only right and wrong ideas (in the sense of corresponding to reality), but also logically correct or incorrect ideas—that these people sometimes apply their knowledge in thinking and in verifying conclusions. It is no less evident that logical knowledge of thinking is not found in all cultures, and for this reason, it cannot be applied everywhere. Leibnitz carefully noted that "in Asia, Africa, and America among peoples independent of Europeans, almost never has anyone heard syllogisms mentioned" (Leibnitz, 1983, p. 492). If there is no knowledge of thinking in one culture or another, then a person belonging to that culture cannot in principle explicitly consider his own and others' conclusions from the point of view of their logical correctness. He evaluates them by a different method than people use who have such knowledge.

In other words, general knowledge of thinking present in different cultures, like particular devices for solving some concrete types of problems, are used as a means of thinking by those belonging to the cultures. How people in different cultures realize, regulate and verify the course of thought depends specifically on the means used which they assimilated from their cultures. The English anthropologist, R. Horton (1967) convincingly demonstrates that in traditional cultures of Africa, there is no explicit knowledge of thinking (see 3.3.2 below). If Horton is right, then we must assume that it would hardly be possible to find reflection, conscious regulation and verification of the course of thought in those cultures. In this case, it would be natural to pose a concrete question about the time and causes of the appearance in history of the ability to realize, consciously regulate and verify the course of thought.

The study of corresponding experimental data obtained in cross-cultural studies of thinking may help answer the question which research done in Europe and America failed to answer: is it actually schooling, systematic mastery of scientific knowledge and solving corresponding problems as a special type of activity that is the *sine qua non* condition for the emergence of those abilities, the appearance of which Vygotsky connected with mastery of scientific concepts? If this is so, then in subjects from traditional cultures and groups, we cannot expect to find conscious realization of their own thoughts (as distinct from realization of things), or operations that require movement along a "line of generalization" between concepts, which, according to Vygotsky, is possible only for scientific concepts, etc.

The new doctrine of "psychic unity of humanity" considered above (1.4), developed in the works of Levi–Strauss, is constructed on the assumed universality of the unconscious structures of thinking. The data and hypotheses cited above, however, speak of the actual role of conscious realization of thoughts in thinking itself and of the cross-cultural differences in means of this realization, regulation and verification of the course of thought. For this reason it seems incorrect to ignore the role of consciousness in thinking and its development. It would make sense in constructing theoretical conceptions of the historical development of thinking, just as in the interpretation of experimental data on cross-cultural differences and historical changes in thinking, to consider the possibility that in the history of a culture, the appearance of various forms of knowledge of thinking and the ability of consciously realize, regulate, and verify the course of thought may involve changes in the very processes of thinking.

2.5. Why Thinking Must Change through History and What Must Change in It (Conclusions). Before we move to a consideration of experimental data on the historical changes and cross-cultural differences in verbal thinking, we will turn once again to those basic questions, which we tried to answer in Chapter 1 by looking at old and modern theoretical conceptions of the historical development of thinking: why must thinking change through history? what must change in it?

Applying the activity approach to problems of the historical development of thinking compels us to believe that differences in the activity of people in different epochs and in different cultures are the general cause of historical changes and cross-cultural differences in thinking. Different types of activity confront people with problems that are partially different and for this reason require application of different types of thinking. Types of thinking characteristic for certain types of activity appear in history together with those types of activity and are transferred to subsequent generations by training. Since there are universal types of activity, there are also universal types of thinking. With changes in culture, the existing types of thinking are preserved to the extent to which they are functionally necessary under the new conditions. For example, scientific thinking, the function of which, roughly speaking, is explaining phenomena according to certain rules, cannot in principle replace artistic or ideological thinking that fulfills different functions in a culture and for an individual. Thinking in any culture and of any individual is heterogeneous according to the principle that a variety of types of activity and of problems characteristic of it requires a variety in the types of thinking applied.

After all that has been said, connecting the unique features of thinking in one culture or another with the features of the specific activity of the people (and not, let us say, the sensory experience or the structure of the society) may appear to be trivial. It seems natural to think that if we have to construct hypotheses on the nature of thinking in one epoch or another or in one culture or another, we must first of all ask how the people there were occupied, what kind of problems they had to solve, and on the basis of the data obtained, develop a hypothesis on the nature of the units and operations of thinking that they used.

For various reasons such a possible general solution of the problem of determining the historical development of verbal thinking has remained unnoticed by authors whose views we considered in Chapter 1. The most common reason for this is, evidently, that the investigators of historical changes and cross-cultural differences in thinking were rarely interested in what kind of functions verbal thinking fulfills or to what it is concretely applied in one culture or another.

Spencer believed that people in any cultures were involved in the struggle for life. Thinking is a means of adaptation to the environment and it changes to the extent that the environment changes. Spencer did not pose the question as to what people really do in one culture or another to determine specifically to what kind of problems they apply thinking. He approached the problems of the historical development of thinking from the sensualist position. An object exists that can be sensed; sensations are made into a perceived image; from the representations, a thought about the object is formed. How an object is thought of depends on the object itself. How people think in one culture or another depends on the materials and objects that surround them.

Absence of a functional approach to thinking is also characteristic of the ideas of Levy–Bruhl where they pertain to the reasons for the historical development of thinking. For Levy–Bruhl, thinking is not so much solving problems as man's producing and maintaining collective representations of his culture. Levy–Bruhl was not interested in cognitive functions of collective representations. Correspondingly, he did not succeed in explaining the reasons for the historical development of thinking.

In Vygotsky, we can find thoughts about the functional connection between features of thinking and the nature of the activity and the problems whose solution required the use of one type of thinking or another. However, he did not especially consider the problem of reasons for social-historical development of thinking and of the function of thinking in different cultures. The functional approach to the mind in Vygotsky's school was systematically developed in the works of Leont'ev.

We have seen that Levi–Strauss connected "wild" thinking with certain types of activity and "domesticated," with other types. Neither Spencer nor Levi–Bruhl nor Vygotsky cited this number of concrete types of activity as did Levi–Strauss. However, the connection between activity and thinking does not appear in the representation of Levi–Strauss as a causal connection. His conception does not permit explaining thinking through activity. We have also seen that Levi–Strauss considers the various types of thinking outside their historical development, deducing substantive traits of thinking from assumed principles of the working of the brain.

To Piaget, on the other hand, the idea of development was dear, but he was not at all interested in the concrete functions of thinking. For this reason, neither did he ascribe to culture any important role in the determination or development of thinking.

In studying the historical development of thinking, Bruner proceeds not so much from the function of thinking as from those means that thinking uses in any given culture.

The position of Cole is closest to that described in the present chapter. Cole believes that the situation determines the kind of thinking that will be used. For Cole, however, the idea of historical development of thinking is unacceptable just as is the idea of the existence of any substantial intercultural differences in thinking is not accepted. According to Cole, any person in any culture has available any operations of thinking and the differences consist in whether or not he applies them in solving one concrete problem or another. By the same token, activity determines applying or not applying thinking and not thinking itself with its units and operations.

We will turn to the problem of what must of necessity change in verbal thinking in the course of its historical development. Considering Vygotsky's typology, we saw that words are used variously in various types of activity. We might expect that in connection with the appearance of schooling in a culture, a qualitatively new type of verbal thinking would appear, which Vygotsky designated as thinking in scientific concepts. We must assume that reflection in thinking occurs only in those cultures in which science and schooling exist (since no indispensable connection between reflection and other than scientific types of activity has been established). Finally, there is no basis for believing that in the course of historical development, thinking had to change as a whole—it had to change only to the extent and in the part where this was required by new types of activity, new problems.

Naturally, questions concerning the reasons for and content of historical development of thinking can in fact be answered only on the basis of appropriate empirical data. We will now approach the consideration of these data.

CHAPTER 3

Schooling and the Development of Verbal Thinking: Toward an Interpretation of Results of Comparative Experimental Studies of the Thinking of People from Different Cultural Groups

Formerly, investigators of the historical development of thinking depended on indirect data on the nature of thinking of people from traditional cultures, on data on language, beliefs, folklore, pronouncements of people on various occasions, on their behavior. On the basis of these data, they made judgments about the processes of thinking, how concepts are formed, how the course of thought is structured. As early as the 1900s, certain experimental methods were applied in ethnopsychology that provided more direct access to the processes of thinking. In 1906, R. Thurnwald studied counting, verbal associations, and retelling of short stories among the Melanesians (Thurnwald, 1913, p. 20–42). If Thurnwald's experiments had a tentative and preliminary character, and if it was not clear why there must be differences in thinking and what caused them, then during the expeditions of A. R. Luria at the beginning of the 1930s, verbal thinking of people from traditional cultures was subjected to more purposeful and systematic experimental study on the basis of a specific theoretical position. Intensive study of the thinking of people in different cultures and cultural groups, using various experimental methods, began in the 1960s when cross-cultural studies split off into an independent branch of psychology.

Since that time, the methodological circle has been expanding, the number of studies has grown involving ever newer cultures and cultural groups. The existing experimental material in some cases already makes it possible to construct generalizations and to confirm certain general ideas about the reasons for and mechanisms of certain historical changes and cross-cultural differences in the processes of verbal thinking. In this chapter, on the basis of existing data (including our own experimental results), we will discuss certain changes in the verbal thinking of people from traditional cultural groups generated by schooling.

Among the various experimentally established differences in verbal thinking of people in different cultures and cultural groups, according to the unanimous opinion of investigators, the most substantial are the differences between subjects who attend school and those who do not. Schooling more than any other now known separate cultural factor transforms thinking and engenders intergroup differences in it. We will note only that to some extent the exclusive role of schooling in transforming thinking (as it enters into these studies) may be advanced also by the circumstance that most of the methods currently used in cross-cultural studies were initially developed for studying the development of children's thinking in "modern" cultures. The development of a child's thinking in these cultures is inseparably connected with schooling. Moreover, in child psychology, the object that gets the most attention, somewhat one-sidedly it seems to us, is the development of scientific thinking, that is, of a process in which school plays the major role. Accordingly, these methods when used in cross-cultural studies are most sensitive with respect to those changes and differences in thinking that are promoted specifically by schooling, and not by other cultural factors.

Being interested here primarily in the effect of schooling on thinking, in the thinking of adults from traditional groups, we will look more for what is lacking rather than what is there. The center of our attention will be not that thinking which people in cultures and cultural groups who have not attended school use in their various forms of practical and theoretical activity, but mainly those changes that the thinking of an adult or child from a traditional culture undergoes when he finds himself in school. Such a subject for study seems to be no less significant than thinking which these people used before schooling and which fellow-tribesmen who have not gone to school use. Positive experimental data on the latter are relatively sparse at present. We know more about its "deficiencies" in comparison with scientific thinking than about the patterns of formation, development and functioning of its units and operations. The existing data on the thinking of people from traditional cultures and groups will serve as a background for our study of changes in thinking and not as a basic object of study. This can be explained by the fact that we are interested primarily in problems concerning the reasons for and content of development of verbal thinking affected by schooling.

M. Cole (1985, pp. 150–152) reproaches Luria because in his studies at the beginning of the 1930s, he paid no attention to the concrete types of activity and forms of socializing of traditional groups. As we have seen (1.5.2), Cole believes that features of people's thinking may be established only by detailed knowledge and consistent consideration of the cultural context in which it is actually applied. This observation is absolutely correct. However, Luria's purpose was to study not so much the character of the thinking of people in traditional groups, as its transformation resulting from social and cultural changes. It is understood that this assumes also the study of thinking in traditional groups, but in his work Luria deliberately placed the emphasis specifically on establishing the changes taking place. Our work in this sense continues Luria's work in the direction of a more precise disclosure of the character, dynamics and function of the changes that occur in thinking under the influence of schooling. We might say that in this chapter, we will consider the thinking of people who have not attended school only to the extent necessary for understanding the origin, function and character of certain substantial features of verbal thinking of people who have attended school.

In school, an individual assimilates, first of all, scientific knowledge and habits of solving "scientific" (school) problems. For this reason, the data considered in this chapter enable us to explain the role of specifically those factors in the formation of thinking. Studying the changes in the thinking of children and adults, who had no contact with scientific knowledge before schooling, we learn which features of the thinking of people in "modern" societies owe their existence to the circumstance that science plays so important a role in these societies. Such studies could have been done in Europe or America if there had been a sufficient number of mentally healthy subjects who had not attended school and had never been in contact with scientific information, discussions, or problems. But these differences in thinking can be studied in a more "pure form" in people from traditional cultures who knowingly come into contact with scientific information and problems in school for the first time.

In this chapter, we have in mind schooling of the European type. It would be extremely interesting to compare its effect on verbal thinking with the effect of other systems of schooling, for example, the Islamic. Unfortunately, experimental data on the effects of alternative systems are at present inadequate for a systematic comparison.

For various reasons, our subject for detailed discussion will be those changes in solving simple syllogistic problems and in units of verbal thinking that are the result of schooling.

3.1. The Origin of Syllogistic Reasoning. For a number of reasons, it seems expedient to consider the effect of schooling on operations of verbal thinking primarily on the basis of changes that occur in the processes of solving simple syllogistic problems.

First, beginning as early as with the expeditions of A. R. Luria, these problems were used more than any others in comparative studies of verbal thinking in various cultures. Because of this, we have a sufficient amount of experimental data to use as a basis for some generalizations and for confirming some hypotheses on the reasons for and nature of changes that occur as a result of schooling. Syllogistic reasoning has long been a popular subject for study in general and child psychology, and for this reason there is a certain theoretical and experimental background for interpreting cross-cultural differences and historical changes.

Second, it is exactly in solving syllogistic problems that the most substantial differences were found in responses, in methods of solving, and in methods of providing a basis for the solutions between those attending and those not attending school. In other words, syllogistic problem solving is material that is particularly sensitive with respect to schooling.

Third, in primary school, logic is not taught as a school subject. For this reason, neither the subjects from traditional groups not attending school nor those attending school have special knowledge of logic nor have they been taught to solve syllogistic problems. Thus, there is no need to establish and "subtract" explicit, special knowledge that some might have and others might not have. Syllogistic problems differ in this from many other problems that pupils are taught to solve in school (problems in mathematics, physics, or chemistry, for example).

Fourth, regardless of the many works studying the solution of verbal-syllogistic problems by European and American children of various ages, thus far no light has been cast on the question of exactly what kind of factors engender and develop the ability to solve these problems. Some investigators see this ability as the result of general practical experience of the child, others stress the role of socializing with adults or, conversely, with peers, and still others stress the role of schooling in the formation of this ability (see the review: T. Tulviste, 1985). Nor is the status of syllogistic reasoning clear—are we dealing with universals, with an indispensable basic part of human thinking, or is it a specific thinking operation typical for scientific thinking? In cross-cultural studies, a comparison was made between experimental results of people having no contact and those having various degrees of contact with schooling and other cultural factors. It might be expected that these data would make it possible to identify precisely the potential role of separate factors in the establishment and development of the ability to solve simple syllogistic problems and in determining the status of syllogistic reasoning.

Fifth, as we have seen in Chapter 1, since the time of Levy–Bruhl, there have been endless arguments on the logic, prelogic, and alternative logic of thinking in traditional cultures. This most knotty circle of problems can also be approached by considering the results of experiments in which people from traditional and "modern" cultures solved simple logical problems.

Sixth, it was established in child psychology that children of different ages realize different aspects of simple syllogistic problem solving to varying degrees, and the degree of realization is significantly related to a correct solution (see T. Tulviste, 1985). Thus, we are dealing with problems in the solving of which reflection is known to play an effective role, and, according to the views of L. S. Vygotsky (see 2.4), reflection appears in thinking specifically as a result of schooling. This makes it possible to consider the problem of the connection between schooling and the appearance of reflection in thinking on the basis of this experimental material.

3.1.1. Basic Data on Simple Syllogistic Problem-Solving by People from Different Cultural Groups. Suggestions Regarding the Reasons for the Differences.
The first comparative study of the solving of syllogistic problems by people belonging to different cultural groups was conducted by A. R. Luria at the beginning of the 1930s (Luria, 1971, 1974). It was included in the program of studies, developed by Luria and Vygotsky, on changes in the minds of people that were caused by social and cultural transformations in Central Asia. Under

the direct influence of Luria, subsequent studies were done in the 1960s and 1970s in Liberia (Cole et al., 1971; Cole and Scribner, 1977; Scribner, 1975, 1977), in Taimur (Tulviste, 1978, 1979), in Yucatan (Sharp, Cole and Lave, 1979), in isolated mountain regions of Kirghizia (Tamm, Tulviste, 1980; T. Tulviste, 1985), and again in Liberia (Scribner and Cole, 1981). The results of this work can be compared relatively easily since all the investigators used simple syllogistic problems with supplementary questions and required the subject to give not only the answer, but also a basis for it.

Two experimental protocols will serve as an example. "A syllogism is presented: in the Far North where there is snow, all the bears are white. Novaya Zemlya is in the Far North and there is always snow there. What color will the bears be?

—There are different animals there. (The syllogism is repeated.)
—I don't know, I saw a black bear, I didn't see any others... Each place has the same kind of animals: if it's white, then the animals are white, if it's yellow, then the animals are yellow.
—But what kind of bears are there in Novaya Zemlya?
—We always talk only about what we see; what we don't see, we don't talk about.
—What follows from what I have said? (The syllogism is repeated.)
—This is the problem: our czar is not like your czar, and your czar is not like our czar. What you have said can be answered by someone who has seen, and someone who has not seen can say nothing about it.
—But according to what I have said, that in the north where there is always snow the bears are white, is it possible to figure out what kind of bears there are in Novaya Zemlya?
—If a person is 60 or 80 years old and has seen a white bear and tells about it, then we can believe him, but I never saw and so I can't say. This is my last word on this. If any one has seen, then he will say, if he has not seen, then he can't say anything! (A young Uzbek comes forward and concludes: 'From what you say, the bears there are white.')
—Well, which one of you is right?
—A rooster does what he knows how to do. What I know, that I say, and I can't say anything else!" (Luria, 1974, pp. 112–113).

The second protocol: "Experimenter: At one time a spider went to a feast. He was told to answer this question before he could eat any of the food. The question is: Spider and black deer always eat together. Spider is eating. Is black deer eating?

Subject: Were they in the bush?
Experimenter: Yes.

Subject: Were they eating together?

 Experimenter: Spider and black deer always eat together. Spider is eating. Is black deer eating?

Subject: But I was not there. How can I answer such a question?

Experimenter: Can't you answer it? Even if you were not there, you can answer it. (Repeats the question.)

Subject: Oh, oh, black deer is eating.

Experimenter: What is your reason for saying that black deer was eating?

Subject: The reason is that black deer always walks about all day eating green leaves in the bush. Then he rests for a while and gets up again to eat. (Cole and Scribner, 1974, p. 162)

In the first case, the subject was a 37-year-old illiterate peasant from a Kashgar village (Central Asia), in the second case, a village chief from the Kpelle tribe in Liberia. In the first case, when the facts referred to were not familiar to the subject through personal experience, the responses were never appropriate. In the second case, the response in the final analysis was right specifically because of the subject's knowledge of the reality with which the problem was concerned. Of course, what is of interest here is not so much that the answer is right or wrong, as how it was arrived at.

Such results are typical for all traditional cultures and groups in which experiments with syllogistic problems have been done. S. Scribner writes: "... certain qualitative aspects of performance are so similar that it is often difficult to distinguish the translated interview protocol of an Uzbekistanian from that of a Vai–cultural and geographical distance notwithstanding" (Scribner, 1977).

The differences between subjects from different traditional cultures appear insignificant while substantial differences are found (including within specific cultures) between experimental results of two groups of subjects: traditional (i.e., those with a traditional culture and economic activity not exposed to schooling, literacy and economic innovations) and the "advanced" (literate, with some schooling, involved in "modern" economics).

The results of these experiments usually evoke two different, typical reactions. Some see in them evidence for the underdevelopment of thinking in people from traditional cultures, their low mental abilities. Others reject these results maintaining that the methodology of the experiment is evidently not suitable for use in traditional cultures, that the subjects do not understand what is expected of them, etc.

Reference to underdevelopment or low capabilities explains nothing. The same subjects cleverly and successfully solve other experimental and nonexperimental problems. Moreover, it isn't as if they were trying to solve these problems in the same way as educated people (that is, people with schooling), but do it less well. No, they try to reach a solution by a different method not expected from the point of view of an educated person. But why?

Maintaining that syllogistic problems are not suitable for use in the study of the thinking of people from traditional cultures is, in a certain sense, true. These problems clearly are strange to the subjects, not in content, but in their type, their form. All investigators evidently sensed this inadequacy even before doing the experiments, for they used the most simple syllogistic problems and not problems, let us say, of the type: "Some academics are parents. All parents are drivers. What conclusion can you reach?" (example from a study done with American subjects—Johnson–Laird, 1982). It is intuitively clear that even if we make the task more suitable in content for traditional subjects (replacing academics with peasants and drivers with hunters), the form will still not be suitable for them. So in a certain sense, the methodology has already been adapted for traditional subjects in syllogistic problems that are the simplest in form. With problems that are more complex in form, the differences between the results of those attending school and those not attending school would be definitely much sharper. But, as we have seen, even simple problems were not suitable. It seems to us that it is exactly this inadequacy that is of primary interest. Why are these problems strange to people who had not attended school, but suitable for people of the same cultural group who had attended school for two or three years? We believe that in cross-cultural studies of thinking, the suitability of experimental tasks does not always appear as a prerequisite preliminary condition of research, as must be the case, for example, in measuring intelligence, but itself comprises part of the object of the research. If we know which problems are suitable and which are not from the point of view of the thinking of people in a certain culture, then we already know quite a bit about their thinking. Of special interest are the reasons for suitability or lack of it of one set of problems or another to the thinking of people in different cultural groups. Why do people who easily contend with much more "complex" problems in life such as resolving social conflicts, treating somatic and mental illnesses, etc., only by chance solve syllogistic problems, simplest from the point of view of an educated person, whose content is familiar to them from personal experience, but do not at all solve problems that are similar in form if they have no experience with the reality referred to in the problems? Using special experiments, Luria (1974) and Scribner (1975) established that subjects from traditional cultures do not remember correctly the premises of a syllogism and the supplementary questions presented to them. On the basis of data obtained on these subjects' solving and remembering syllogistic problems and on the way they explain their solutions, Luria established the following reasons that interfere with their verbal-logical thinking: 1) they do not trust the initial premises if these do not reproduce their personal sensual experience, and they refuse to "accept" them; 2) for the subjects, premises do not have a general character, but are perceived by them more as particular, isolated information that does not form a single logical system,—accordingly, the thinking of the subject cannot move within this system that is so clear to the educated person (Luria, 1974, pp. 119–120). What is the reason for these characteristics of the thinking of traditional subjects in solving simple syllogistic problems?

It would probably be more correct to pose the question differently: in solving such problems, what is it that compels and allows passage beyond the bounds "of direct practical experience?"—as Luria puts it (Ibid.).

At the level of sociological correlates, the answer to this question is already contained in Luria's work: foremost is schooling. The results of later studies confirm this (other factors of culture sometimes also play a certain role, but by no means as important a role as schooling). Two or three years of schooling seems to be sufficient for the following two changes in solving verbal-syllogistic problems: 1) the percentage of correct responses increases significantly. As a rule, subjects from traditional groups solve problems with a content familiar to them at the level of chance (that is, they solve approximately half the problems correctly). In school, the percentage of correct responses begins to increase until practically all simple syllogistic problems are solved correctly; 2) the subjects begin to provide "theoretical" explanations for their responses. Beginning with the work of Luria in cross-cultural studies, two types of explanations for responses were distinguished: a) "outside the syllogism" (Luria) or "empirical" (Scribner) in which the subject explains his conclusion through actual correctness of the premises and conclusion, which assumes knowledge of the reality involved in the problem, and the subjects frequently bring in additional data about the reality that the problem itself does not contain; b) "within the syllogism" (Luria) or "theoretical" (Scribner) in which the subject draws only on the data contained in the problem and on the logical correctness of the conclusion from the given premises. For subjects from traditional groups, "empirical" explanations for responses are characteristic while "theoretical" explanations begin to predominate as a result of schooling (Scribner, 1975, 1977).

The explanations specifically are used to evaluate whether the subject solved the problem through "real" syllogistic reasoning, that is, on the basis of its form and logical relations between the premises and conclusion, or whether he based his response on his previous knowledge of the reality involved in the premises and in the supplementary question.

The results of experimental studies indicate that the "theoretical" explanation is almost always accompanied by a correct response while the "empirical" explanations are connected at random with correct and incorrect responses as well as with refusals to solve the problem (Scribner, 1977; Tulviste, 1978; Sharp, Cole and Lave, 1979; Tamm and Tulviste, 1980).

Beginning with the work of Luria on the study of verbal syllogistic problem-solving by people from traditional cultures and groups, together with problems with a content familiar to the subject, problems were used in which reality and circumstances were unfamiliar. As we have seen in the first protocol cited, the subjects sometimes refused to solve such problems. They solve problems with a content familiar to them from personal experience and give an "empirical" explanation for their responses. As distinct from this, "advanced" subjects solve problems with any content, and their responses are usually accompanied by "theoretical" explanations.

Thus, together with an increase in number of correct solutions and predominance (or emergence) of "theoretical" explanations, yet another substantial change can be identified that occurs in the solving of syllogistic problems under the influence of schooling: ability to solve syllogistic problems with any content emerges. Finally, the results of people from traditional backgrounds attending school do not differ any more from results of people from "modern" cultures in these experiments.

Why does schooling evoke such changes in the solving of syllogistic problems? How do these changes occur and what is their nature—are we dealing here with a transfer of skills the subject is already using from familiar material to unfamiliar material (that is, to problems in which the content is unfamiliar to him from personal experience) or with the emergence of a qualitatively new skill, new method of solving these problems?

Luria (1974) links the differences in experimental results of traditional and "advanced" subjects to a transition from practical to theoretical activity resulting from social and cultural transformations. However, theoretical (or "non-practical") types of activity undoubtedly also exist in traditional cultures. In their folklore and beliefs, people from traditional cultures consistently go beyond the limits of "immediate practical experience," although they do not do this in solving syllogistic problems in experimental situations. Possibly the differences in experimental results might be explained by differences between the types of theoretical activity that are common in traditional and "modern" societies and by the different functional significance of the syllogistic conclusion in these types of activity. On the basis of experimental data, we may assume that the types of activity common in traditional cultures compel people to relate both the premises and the conclusions to their own knowledge or notions of external reality and do not require them to reach conclusions from premises whose content is not familiar to them from personal experience and in the truth of which they have no confidence. On the other hand, in "modern" societies there evidently exist types of theoretical activity and problems that require relating deduction to premises and drawing conclusions from premises based on a reality with which the subject is not familiar from personal experience.

Scribner (1977) links the differences between results of subjects attending and not attending school with the circumstance that in school problems must be solved, in arithmetic, for example, in which the "empirical" approach characteristic of people from traditional groups does not lead to a solution. "We might say that the areas in which special sign systems are used present a person with 'arbitrary' problems, that is, problems that flow from a system that lies beyond the bounds of the pupil's personal experience and which must be accepted as a given." Scribner also indicates that further research must show which "nonschool" types of activity and, specifically, which types of activity common in traditional cultures develop a logical method of reasoning.

Actually, if only from the experimental protocols presented at the beginning of this chapter, it is quite evident that school problems cannot be solved and the correctness of the solution cannot be confirmed in the way subjects from traditional groups did it. If they had tried, for example, to solve problems of the type, "One train leaves town A to go to town B at a rate of 60 km per hour, and another ..." etc., depending on personal experience and knowledge of railroads, their responses would probably be something like: "I don't know. I have never been in town A." Or: "No train travels from A to B at that speed." Or: "The trains meet at 6:00 p.m. at station B; I was there and saw it, so I know." Such attempts at solution would be meaningless and unsuccessful. Problems of this type can be solved only on the basis of data presented in the problem itself and introducing other data on the reality involved in the problem only confounds the solution. Relating the data presented in the problem and the solution to reality does not help here, elements of the data must be related to each other. In other words, such problems assume controlling the correctness of the course of solution, that is, the course of thought. This, it seems to us, is an essentially new method of obtaining and confirming knowledge, and must not be considered as a higher stage in the development of the method of solving problems applied by people from traditional groups in experiments with syllogistic problems. There is some basis for assuming that the "school" method of solving problems is not simply a transfer of an available skill to new material that is not familiar to the subject from personal experience, as M. Cole and his colleagues believe. In both cases the subjects proceed from completely different knowledge. Traditional subjects proceed from knowledge of the external reality and confirm the truth of the premises and deduction, that is, their correspondence to reality, while in the "school" method of solving the problems, the subjects proceed from some knowledge on the method of solving the problems, that is, on thinking, and they confirm not the truth, but the logical correctness of the deduction (regardless of the fact that the words, "logic" and "logical" are unknown to them).

Now we can ask the question as to why pupils in school are being taught to solve problems that require new methods of solution which are typically confirmed not by validity, but by logical correctness of the solution. Knowing how to solve "school" problems is, of course, not an end in itself. In school, pupils are taught primarily scientific information and scientific thinking. It would be impossible to create, confirm and use scientific information if every separate deduction had to be compared each time with reality or with available information on reality. It would be impossible to imagine constructing a scientific theory or even solving a small problem in applied science if all intermediate results would have to be directly verified. There is another possibility: students are being taught to confirm whether or not the course of thought is proper, whether the conclusion follows from the premises, and the solution, from the data presented in the problem, etc. In other words, the correspondence of the process of solving the problem to certain laws of thinking must be confirmed. N. Minick (1980), supplementing our ideas (first proposed in Tulviste, 1978), indicates that this type of reasoning fulfills still other functions in scientific activity. For example, on the basis of hypothetical premises conclusions are drawn, the validity of which are subject to confirmation (through observation or experiment) so that a judgment on the correctness of the original premises might be made subsequently, based on whether the conclusion was or was not valid.

Apparently, we might go even further and assert that only in this way can we imagine the movement of thought in the ideal worlds constructed in various sciences in which there are only ideal objects and ideal relations between them modelling certain aspects of the real world. Obviously, these ideal objects and relations, for example, in mechanics, cannot be "known" through direct experience. It is appropriate to recall the words of A. N. Leont'ev (1964, pp. 92–93) cited above (2.4) that in view of the certain detachment of scientific thinking from the material world, it needs certain rules that allow controlling and regulating the process of thinking. Thus, we may assert that school problems are used to engender and develop in the pupils a method of obtaining, confirming and applying information specific to science. (It is perfectly obvious that what has been said is not a characterization of all thinking used in science. For us, it is important here to indicate only one essential difference between scientific and everyday thinking.)

On the basis of the described, characteristic trait of scientific thinking, we can deduce a hypothetical explanation of the difference between the results of traditional and "advanced" subjects in experiments with syllogistic problems. Why, specifically, do those attending school solve syllogistic problems with any content while subjects from traditional groups do not attempt to solve problems with a content that is not familiar from personal experience? This may be explained by the fact that traditional subjects can rely only on information about the reality specified in the problem, while subjects attending school rely on their knowledge of thinking, on the laws of deduction. The latter method of solving problems does not assume a knowledge of the realities involved in the problems. The subjects who attended school solve similar problems even if they are constructed not of words, but of symbols which represent no specific reality. Such problems are frequently used in studies with

European and American subjects, but they have never been used in cross-cultural studies.

Experimental data show that traditional subjects solve simple syllogistic problems with a familiar content correctly in half the cases on an average, that is at a chance level, while the educated solve them with almost no errors. We may assume that this difference can also be explained by the difference in methods of solving the problems. Educated subjects apply the "school" method here also, which ensures independence of the answer from the "actual situation." Although the answers of the two groups of subjects in half the cases were the same, they could be obtained by different methods. This hypothesis is supported by questions traditional subjects asked the experimenter and the basis they gave for their solutions.

Thus, we may assume that the differences in experimental results of traditional and educated subjects in solving simple syllogistic problems are due to the circumstance that in the latter, the school engendered a new type of verbal thinking corresponding functionally to working with scientific information and solving scientific problems. However, this point of view requires proof.

It is unacceptable to psychologists and ethnologists proceeding from the doctrine of psychic unity of humanity. In their opinion, there are no qualitative differences in the thinking of people of different cultures, including those attending and not attending school. These authors perceive the manifestation of Eurocentrism in the identification of qualitative differences in thinking. They believe that all people have identical thought processes, and the difference consists only in whether these are or are not used in solving one set of concrete problems or another. The role of schooling is reduced in this case to this: the person from a traditional culture attending school learns to apply his already existing thinking operations to new material in solving problems that he never encountered in a traditional environment. We have seen that in approximately half of all cases, traditional subjects correctly solve simple syllogistic problems with a familiar content. From the point of view under consideration, the changes in solving these problems resulting from school influence can be explained by the fact that a person begins to solve problems with a familiar content ever better and transfers his skills to problems with an unfamiliar content.

If we consider only the responses of subjects to syllogistic problems (but not their questions to the experimenter and not the basis for the answers that they put forth), then such an explanation would agree with experimental data as well as the hypothesis on the qualitative transformation of thinking under the influence of schooling. And the preference in this case would, of course, have to be given to the simpler explanation that does not assume the existence of qualitative differences between the thinking of people from different cultural groups.

How can we determine which of the two ideas about changes occurring in the thinking of people from a traditional culture who are influenced by schooling is correct? Apparently, to do this, we need to try to study the changes themselves in the dynamics with a group of subjects who are already in school, but do not yet solve simple syllogistic problems of any content without errors. As a rule, in cross-cultural studies, solving syllogistic problems was limited to comparison of results of traditional subjects with those of subjects attending school who no longer experienced difficulties in solving the problems.

3.1.2. A Study of How School Children Coming from a Traditional Environment Solve Simple Syllogistic Problems. The two general ideas described above about changes occurring in simple syllogistic problem solving by people from traditional cultures when they attend school assume different dynamics of change in thinking. If the effect of schooling only extends the sphere of application of already existing thinking operations, then we may assume that a child from a traditional culture first begins at school to solve syllogistic problems with a content familiar to him from personal experience with greater success, and then (as he becomes familiar with new "school" information) gradually begins also to solve problems with school realities. After two or three years of schooling, as existing data indicate, he can solve simple syllogistic problems with any content equally well. However, there cannot be an instant in which he would be able to solve the problems of unfamiliar, school content better than problems with a familiar content.

If we adopt the second point of view described above, then a different picture appears. In school, a person is confronted by problems that cannot be solved with the types of thinking that he has. For this reason, a new type of thinking is formed, functionally appropriate to these problems. Most likely, the acquired type of thinking is initially applied specifically to the new problems for the solving of which it is intended since they could not be solved otherwise. "Old" problems, that is, those that could be solved by previously existing types of thinking will still be solved with these types. Later the new type of thinking may in principle be used with respect to them also.

In order to confirm which of these two representations is correct, we can do the following experiment. We will present children from a traditional culture attending school with syllogistic problems of everyday content and school content, and we will see which they will solve better. If the first point of view—a change in thinking pertains only to the sphere of its application—is justifiable, then the subject will not solve problems with a school content better than those with an everyday content. The second point of view, on the other hand, compels the assumption that to problems of school content, unfamiliar from personal experience, the subject will apply the just acquired, new method that will ensure relatively successful solution of the problems, and to problems of everyday, familiar content, he will apply the old method which, as we have seen, frequently leads to errors. Thus, the subjects who have mastered the new method of solving problems, but have not yet applied it to problems of both contents, must solve problems with unfamiliar content better than those with familiar content.

V. I. Shestakov and I did an experiment of this kind in the spring of 1977 on the Taimur Peninsula in the village of Volochanka (the Taimur [Dolgano Nenets] Autonomous Region). (The results of this work are treated in detail in Tulviste, 1978, 1979; a short review in Tulviste, 1981b). Our subjects were 35 pupils of grades II–VI. Most of them were Nganasans. This is a small nation (approximately 1000 people), the northernmost in Eurasia, occupied almost exclusively with their traditional types of economic activity: hunting, fishing, and reindeer herding. (An ethnographic description is contained in Popov, 1948, 1984). Attempts to make the Nganasan people give up their nomadic life had no success and they are still nomads. Children learn traditional types of activity and traditional intellectual culture at home.

The experiments Shestakov and I did with adult Nganasans showed that they solve simple syllogistic problems with the same results as people in other traditional cultures. Attending school, the child finds himself in a cultural environment completely new to him and is exposed for the first time to scientific information and scientific thinking. (In recent years, in conjunction with universal schooling, such a sharp contrast probably does not exist.) For this reason, it was possible here to study in a quite pure form the changes that take place under the influence of schooling in the solving of syllogistic problems by children from a traditional culture.

The experiment consisted of orally presenting to each subject 10 simple verbal syllogistic problems; each problem of everyday content (for example: "Saiba and Nakupte always drink tea only together. Saiba drinks tea at three in the afternoon. Does Nakupte drink tea at three o'clock or not?") was followed by a problem of "school" (scientific) content (for example, "All precious metals do not rust. Molybdenum is a precious metal. Does molybdenum rust or not?"). After the subject solved the problem, we asked him for the basis of his solution ("Why do you think so?").

The experiments were done in Russian. The children know the names of both home and school objects very well, but for many of the school objects there are no Nganasan names. Lessons in school are conducted in Russian from the very beginning.

Of the 35 subjects, judging by the explanations or justifications or bases they offered for their answers, 9 solved all 10 problems using the "school" method, and 4 did not use it at all. We were interested in the results of the other 22 subjects who solved some of the problems with the "school" method and some with the "everyday" method. This group of subjects could literally be called transitional. (Outside the group, on the one hand, fall subjects who simply did not use the "school" method, and on the other hand, those pupils in the higher grades (and some in the lower) who solved all problems with the "school" method.)

Which problems did subjects in this "transitional" group solve more successfully, those with an everyday content or those with a school content? We proceeded from the conception of Vygotsky that in school, an essentially new type of thinking emerges, thinking in scientific concepts. Our hypothesis presupposed a somewhat unnatural result: the children would have to be more successful in solving a problem that involved an object as strange for them (and for the experimenters [1]) as molybdenum than a problem that involved a matter as familiar and everyday for the Nganasan children as tea drinking.

In 90 cases of 110, subjects from the "transitional" group gave correct solutions to problems with a "school" content, and based their solutions "theoretically" in 59 cases. (In the remaining cases, the bases were of an "empirical" type or were absent.) Problems with an "everyday" content were solved correctly in 81 cases of 110, and 26 "theoretical" bases were provided. In all cases, "theoretical" bases accompanied only correct answers.

Thus, the subjects from the "transitional" group gave significantly more "theoretical" bases for solving problems of the "school" type than those of the "everyday" type. Table 1 shows that of 22 subjects, only 2 gave more "theoretical" bases for solving "everyday" problems than "school" problems, and 3 gave the same number of "theoretical" bases for solving both "school" and "everyday" problems. The other 17 subjects gave more "theoretical" bases for "school" problems than for "everyday" problems.

These results lead to the conclusion that practically error-free solution of simple syllogistic problems based on relating deduction to premises initially emerges in the sphere of school (scientific) information and is transferred only later to the everyday sphere. First, children successfully solve the problem with molybdenum, and only later the one involving tea drinking.

The data presented contradict the idea, common in both child psychology and comparative studies of the thinking of people in various cultures and cultural groups, that subjects would always solve—and must solve—problems with a familiar content more successfully than problems with an unfamiliar content. A considerable number of comparative studies have been done (including studies with syllogistic problems and with classification) in which the experimental material was specially manipulated to establish the connection between successful solving of problems and the degree of a subject's familiarity with the experimental material. Sometimes the subjects solved problems with a familiar content better, and sometimes the degree of familiarity with the material was not reflected in the results (see a discussion of these problems in Glick, 1975; LCHC, 1983). However, we do not know of a single work in which subjects would solve problems with an unfamiliar content more successfully than problems with a familiar content.

Tabel 1. Results of experiments with syllogistic problems with pupils from the Village of Volochanka

Number of "theoretical" bases for solving problems with a "school" content	Number of subjects	Average number of "theoretical" bases for solving problems with an "everyday" content, same subjects
5	2	2
4	5	1
3	5	1.6
2	5	0.6
1	4	1.25
0	1	1
	22	

Number of "theoretical" bases for solving problems with an "everyday" content	Number of subjects	Average number of "theoretical" bases for solving problems with an "school" content, same subjects
5	0	–
4	1	5
3	2	3.5
2	4	1.9
1	8	1.9
0	7	3
	22	

According to Piaget, formal operations appear in a person's thinking first in the area with which he is very familiar: in a scholar, in solving scientific problems, and in an auto mechanic, in repairing a car. In experimental studies of Piaget's phenomena in different cultures and cultural groups, investigators looked for concrete and formal operations in areas of knowledge and skills familiar to the subjects. It seems to us that this procedure is justified only to the extent that solving problems related to these areas presupposes the inevitable use of this kind of operations. It is apparent that many types of activity can be carried out without using such operations. Quite probably in some concrete traditional cultures not one of the types of existing activity requires using formal operations. In this case, there is evidently every reason to expect the emergence of this qualitatively new stage in the development of thinking, as Piaget describes it, not in areas familiar to the subject, but conversely, specifically in that "unfamiliar" area where the use of formal operations is functionally indispensable. At this point, without discussing the problem of the expediency of using such categories as concrete or formal operations in describing the changes in thinking that occur in school, we will note that in a certain sense, the new thinking operations that emerge under the influence of schooling emerge specifically in order to facilitate operations with objects unfamiliar to us from personal experience: free-falling bodies, atoms and electrons, rare metals, the number π (0.314...), etc.

The position of M. Cole, as we have seen above (1.5.2), is in many respects opposite that of Piaget. However, it also leads to the conclusion that functional systems are initially applied to objects familiar to the people of the given culture. Later they begin to apply them to new, less familiar objects, which constitutes development of thinking. Common to the representation of Piaget and Cole is the fact that both consider as natural the presence of any thinking operations in people engaged in any spheres of activity and belonging to any cultures—without, it seems to us, sufficient theoretical bases for this. There are reasons for doubting the identity of thinking operations of the people for whom "going beyond the information given" (Bruner) means entry into the world of myths and tales and of those for whom it also means entry into the world of science.

It seems to us that the approach outlined here, leading to the work of Leont'ev, differs advantageously from the approaches of Piaget and Cole in that it allows constructing a basis for a hypothesis on the cases in which one type of thinking or another "must" emerge, and in which it need not. There is scarcely any basis for believing that the more familiar we are with one reality or activity or another—no matter how simple these might be—the more "complex" will be the type of thinking we will use.

The experimental results presented cannot be explained if we proceed from the assumption that development of thinking under the influence of schooling is reduced to extending the area of applying existing thinking operations from the familiar realities to the unfamiliar. The results confirm the second hypothesis described above according to which a substantially new method of thinking emerges in the sphere of scientific information and problems which is functionally appropriate to them and can later be applied also in the sphere of everyday information and problems.

Can we, however, assert that the "school" method of solving simple syllogistic problems actually is unequivocally connected with schooling? Is it really true that not one person from a traditional culture, not attending school, has never solved syllogistic problems with a similar method? The experimental data of Scribner (1977) speak against this. Subjects not attending school also gave "theoretical" bases for solutions, although significantly more rarely than those who had attended school. Some of Scribner's subjects from traditional groups even gave "theoretical" bases for <u>all</u> of their solutions. At the same time, she admits that under conditions of "extreme isolation of the village," it is possible to find exclusively "empirical" bases also. This can be understood thus: if any group is a strictly traditional group, that is, one with no contact with social and cultural innovations, then in similar experiments, we would obtain only "empirical" bases. Sharp, Cole and Lave also admit a similar "gradation" of traditionality (1979, p. 54): "Adult Maya from Ticul respond significantly better than a similar group from the smaller and more traditional town of Ramonal" (authors' emphasis, P.T.)

How can we deal with those "less traditional" subjects who had not attended school, but, regardless of this, gave "theoretical" bases? Two circumstances compel us to believe that between the "theoretical" bases and scientific information and problems there may nevertheless be a definite connection as follows from the discussion presented in this section.

First, scientific information and scientific thinking is spread not only through school, but also outside school. Because of this, in "modern" cultures, six- or seven-year-old children who do not yet go to school solve syllogistic problems with content unfamiliar to them from personal experience and provide "theoretical" bases for the solutions (for example, see Tamm, 1977). We may assume that subjects from traditional groups sometimes give their solutions "theoretical" bases because they came into contact with the scientific method of thinking outside school. Here particularly we have in mind contacts with educated adults. We know nothing about the significance of these contacts for the thinking of people from traditional cultures and for that reason will limit ourselves to indicating a possible parallel to the development of logical thinking in the child. According to J. Dollard and N. Miller (see Henle, 1962, p. 367), adults rebuke a child for logically contradictory and absurd thinking, for illogical and contradictory plans of action. As a result, as these authors assume, the children strive to form their explanations and plans so that they would appear logical. It is also possible that something similar occurs in contacts of people from traditional groups with their fellow-tribesmen who had attended school or with other educated people.

Second, there is some basis for the assumption that sometimes the "theoretical" bases for solutions proposed by traditional subjects are actually not "theoretical." Let us assume that we present the following problem to a Nganasan subject: "All men go hunting. Kyudapte is a man. Does Kyudapte go hunting?" If the subject responds: "Yes, because he wants to shoot a fox," we classify his basis as empirical. However, if he responds: "Yes, because he's a man," we consider this basis theoretical since the subject remains within the framework of the problem and bases his solution on relating it to the premises. Actually the second basis may just as easily be a reference to the cultural norm: among the Nganasans, all men go hunting. Consequently, using only this one basis, we cannot conclude that the subject actually relates the conclusion to the premises. He may be responding on the basis of his own general information.

Such a possibility seems to be especially probable if the subject does not refer to the premises as a basis for the solution of problems with content unfamiliar to him from personal experience. In all cross-cultural studies on solving syllogistic problems thus far, including our studies in Volochanka, problems can be found, for whose solution subjects provide bases that cannot confidently be described as either empirical or theoretical. Sharp, Cole and Lave (1979, p. 55) specially examined their own experimental problems for which traditional and educated subjects gave approximately the same number of theoretical bases. They established that these were "exactly those problems for which the correct response was in complete agreement with the experience of the subjects." It is very likely that in essence, in the case of traditional subjects, we are dealing not with "theoretical," but with "empirical" bases. The difficulty of separating the two types of bases appears to be surmountable with further research. The experimenter must not limit himself to the subject's response to the question, "Why do you think so?" but must pose further questions until it becomes clear what the actual nature of the proposed basis is.

Naturally, from the results of a single, solitary experimental study, we cannot make far-reaching conclusions. Nevertheless, we now have a broader basis for believing that in an experimental situation, traditional and educated subjects solve simple syllogistic problems by various methods, and that the method with which the conclusion is related to the premises and which ensures practically error-free solution and a theoretical basis for the solution of similar problems of any content first emerges in school. Its emergence is connected with the need to solve problems of a new type resembling in certain essential aspects the problems characteristic of science.

Considering the data obtained, we cannot agree with the recommendation given by Cole and Bruner in 1972: "... the teacher should stop laboring under the impression that he must create new intellectual structures. He should start concentrating on how to get the child to transfer skills he already possesses to the task at hand." Here, as the authors believe, the teacher should rely on materials or content "to which the child already applied skills the teacher seeks to have applied to his own content" (Cole and Bruner, 1972, p. 176). It is understood that in many cases this is exactly so. But we have seen that under the influence of schooling, changes in thinking also occur that cannot be reduced to an application of old skills to new material. The danger arises that the teacher, if he follows the advice of Cole and Bruner, will have nothing to rely on. In a classroom in the Volochanka school where we did a study, above the blackboard hung a square, a circle, and a triangle cut from cardboard. The teacher told us that when she was a pupil, she found it very difficult to understand what geometric figures represent, what kind of objects or things they were. She did not know such "things" at home. Now, having hung them above the blackboard, from time to time she repeated their names and descriptions for the pupils, beginning with the first grade, so that they would get used to the existence of "things" of this type, ideal objects that can be described only within a specific system of concepts, and not by reference to immediate reality.

3.1.3. A Study of Simple Syllogistic Problem-Solving by People Returning to a Traditional Environment after Schooling. If the new method of solving syllogistic problems that emerged in school is linked functionally primarily with managing scientific information and with solving scientific problems, then it would be reasonable to assume that it should recede when people who had attended school do not have to manage this kind of information and solve this kind of problems. Under those conditions, a method of solving problems probably takes over that is characteristic for people from traditional cultures who had not attended school, a method functionally appropriate to the problems that these people have to solve in their real activity. This hypothesis conforms to the activity approach which emphasizes the functional correspondence between mental processes and activity. The activity approach, as we have seen in 2.1, differs in this substantially from the evolutionary approach which evaluates mental processes not from the point of view of the functions they fulfill, but from the point of view of which level of development they represent: "low" or "high."

Among the adult population in some isolated regions in which traditional types of economic and cultural activity predominate, it is possible to study syllogistic problem solving by people who have had various amounts of schooling, and then returned to the traditional environment, to accustomed types of activity. It is possible to establish which of the two methods of solving syllogistic problems they will apply. By the same token, we study not the development of syllogistic reasoning in people from traditional cultures as affected by schooling and other cultural factors, as had been done thus far in cross-cultural studies, but on the contrary, we study its possible deviation, possible regression under the influence of "post-schooling" activity factors. Of course, such study could be done in Europe or America also. However, it is more expedient to do it under conditions where there is maximum contrast between school and everyday problems and information.

Experiments were done in the summer of 1977 in some isolated regions of Kirghizia with the help of a translator competent in the Kirghiz language. (The results of this work were published in Tamm and Tulviste, 1980, and T. Tulviste, 1985). The syllogistic problem and supplementary question were presented orally to the individual subjects. The subject was asked to give a basis for his response ("Why do you think so?"). If there was no answer or basis, the problem was repeated. In the present work, data are used on the solution of the following syllogistic problems:

1. Asan and Kenesh always drink tea together. Asan is now drinking tea. Is Kenesh drinking tea or not?

2. Anara invites Damira for a visit every Thursday. Tomorrow is Thursday.Will Anara invite Damira for visit tomorrow or not?

3. In one mountain village, each person has a dog. My friend lives in that village. Does he have a dog or not?

The experiments were conducted with shepherds and other villagers age 25 to 87 years. The average age of the subjects was 52.7 years; most of them were between 30 and 70. Of these, 18 were illiterate and the other 52 had had various amounts of schooling. The average school attendance was 4.5 grades. There was a high negative correlation between age and education: –0.7, statistically significant at a significance level of 0.001. This relation was as follows: subjects age 25–30 years had finished at least 7 grades; for older subjects, the level was lower. All those older than 70 were illiterate. Including those who had not attended school allowed us to compare their results with the results of those who had attended school. Since other cross-cultural studies of verbal-syllogistic thinking included individuals attending school during the experiments as subjects "who had attended school," and our subjects had been occupied with traditional types of economic and cultural activities for some time after schooling, there was a basis for assuming that the results of our subjects would be "weaker" than those described in other work.

Following Scribner, we divided the bases for responses into "empirical" and "theoretical." Examples of "empirical" bases are: "I don't know. I am not familiar with those people;" "I don't know. I didn't see it myself;" "I don't know. Maybe he got sick or went somewhere. If I'd been there, I would know" (Problem No. l); "If Anara has something to offer her friend, then she will ask her to come" (Problem No. 2). An example of "theoretical" bases is: "She will invite her. On Thursday she always invites her" (Problem No. 2). We considered the "theoretical" basis as indicating the "school" method of solving syllogistic problems.

The results were as follows. The correlation between number of correct responses and educational level of the subjects was 0.493; statistically significant at a significance level of 0.001 (Table 2): 1) the higher the educational level, the smaller the number of cases in which the subject does not give a substantive response (most likely, the fact is that these subjects begin to perceive the syllogism as a problem); 2) the higher the educational level, the more correct responses there are; 3) in those who had attended school, the percentage of correct responses is significantly higher than in those who are illiterate (61.5% and 30%, respectively, $t = 2.47$; $p < 0.05$).

Table 2. Relation between correctness of solving syllogistic problems and subject's level of schooling (2)

Solution Education, in grades	Refual to answer Number	%	Incorrect Responses Number	%	Correct Responses Number	%	Total number of Responses
0	30	55	8	15	16	30	54
1	2	67	–	–	1	33	3
2	2	17	2	17	8	67	12
3	1	7	6	40	8	53	15
4	–	–	6	67	3	33	9
5	2	11	5	28	11	61	18
6	1	5	2	10	18	86	21
7	8	22	10	28	108	50	36
8	1	7	3	20	11	73	15
9	–	–	4	33	8	67	12
10	2	13	3	20	10	67	15
Total	49		49		112		210

$x^2 = 67.9$; df = 20; $p < 0.001$; r = 0.49; $p < 0.001$

These generalizations correspond to those made in other cross-cultural studies of solving simple syllogistic problems. There is something else that is important and unexpected. While it is well known that two or three grades of schooling are enough to teach a person to solve simple syllogistic problems with practically no errors, for our subjects who were in school for 4–5 years, only 52% of the responses were correct and only 15% of the bases were "theoretical." In other words, the problems were solved at the level of chance success. Even in subjects with 10th grade schooling, only 67% of the responses were correct, which differs only slightly from indices in similar studies of traditional subjects who had not attended school. In many cases, the protocols of the subjects who had attended school for quite a long time and those who had not attended school at all were practically identical.

As examples, we will give segments from the protocol of a 26-year-old woman who had finished 10 grades. According to her own statement, she was an average pupil in school. After schooling, she returned to her village. She works on the kolkhoz; she has borne and is bringing up seven children.

Experimenter: We have several problems here that people in different places solve in different ways. We would like to find out how you would solve these problems. The first is: every morning Asan plays on the kamuz [a Kirghiz musical instrument]. Did Asan play his kamuz yesterday morning or not?

Subject: How should I know? (The problem is repeated.) Maybe he did play.

—Asan and Kenesh always drink tea together. Asan is drinking tea now. Is Kenesh drinking tea now or not?
—No, he's not.
—Why do you think so?
—Because he may not be there now.
—Kadyr goes to bed at exactly 10 o'clock every night. Will Kadyr go to bed at 10 today or not?
—This evening? We all go to bed. (The problem is repeated.) Maybe he won't go to bed. Maybe he went to visit someone. And so on.

Table 3.. Relation between type of basis for solutions of syllogistic problems and subject's level of schooling

Types of bases	Refusal to state basis		Empirical		Theoretical		Total number of responses
Schooling in grades	Number	%	Number	%	Number	%	
0	18	33	30	56	6	11	54
1	1	33	1	33	1	33	3
2	1	8	9	75	2	17	12
3	2	13	9	60	4	27	15
4	–	–	9	100	–	–	9
5	2	11	12	67	4	22	18
6	1	5	11	52	9	43	21
7	5	14	24	67	7	19	36
8	2	13	10	67	3	20	15
9	2	17	6	50	4	33	12
10	2	13	9	60	4	27	15
Total	36		130		44		210

$x^2 = 28.4$; df = 20; $p > 0.05$; r = 0.34; $p < 0.01$.

The results of our subjects with any amount of schooling were significantly "poorer" than the results of subjects with the same amount of schooling in other studies. Since the methodology was the same, the differences in results might logically be explained by the circumstance that in other studies, the group of "educated" subjects was made up of school children, and our group was made up of people who had gone to school at some time, but were subsequently occupied with traditional economic and cultural activity which did not require schooling or the corresponding types of thinking. Table 3 presents the relation between types of bases for solutions of syllogistic problems and level of schooling of the subjects. The correlation here is 0.34; statistically significant at a significance level of 0.001. It is apparent from Table 3 that the basic change that occurs as a result of higher educational level is a decrease in numbers of refusals to respond. The difference in number of "theoretical" bases for subjects attending school and the illiterate was statistically insignificant (24% and 11% "theoretical" bases, respectively; $t = 1.37$; $p > 0.05$). Regardless of the educational level, "empirical" bases predominated among our subjects.

Thus, the level of schooling had a greater effect on the percentage of correct solutions than on the percentage of "theoretical" bases. In other words, under these economic and cultural conditions, first the habit of basing solutions "theoretically" recedes, which, as we know, is almost always found only with correct solutions.

It is curious that sometimes (in seven cases) the subjects gave their responses a combined basis including both a "theoretical" and an "empirical" basis. For example: "If they drank together before, then they must drink, but of course I can't say so exactly because I don't know what kind of people they are"; "If she always invites her, then she'll invite her this time too if she doesn't have something urgent to do and if she has time." In all cases, such bases were found only with a correct response. It seems that such bases are not given by traditional subjects or those who attend school. They are evidently characteristic especially for those who had attended school and had then returned to traditional types of economic and cultural activity.

Table 4 presents the relation between correctness of solving syllogistic problems and age of the subjects. The correlation between these traits is −0.39; statistically significant at a significance level of 0.001. Table 5 presents the relation between type of basis and age of subjects. The correlation here is 0.256; statistically significant at a significance level of 0.05. Thus, both correlations are negative: the older the subject, the lower the results. It was noted above that age and level of schooling of our subjects had a high negative correlation. This is specifically the explanation for the negative correlation between age and successful solving of syllogistic problems and basing of the solutions, that is, there is no contradiction here in the results of investigators who showed that success in solving these problems and type of basis depend not on age, but on level of schooling of the subject (for example, Blackburn, 1984).

Table 4. Relation between correctness of solution of syllogistic problems and subject's age

Age, years	Refusal to solve		Incorrect solution		Correct solution		Total Number of solutions
	Number	%	Number	%	Number	%	
21–30	–	–	4	33	8	67	12
31–40	4	19	5	24	12	57	21
41–50	8	9	20	28	44	61	72
51–60	9	19	8	17	31	64	48
61–70	18	50	7	19	11	31	36
71–80	8	53	2	13	5	33	15
81–90	2	33	3	50	1	17	6
Total	49	23	49	23	112	53	210

$x^2 = 38.2; df = 12; p < 0.001; r = -0.39; p < 0.001$

Table 5. Relation between type of basis for solving syllogistic problems and subject's age

Age, years	Refusal state basis		"Empirical"		"Theoretical"		Total Number of solutions
	Number	%	Number	%	Number	%	
21–30	–	–	10	83	2	17	12
31–40	3	14	14	67	4	19	21
41–50	10	14	45	63	17	24	72
51–60	6	13	28	58	14	29	48
61–70	11	31	21	58	4	11	36
71–80	4	27	8	53	3	20	15
81–90	2	33	4	67	–	–	6
Total	36	17	130	62	44	21	210

$x^2 = 14.9; df = 12; p < 0.05; r = 0.26; p < 0.05$

The relation between number of correct solutions and types of bases for the solutions of syllogistic problems is presented in Table 6. The correlation between them is 0.52; statistically significant at a significance level of 0.001. It is apparent from the table that subjects who gave no correct solutions gave not one "theoretical" basis. Subjects who solved two problems correctly gave no more than two "theoretical" bases, and those who solved one problem correctly, no more than one. Fifteen subjects solved all syllogistic problems correctly, but only two gave a "theoretical" basis for all three solutions. A "theoretical" basis was always accompanied by a correct response.

There can be no doubt that if we had studied the thinking of our subjects while they were in school, there would have been more correct answers and "theoretical" bases. In all likelihood, retention of the ability to solve syllogistic problems correctly and to provide "theoretical" bases for the solutions, requires participation in those types of activity that require applying that type of thinking and support it.

Table 6. Relation between number of correct solutions of syllogistic problems and number of "theoretical" bases

Number of correct solutions	Number of "theoretical" bases				
	0	1	2	3	Total
0	11	–	–	–	11
1	13	9	–	–	21
2	12	5	6	–	23
3	5	4	4	2	15
Total	41	15	10	2	70

$x^2 = 26.14$; $df = 9$; $p < 0.01$; $r = 0.52$; $p < 0.001$

Similar results were obtained by Scribner and Cole (1981, pp. 124, 131) in Liberia: the more time elapsed since persons from traditional cultures left school and returned to their villages, the less their results differed from the results of subjects who had not attended school. Scribner and Cole (p. 131) write: "One of the most important distinctions turned out to be school status at the time of our survey—whether individuals still engaged in schooling as their primary pursuit or whether they were out of school and occupied with daily activities that might or might not call upon the skills they had acquired there.

. . . even if we were to accept as a working proposition that school produces general changes in certain intellectual operations, we might have to qualify the conclusion to refer only to students, recent ex-students, or those continuing in school-like occupations."

If the "school" method of solving syllogistic problems represents a generally higher stage of the development of thinking that makes it possible to solve any problems better, then it certainly would be retained by individuals who had attended school and might even be subject to further development. Absence of this method under traditional environmental conditions, on the other hand, indicates that we are dealing with a specific method of thinking that is functionally appropriate to solving specifically school or scientific problems and does not have a functional significance in the types of activity that do not require applying scientific information and solving corresponding problems.

3.1.4. Two Methods of Solving Simple Syllogistic Problems. The Status of Syllogistic Reasoning. Let us return to the problem of Saiba and Nakupte who always drink tea only together. Without hesitation, we accept as correct the response that Nakupte drinks tea at three o'clock in the afternoon since the problem states that they always drink tea together and that Saiba drinks tea at three o'clock in the afternoon. We consider as incorrect responses in which the subject states that Nakupte does not drink tea at three o'clock since it is possible that he has not yet returned from hunting, or since he may be angry with Saiba and doesn't want to drink tea with him, etc. From the point of view of logic, these responses are, of course, incorrect. On the basis of results obtained, which seem to indicate the "underdevelopment" (or prelogical state) of the thinking of people from traditional cultures, it is easy to reach the conclusion that "we" have one kind of thinking and "they," another, less developed.

However, we have only to look at the method of solving syllogistic problems used by the traditional subjects from the point of view of the functions it fulfills, and the picture changes abruptly. In the concrete case before us, the problem is by no means a school problem, but an everyday problem. Let us assume that we have to meet Nakupte. We know that he always drinks tea with Saiba, and Saiba drinks tea at three o'clock. Before three, we prepare to go to Saiba's. There can be quite a few reasons why Nakupte does not come to drink tea in this specific instance. There are usually exceptions to the general claims about everyday life which should be considered. In other words, in everyday life, we frequently think "usually" when we say "always." If we are to be sure that we will actually find Nakupte at Saiba's, it would be sensible to find out if he is well now, if he hasn't gone somewhere, etc. This is exactly what the traditional subjects are doing in the experimental situation. And this, and exactly this, is what "we" do when we are not solving syllogistic problems, but when we need to find Nakupte or board a train that's leaving point A.

It is generally naive to think that in a culture where people drink tea several times a day, there may be two people who always drink tea only together. It is easy to understand the subjects who asked us if these people promised to drink tea only together.

If we transfer the problems presented to the subjects to everyday life, then even for "us" the truth of the premises and conclusion will be more important in this case than the logical correctness of the conclusion. (It is understood that in many cases they may appear to be both correct and true.) It is easy to guess that any individual in any culture uses with much greater frequency specifically this "incorrect," "underdeveloped" method of solving problems, which only traditional subjects use in an experimental situation. The difference between the traditional and the educated subject consists not in the one having one type of thinking and the other, another, then depending on the activity, the problem, and the situation, the educated subject uses either of the methods described for reaching a conclusion. At the same time, the traditional subject, not having been exposed to schooling, to scientific information and problems, has mastered the one, single method of reaching a conclusion which he uses in solving any problems in any situations.

It is curious that under experimental conditions, those who had attended school usually use the "school" method exclusively for solving simple syllogistic problems. This can probably be explained by the fact that the problem, "liberated" from extraneous details, "extracted" from context, is perceived by them as a school problem. R. Thouless (1959) writes that the subjects are influenced by knowing the fact itself that they are dealing with a psychological test, and this creates in them a special attitude with respect to the problems. "The experimental situation alerts the subject and his thought processes are free from many of the influences which would determine them in the more ordinary situation of listening to a speech or reading a newspaper." We know that if a problem is included in a story, then even educated subjects frequently evaluate not the logical correctness, but the truth of the conclusion, and make mistakes in the solution. M. Henle (1962) presented similar problems to psychology students, most of whom had taken a course in logic. Here is an example from her work: "A group of women were discussing their household problems. Mrs. Shivers broke the ice by saying: 'I am so glad we're talking about these problems. It's so important to talk about things that are in our minds. We spend so much of our time in the kitchen that of course household problems are in our minds. So it is important to talk about them.' (Does it follow that it is important to talk about them? Give your reasoning.) Responses: 'The conclusion does not follow. The women must talk about household problems because it is important to talk about their problems, not because the problem is in their minds.'... 'No. Just because one spends so much time in the kitchen it does not necessarily follow that household problems are in our minds.' ... 'Yes. It seems obvious that problems which are in the forefront of one's mind bring more consideration to them and possibly newer aspects when they are discussed with another. Two heads may be better than one."' And so on. Here educated subjects apply an "everyday" method of problem-solving in an experimental situation.

It is enough also to change or supplement the instruction in order to obtain similar responses. In this connection, it is appropriate to recall the episode described by W. Stern. Studying the development of syllogistic reasoning in Berlin children, he presented the pupil with the problem: "All mammals feed their young with milk. The horse is a mammal. Does the horse feed the colt with milk or not?" The subject responded that it does because the horse is a mammal and all mammals feed their young with milk. Stern asked him, "And what do you think, does the horse really give milk or not?" To this the subject, being a true city person, responded: "No, actually, of course it doesn't." In the first case, the subject proceeded from the logical correctness of the conclusion, and in the second, from his knowledge of horses (which in this concrete case betrayed him).

Actually, it is completely obvious that individuals who have attended school must frequently confirm conclusions by relating them to reality, that is, by evaluating them not from the point of view of logical correctness, but from the point of view of truth. This is characteristic for many types of activity, including science. If, however, subjects who had attended school do not do this in one experiment or another, then it may be assumed that the experiments simulate only separate aspects of the thinking of the subjects and leave other aspects uninvolved.

We also know that in experiments with educated subjects, in which more complex syllogistic problems are used, together with considerations of logical correctness, the subject's representations of the truth of the conclusion also play a certain role in the solving process (Janis and Frick, 1943; Morgan and Morton, 1944; Lefford, 1946; Thouless, 1959; Henle, 1962; Evans et al., 1983). Even in those cases where the subjects were given a detailed explanation that they must specifically reach a logically correct conclusion from the premises presented (and not conclusions which match their representations of truth), and an example was given of the difference between logical correctness and truth of the conclusion, even then their thinking displayed a marked effect of their notion of the correspondence or non-correspondence of one conclusion or another to reality, agreement or non-agreement with a conclusion. "The subjects not only evaluate the correctness of the conclusion (by referring it to the premises); they are also affected by a different, direct evaluation of the truth of the conclusion" (Evans et al., 1983). The authors assume that in solving simple syllogistic problems, there is a constant struggle between logical and "nonlogical" processes—or, using a different terminology, between "school" (theoretical) and "everyday" (empirical) solving methods.

On the basis of the experimental data presented above, and the representations cited, we can conclude that there are two separate methods, qualitatively different from each other, for solving simple syllogistic problems.

The first method is proper to everyday thinking (common sense), which provides for the solution of a broad circle of problems in various forms of practical and theoretical activity in any cultures. Using this method, to answer the question presented, the subject turns to his knowledge about the reality that is involved in the problem. This method of solving problems is applicable only when an individual has appropriate information and considers it reliable. Here, the criterion for evaluating the conclusion is its truth, that is, its correspondence to reality. This method of solving problems can be considered a universal of human thinking, and can be called an empirical method of solving syllogistic problems.

The second method, usually referred to in speaking about syllogistic reasoning or deductive conclusion is characteristic of scientific thinking. It is applied in science, in school, in various types of activity in "modern" cultures, in the processing of information and problems of a scientific type. In order to get an answer, an individual turns in this case to data presented in the problem itself and to his knowledge of correct and incorrect thinking (in whatever form he has this knowledge). The individual realizes the course of solving the problem and confirms it on the basis of this knowledge, comparing the conclusion with the premises. This method of solving problems ensures practically error-free solutions of simple syllogistic problems of any content since the answer here depends neither on the knowledge the subject has about the corresponding reality nor on his conviction or lack of conviction concerning the premises and conclusion. Logical correctness is the criterion for evaluating the conclusion, which, if the premises are valid, ensures the validity of the conclusion. This method of solving problems is mastered in school as a rule and is evidently not found in those cultures in which there is neither science in the modern meaning of the word nor schooling. It can appropriately be called the theoretical method of solving syllogistic problems. Like every skill, it is inclined to regress when not used.

M. Braine differentiates the methods of solving syllogistic problems in a similar way: "Practical (i.e., everyday) reasoning uses all the information at a person's disposal, whereas formal reasoning is concerned with whether conclusions follow from premises. ... formal reasoning makes two demands not made in everyday reasoning: (a) Reasoners must compartmentalize information (i.e., restrict the information used to that contained in the premises) and (b) they must take a special attitude in comprehending the premises, by attempting to discover the minimum commitments of the premises as they are worded" (Braine, 1978).

We cannot now with any precision describe the circle of problems in real life in which individuals in "modern" cultures use one or the other of the described methods to reach a solution. To do so, we would have to have solid empirical material on the solution of problems in various kinds of practical and theoretical activity. Few such studies have been made thus far (see, however, Rogoff and Lave, 1984). Most likely, in many types of activity, both methods are used, depending on which path of ensuring the validity of the conclusion seems possible or more suitable in the given concrete case. We must also keep in mind that the question is still open as to the degree to which syllogistic schemes are suitable for describing the actual processes of thinking (see, for example: Henle, 1962; Johnson–Laird, 1982).

Of special interest is the question concerning the way knowledge exists and the nature of knowledge about thinking applied in the "school" method of solving simple syllogistic problems. It seems obvious that this knowledge is acquired by individuals from traditional cultures in school in connection with mastering scientific information and learning how to solve school (scientific) problems. It is also clear that applying this method does not assume the presence in the individual of explicit knowledge on the logical laws of thinking. In "modern" cultures, necessary knowledge begins to form in children by age six or seven. It may be assumed that for the development of this method of solving problems in an individual, the idea must exist in the culture that there are not only true and false, but also correct and incorrect conclusions. For realizing and evaluating the course of thinking, certain words or terms are indispensable.

Thus far, in determining the method of problem-solving that subjects were using in an experimental situation, the investigator depended mainly on the nature of the bases that they gave for their solutions. If the subject asks a question of the experimenter about the circumstances involved in the problem, this also indicates that he is using the "everyday" method of problem-solving. We have seen (3.1.2) that the basis the subject gives does not always permit determination of the method he used.

Admitting that there are two distinct methods, qualitatively different from each other, for solving simple syllogistic problems makes it possible, it seems to us, to look again at the old problem of the status of syllogistic deductions. We know that in syllogistic deductions, sometimes a "natural" or "spontaneously" arising trait of human thinking has been perceived, and sometimes a thinking operation that appeared late in ontogenesis and presupposed a high level of mental development. If we take the first position, it remains incomprehensible why adults in traditional cultures fail to solve simple syllogistic problems with an unfamiliar content and solve problems with a familiar content only at a chance level (and with a completely unexpected method from the point of an educated person). If we take the second position, it remains incomprehensible why even three-year-old children sometimes solve these problems. Evidently, solving this problem involves the fact that there are two methods of solving these problems—the empirical and the theoretical. The second method may also be called the conscious method.

Previously (1.2), we discussed in detail the hypothesis of Levy–Bruhl on the prelogical state of thinking in traditional cultures. The data cited here on the solving of simple syllogistic problems by individuals who had attended school and those who had not indicate that "logical sense" actually plays a different role in the two methods that we have described for solving these problems. Even if both methods can be described in identical logical formulas, there are important psychological differences between them.

We know that syllogistic problems frequently are considered to be artificial and, for this reason, unsuitable for studying thinking even of subjects who had attended school. P. Johnson–Laird (1982) presents this argument in the following form:

Syllogisms are completely artificial problems.
Psychologists should not study artificial problems.
Therefore, psychologists should not study syllogisms.

As an answer to that argument, he points to a study in which identical premises were presented to a subject once in the form of a syllogism and once in a more natural formulation (probably in the way that appears in the segment from Henle's work cited above). Identical errors appeared in both cases.

We have already mentioned certain similar traits in syllogistic and "school" problems. Both of these require that the individual solving the problem remain within the framework of the problem and relate the components to each other instead of referring to the reality involved in the problem.

We can cite Luria's results as evidence that, in the solving syllogistic problems, general traits of the approach of traditional subjects to "school" problems can actually be found that are typical not only of the solving of syllogistic problems. He gave his subjects simple verbal arithmetical problems. We will present the shortest protocol from Luria's book (1974, p. 126). The subject is a 24-year-old illiterate woman from an isolated Central Asian village.

"Here is the problem: It is a 30-minute walk to village X, and by bicycle, it is five times faster. How long will it take to get there by bicycle?

—My brother in Dzhizak has a bicycle, and he goes much faster than a horse or a man.
—The problem is repeated.

—Five times faster... a verst... If you walk, you get there in 30 minutes, and on a bicycle, then, of course, you will get there faster, probably in a minute or two (the subject refused to continue working on the problem). The fact that the difficulties arising here are not connected with the computation operations is clear since this subject can easily solve a problem in division (30:5) when it is concrete (divide 30 cakes among five people)." Evidently, the approach of the subject to the problem is, in its essential characteristics, the same as in the case of syllogistic problems.

3.1.5. Conclusion. The experimental data, generalizations and arguments presented lead to the following conclusions:

1. The method for solving simple syllogistic problems used by subjects from traditional cultures and groups belongs to everyday thinking (common sense). It provides for solving a broad circle of problems in any culture.
2. When a child or adult from a traditional culture begins to study in school, he forms a new method of solving simple syllogistic problems. The reason for this is that school problems that simulate certain essential aspects of scientific problems cannot be solved by the method typical for everyday thinking. The emergence of the new method signifies the development of thinking that is neither "further advanced" nor "higher," but in a quite specific direction functionally appropriate to science as a type of activity: operating with scientific information and solving scientific problems.
3. The two methods of solving simple syllogistic problems differ from each other primarily in that in the empirical method, the subject tries to get to the truth of the conclusion by direct relation of the premises and conclusion to his knowledge of reality while in the theoretical method, he pays most attention to the logical correctness of the conclusion. In science, it is impossible and unreasonable to confirm all conclusions by relating them directly to reality. The theoretical method of solving problems, in its turn, is not applicable to many other spheres of life where there usually are exceptions to the general claims. The theoretical method which emerges in school cannot, in principle, replace the empirical method which retains its functions (and also participates in real scientific thinking).
4. The hypothetical explanation of the differences in the way individuals attending school and those not attending solve simple syllogistic problems, developed in this chapter, is based on a certain difference between the types of activity in which the two groups of subjects participate. We proceeded from the circumstance established by Leibnitz that scientific thinking must be based on certain rules of thinking that ensure the correctness (and, correspondingly, the truth) of the conclusion while common sense and, evidently, other types of verbal thinking do not require such

rules. Since traditional cultures do not have science or school, there is no basis for assuming that the corresponding type of thinking exists there.

5. Empirical and theoretical methods of solving simple syllogistic problems differ from each other also in that wholly different realities are realized in them. In the first method, only external reality involved in the premises and conclusion is realized. In the second method, the relations between separate concepts and assertions are perceived, that is, thinking itself is realized. The theoretical method of solving problems presupposes the presence in the culture of certain knowledge about thinking, including the rules of thinking. We do not know in what forms this knowledge exists and is applied.

3.2. The Development of Units of Verbal Thinking. In Chapter 1, we saw that the first investigator of the historical development of thinking, H. Spencer, believed that in the course of the development of thinking, its units, that is, its concepts changed. Wundt maintained a similar point of view: "In primitive logic there are no abstract concepts and very few general concepts. It is wholly concrete and particular. There are concepts in it for specific types of activity such as 'to go,' 'to stand,' 'to beat,' 'to push,' but there is no general concept 'to do'; there are concepts for separate species of trees, but no general concept, 'tree' etc." (Wundt, 1914, pp. 127–128). Among the ethnographers, R. Thurnwald noted unique units of thinking in people in traditional cultures: "We must admit that all people are inclined toward logic. At the same time, the units the primitive individual uses are different in nature from the units of analytical thinking" (Thurnwald, 1922, p. 297). He assumed that the "primitive" thinks more in representations than in concepts.

These and certain other investigators considered the changing value in the historical development of thinking to be specifically its units while the operational side of thinking seemed to them to be universal, identical in all people (laws of association and/or logic). Levy–Bruhl, on the other hand, assumed that it was specifically the operations of thinking that changed—and changed qualitatively (cf. 1.2), and he paid little attention to possible changes in its units.

Vygotsky, it seems, was the first to note that in the course of the historical development of thinking both its units and its operations change, and that there is a functional connection between the change of the one and the other. We quoted him previously (1.3) on the fact that "... primitive man ... uses a word differently than we do. A word may assume a different functional usage. Depending on how it is used, that thinking operation will be in effect which is carried out by means of this word" (Vygotsky and Luria, 1930, p. 97). Vygotsky believed that in people from traditional cultures, thinking proceeds in complexes, and they do not use scientific concepts and corresponding operations. This idea followed from another idea of Vygotsky according to which the so-called thinking in scientific concepts is functionally connected with the mastery of scientific concepts in school. If there is no science or school in some culture, then there are no scientific concepts. Thus, if one proceeds from Vygotsky's position, then the assumption follows that the basic change in units of thinking in people from traditional cultures occurring under the influence of schooling consist in the emergence of scientific concepts as a new method of using the word in thinking. Scientific concepts, as we have seen (2.3) differ from everyday or pseudoconcepts primarily in that l) they are defined through other concepts and are part of a conceptual system; 2) they are realized as concepts, that is, the concept is realized apart from its referent; 3) "super-empirical" connections are possible (and obligatory) for them, that is, connections which occur only between concepts themselves, but not between their referents. These features are connected with the use of scientific concepts in a specific sphere of activity, in science. Everyday concepts, used in everyday life (by "everyday life," Vygotsky means practically everything except science) do not require definition and realization separately from their referents and for them, only such connections are possible as prevail in the external world, that is, in the world of referents.

In this section, among existing experimental data on cross-cultural differences and historical changes in verbal thinking, we will try to find data which would confirm or refute the hypothesis that, under the influence of schooling, a new type of units of verbal thinking, scientific concepts (according to Vygotsky), emerges in people from traditional cultures. With the exception of A. R. Luria, none of the investigators has set himself such a goal, and for this reason existing data have only an indirect relation to the stated hypothesis.

Even the first systematic experimental data collected by Luria in 1931–1932 in Central Asia (Luria, 1974) showed that historical changes in units of verbal thinking cannot simply be reduced to a change in the volume of concepts, as investigators had earlier assumed on the basis of linguistic data, but are much more interesting and diverse.

3.2.1. Experiments on Concept Definition .

From the point of view of studying concepts, the concept definition method was often considered artificial and inadequate because proper application of many concepts does not assume their definition, and the definition method says little about the real functioning of the concept in thinking (For example, Sakharov, 1930). If, however, we proceed from Vygotsky's views of the uniqueness of scientific concepts, then this method must be recognized as adequate in the study of scientific concepts and in establishing what kind of concepts we are dealing with in one specific case or another—with everyday or scientific concepts. It is perfectly obvious that in solving physics problems in school, the definition of such concepts as "speed" or "mass" is a *sine qua non* condition for the solution. Outside of science and jurisprudence (which may be considered as applied science), in modern cultures it is difficult to name a type of activity that presupposes operating with strictly defined concepts. Since in traditional cultures, there is no science or law in a form like that in "modern" cultures, then neither is there any apparent reason for people in those cultures to define concepts.

Moving on to presenting the results of experiments in which subjects who had attended school and those who had not were asked to define concepts, Luria (1974, p. 93) refers to the distinction between everyday and scientific concepts introduced by Vygotsky. Luria's data are of great interest since they represent a direct study of one of the basic differences between two types of units of verbal thinking.

The results of traditional subjects were very similar. In the protocols, refusals to do the experimental problem alternate with enumerations of separate external characteristics of the referents of the defined concepts. What is lacking in these protocols is an attempt to indicate the genus-species relations that make up an important component of the definitions applied in science. We will present excerpts from the protocol of a 22-year-old illiterate peasant (Ibid. pp. 94–95):

—Tell me, what a tree is.
—Why should I tell you, you know everyone knows what a tree is. ...
—But there are some people who have never seen trees, so you would have to tell them. How would you tell them what trees are? ...
—All right ... then I would tell them how we sow beets with seeds, how the root goes into the ground and the leaves grow up, and we plant trees in the same way, the roots go down ...
—But how would you tell us in a few words what a tree is?
—In a few words, you can say: apple tree, elm, poplar.
—And what is an automobile? Tell me what it is.
—Fire makes it move and a person makes it move ... If oil isn't poured in and there are no people there, it won't move ...
—But suppose you would have to explain what an automobile is if you came to a place where there are no automobiles, how would you define it?
—If I get there, I'll tell them that buses run, they have four legs (wheels), front seats for sitting, a roof for shade and a machine... In general, I'll say: if you sit down in one, you'll know what it is."

Luria generalizes the results of the traditional group of subjects in the following way: they "either reject the problem of literal definition of the concept entirely, or replace it by a visual description of isolated objects" (Ibid., p. 98).

These experiments are not free of weaknesses. We do not know whether the subject knew the words "plant" (in order to define the word, "tree"), "means of conveyance" ("automobile"), and "heavenly body" ("sun"). Second, in any culture, people undoubtedly know that a dog is a four-legged animal and a sparrow is a bird. In this protocol, when the subject, instead of defining the concept, "tree," says that it is an "apple tree, elm, poplar," the conclusion suggests itself that if he had been asked what an apple tree is, he would probably have said that it is a tree, and he might also name its apparent or functional characteristics that distinguish an apple tree from other trees. [Translator's note: in Russian, the word for apple tree is one word which, like elm or poplar, does not include the word, "tree."]

Luria's protocols leave no doubt that the method of defining concepts is inadequate for use with subjects from traditional groups. The problem seems nonsensical to them, although they do try to solve it. Luria tries to make them think about it, presenting the subject with the artificial situation of having to explain what a tree is to a person who has never seen trees. Actually, it is difficult to think of a natural situation here, that is, a situation in which a traditional subject would really have to define a concept. If this problem is somewhat less nonsensical to persons who had attended school, it is evidently only because they have learned how to define concepts in a more natural situation where this is necessary and where it is impossible to replace the definition with reference to reality, that is, in a situation involving mastering scientific information and solving school problems.

The only other comparative work in which the method of defining concepts was used is Scribner and Cole's study (1981, pp. 150–151). Three groups of subjects who had not attended school participated in the experiments: subjects in the first group were illiterate; in the second, subjects used a syllabic system of Vai writing (Liberia); and in the third, they were able to write in both Vai and Arabic script. Among these groups, no difference was found in defining concepts, which seems natural—there is no obvious reason to expect that becoming literate would have to engender knowing how to define a concept and operate with definitions of concepts. The method of processing the data from this experiment does not provide a basis for stating to what extent the subjects' responses were similar to school definitions.

There are no data about which concepts people from traditional cultures begin to define first in school, those pertaining to everyday life or those pertaining to information learned in school. We might assume that it would be the latter since it is here that definitions have a functional significance.

3.2.2. Experiments on Detecting Similarities. Like defining concepts, finding similarities between their referents (as distinct from enumerating the differences) requires using interconceptual relations, naming a concept of a higher order that encompasses both the concepts being compared. In comparing concepts, Luria's subjects from a traditional group did not try to find a concept of a higher order:

—What do a chicken and a dog have in common?
—They're not alike ... a chicken has two legs, a dog has four; a chicken has wings, a dog doesn't; a dog has large ears, a chicken has small ears.
—These are all differences, but what is it about them that is the same?
—They're not at all alike...
—And could you use one word for both of them?—No, that would be impossible!
—Which word can be true for both the chicken and the dog?—I don't know.
—Well, how about the word, 'animal?'—Yes, that word fits." (This is the protocol of a 38-year-old illiterate woman, Luria, 1974, p. 91).

Without discussing the problem whether a chicken can be called an animal, we will note that this problem is clearly unexpected and beyond the ability of the subjects. Of course, similar problems ("What do a poplar and a mountain have in common?") are also unexpected even for educated subjects, but nevertheless, we purposefully try to find concepts of a higher order no matter how absurd the pair of concepts is. Evidently, the reason for this is that in school we got used to putting concepts into more general categories, which in its turn allowed us learn more about the denotations of these concepts. If we know that a whale is a mammal, then we already know quite a lot about the whale with which most of us are not familiar from personal experience. In the same way, the knowledge that a square is a geometric figure allows us to extend to it the general characteristics of geometric figures, etc. Such an explicit transfer of information is hardly characteristic for traditional cultures.

Sharp et al. also used this methodology in studies done in Yucatan (1979, pp. 32–34). As distinct from Luria, they found no clear differences between groups of subjects differing in age and educational level, although those with more schooling generalized more often than subjects of other groups. The probable reasons for the discrepancies between Luria's results and those of Sharp et al. are as follows: 1) in the experiments of Sharp et al., no clear distinctions were made between semantic and functional similarity (cf. Ibid., p. 80); 2) in these experiments, an answer would be considered correct if the subject said that a pineapple and a banana are both fruits, while Luria asked his subjects to find a common feature, e.g., of a poplar and a mountain; 3) Sharp et al. did not help those attending school (or those who had attended school) with the supplementary question, "Can you use one word for these things?" which Luria consistently asked his subjects in order to nudge them toward using a concept of a higher order.

Generally speaking, it is perfectly normal that schooled subjects do not exhibit thinking in scientific concepts in all concrete experiments. This is linked to the heterogeneity of thinking. More and more psychologists agree that thinking of an educated person can by no means be wholly identified with certain operations characteristic of scientific thinking. There is no doubt that in a certain selection of experimental problems and with certain instructions to the subject, it is possible that a subject who had attended school might come to thinking in scientific concepts (3). From the point of view of the hypothesis under discussion concerning the nature of changes in thinking resulting from schooling, another problem is important: is it really true that traits characteristic for scientific concepts (according to Vygotsky) appear for the first time only in the course of schooling, is it really true that they do not exist in the units of verbal thinking of traditional subjects?

The summarized results presented in the work of Sharp et al. do not permit us to determine whether the traditional subjects proceeded from interconceptual, "superempirical" relations that Vygotsky considered to be characteristic only for scientific concepts. We think that interconceptual relations are used even in traditional cultures. At the same time, it is intuitively clear that the similarity between a boy and a woman (both are people, an example from the work of Sharp et al.) is different from the similarity between a square and a rectangle. The first similarity provides no new information about the boy, but certain substantial properties of the square become evident from the second.

3.2.3. Experiments on Classification. As distinct from Vygotsky, who in his experiments on the development of concepts in the child used Vygotsky and Sakharov's well-known modification of Ach's method, Luria, in his research with adults in Central Asia, decided to use classification not of geometric figures, but real objects and pictures of real objects. He believed that with this method, the possible influence of the subjects' previous experience on the method of classification would be more clearly evident (Luria, 1974, p. 67). "Pictures of four objects were presented to the subjects; of these, three belonged to one category, and the fourth did not and clearly belonged to a different group. The subject was asked to tell which three objects were 'similar' and 'could be placed in one group,' 'could be named by one word,' and which 'did not fit,' 'could not be named by the word that was common to the other three objects'" (Ibid., p. 60). Luria drew the following inferences from the results of a group of traditional subjects: "... they did not operate with the category 'tool' (although, as Luria established, they knew this word - P.T.) and they did not proceed along the path of abstracting essential traits and combining the objects in an abstract concept. Their operations were quite different: they reproduced the visual, practical situation in which the three objects were included, excluding the object that had almost no part in that situation. They said, 'It's clear that the log, saw and ax belong together: the log has to be sawed, then chopped, and a spade is not used here, it's needed in a garden...' Our subjects were not receptive to hints of the correct solution. If we told them that the pictures could be divided into other groups, that 'one person said that an ax, saw, and spade must be placed together, that they are similar to each other,' that they could be named with one word, and that a log is not a tool, that it does not belong here, our subjects did not accept this solution, did not consider it correct, and frequently told us: 'No, this person wasn't right; he doesn't know the situation: you know, what can you do with a saw and an ax without a log? ... and as to the spade, it's not needed here!'" (Luria, 1971, pp. 51–52).

According to Luria, in classification experiments, the most significant differences between the behavior of subjects attending school and those not attending pertained to the basis of classification: the first constructed classes on a semantic basis (nominal, taxonomic), and the second on a functional basis.

It is clear that the differences in classification behavior between subjects attending school and those not attending cannot consist in that the first are capable of taxonomic classification, and the second are not, as follows from Luria's results. Earlier (Tulviste, 1975), we wrote that if in traditional cultures only generalizations on a perceptive and functional basis were possible, then we could not explain the existence in these cultures of general concepts of the type "tools for work"; there would have to be general concepts of a different type (for example, including a saw, ax and a log, and not a saw, ax, hammer, etc.). As soon as generalizations of a taxonomic type exist in a language, there is no doubt that with an appropriate design of the experiment, those using the language would exhibit an ability for taxonomic classification. After the work of Cole and his colleagues (Cole et al., 1971; Cole and Scribner, 1977; Sharp et al., 1979), it became clear that the exclusively functional nature of the classes produced by Luria's subjects would be due to the circumstance that they were presented with only conflicting selections of objects that could be classified either functionally or semantically, and from this conflict, the functional method came out clearly ahead.

If we proceed from the typology developed by Vygotsky, then we must not expect the appearance of a difference between thinking in everyday concepts and thinking in scientific concepts in the subjects' classification itself. The referents of everyday and scientific concepts are identical (Vygotsky, 1956, pp. 180, 191–192 et al.), and classification methods (particularly the method of Vygotsky–Sakharov) do not distinguish between them. At the same time, thinking processes in classification must be different in everyday concepts and in scientific concepts: in the first case, the subject operates with interconceptual relations, without realizing them explicitly, and in the second, the relations between the general and the particular concepts are realized. According to Vygotsky, there is a basis for expecting the emergence of differences not in the classification itself, but in the subjects' verbalizing the basis for the classification formed or not formed: schooled subjects, as distinct from those who had not attended school, must base the semantic groups they form on general concepts that correspond to the groups.

Let us turn to data of new experimental studies. Classification methods are widely used in cross-cultural studies (see the reviews of Cole and Scribner, 1977;

Rogoff, 1981). The way an experiment is set up and the character of the experimental material and instructions are quite varied, and this complicates generalizing the results. The dependence of the results on the character of the objects presented for classification is emphasized by several authors (Sharp et al., 1979; Rogoff, 1981, for example). The same thing can be said with respect to the instructions and additional information given the subjects, although their effect on the results has not been specially studied thus far.

The data accumulated leave no doubt that people from any cultural group, given appropriate experimental material and appropriate instructions, will come to all the principal known types of classification: perceptive, functional and semantic (taxonomic). This circumstance, established primarily by the work of Cole and his colleagues, is a substantial improvement over the earlier results of Luria. It corresponds to the agreement of everyday and scientific concepts according to referent mentioned above; the difference between thinking in everyday concepts and thinking in scientific concepts is not disclosed in the classification itself. But in the experiments, differences were discovered in the preferred basis for classification, in the facility with which it was replaced at the request of the experimenter, and in its verbalization (with the same experimental material and the same instruction for various groups of subjects). Here also, the most substantial differences were found between subjects who had attended school and those who had not. In contemporary works, however, these differences are described purely quantitatively: subjects who had attended school <u>more often</u> classify objects on a semantic basis, change the basis of classification according to the request of the experimenter and verbalize it <u>more easily</u>. Are there qualitative differences in verbalization, specifically differences that would be found if the difference between units of thinking in subjects attending school and those not attending school consisted in the presence of scientific concepts in the schooled subjects that were presumably absent in the others?

Let us turn to data on the subjects' verbalization of the basis for the semantic classes they produced. In many cases, the experimenters asked the subjects not only to classify the objects, but also why they used their method of grouping. Of course, this is not a direct method of studying the thinking used in classification: the bases are given in retrospect and there is no guarantee, for example, that if the subject operates with a general concept in verbalizing, then he operated with it when he was classifying. The probability of this is, nevertheless, quite high. If, however, the subject did not operate with a general concept for his basis, then the probability that he consciously operated with it in classification is low. Moreover, the bases are of separate interest: in forming a basis for the grouping, does the subject operate with general concepts or not, does he refer to relations that occur only between concepts, but not between their referents?

An analysis of data in the literature of subjects' verbalizing the basis for classification leads to the conclusion that the question of possible qualitative differences between the bases of those who had attended school and those who had not is still open. We will cite some reasons for this. First, the instructions do not lead schooled subjects to use taxonomic classification and for this reason, they frequently do not apply it; consequently, they do not provide a taxonomic basis. For example, in an experiment of Sharp et al. in Yucatan (Mexico), the subjects were asked to which of three objects a fourth object is similar (Sharp et al., 1979, p. 25). The results showed that taxonomic classification was almost never found in any of the groups of subjects (Ibid., p. 27). We may assume that if the experimenters, following Luria, had asked the subjects to say which of the objects presented could be named with the same word, then this would nudge the subjects who had attended school toward taxonomic classification and the appropriate bases. The same thing can be noted also with respect to the experiments of Scribner and Cole with subjects of the Vai tribe in Liberia in which no influence of schooling on classification was noted (Scribner and Cole, 1981, p. 123). Second, the boundary between semantic and functional bases is very frequently imprecise. For example, in the same work of Sharp et al. (p. 29), as an example of semantic basis, "These are food" is given, and as an example of functional basis, "People drink these."

In experiments on classification of geometric figures differing from each other in color, form and number of elements, Scribner and Cole established that among the many social and cultural factors they considered, only schooling was significantly connected with verbalization, with the subjects' basis for the groups they produced. In verbalization, the influence of school is felt more strongly than in classification itself (Scribner and Cole, 1981, p. 121). Only further experimental studies will answer the question: do the bases of subjects attending school differ from the bases of traditional subjects only quantitatively or do they also differ qualitatively?

3.2.4. Differentiating between Concept and Referent. According to Vygotsky, differentiating between the concept and the referent is characteristic for thinking in scientific concepts, that is, the concept is realized as a separate, independent reality. The significance of this differentiation for constructing the conceptual systems of modern science is obvious. Do adults from traditional cultures differentiate between the concept and the denotation? The only direct data that we have on this were obtained by Scribner and Cole in the extensive study cited above, which they did among the Vai tribes in Liberia. In view of the conflicting initial results, the authors organized a discussion among the subjects, presenting Piaget's well-known problem for them to discuss: can the moon be called the sun, and vice versa? The participants either admitted or rejected the possibility of such renaming and presented the basis for their point of view. It was established that, first, subjects who had not attended school in some cases do differentiate the concept and the referent; second, their bases differ sharply from those given in similar experiments by European and American children. One of the subjects disputed the possibility of such renaming in a way that would have earned him the title of nominal realist in an ordinary experiment. It developed, however, that he rejected the renaming on the basis of theological representations ("One must not change the names that God gave the objects"), but he completely differentiates between the concept and the referent (when the question was raised as to whether he could buy a fruit drink for the name of a ten-cent coin, a dime, he said, "I can buy a fruit drink for the coin itself, but not for its name"). Scribner and Cole state the basic conclusion: "... the Vai can easily distinguish between word and referent. But acceptance of the notion that names are arbitrary is another matter. During the course of our research, we came to learn that certain classes of names among the Vai are in fact nonarbitrary. These include personal names, which are often selected to reflect individual characteristics ("firstborn," for example), and names of towns ("by-the-waterfall"). Consideration of these Vai naming practices and theological beliefs suggests that people's attitudes toward names need to be assessed in the wider context of cultural belief systems and the rules by which new words enter the lexicon, and not simply as an index of cognitive development" (Scribner and Cole, 1981, p. 157, and pp. 128–129, 140–142).

The data of Scribner and Cole contradict the assumption that a concept and its referent are differentiated only in scientific concepts.

We transferred to the thinking of people from traditional cultures the features of thinking in everyday concepts as they were described by Vygotsky on material from children's thinking and provided a basis for the correctness of this transfer (2.3.3). However, in that section, we also mentioned that the parallels between the ontogenesis of thinking and its cultural-historical development are only partial. In the given, concrete case, we did not consider certain significant circumstances: first, adults in traditional cultures themselves thought of names for children, animals, etc., that is, they had the practice of naming (4); second, they quite likely met with cases where any objects brought into the culture from outside were first called by the English word, and then a native word was devised; third, the problem of naming objects and living beings, as we have just seen, is discussed in religion (the Vai are Moslems). It is also discussed in the folklore of many peoples.

Here we are concerned with a significant correction of the initial hypothesis that ascribes differentiation between concept and referent only to scientific concepts. In whatever form, this differentiation is already assumed in such a universal phenomenon as naming children, places, animals, etc. With respect to this problem, a more detailed analysis of the function of differentiating a concept from its referent in science may possibly permit the disclosure of even finer differences between subjects who had attended school and those who had not. The data of Scribner and Cole, however, compel us, first, to formulate more precisely the characterization of scientific concepts developed by Vygotsky; second, in the spirit of Cole, to search more carefully in traditional cultures for possible forms of activity which might engender one trait or another that at first glance would seem to be present in scientific concepts alone.

3.2.5. Conclusion. We tried to find in extant literature data confirming or refuting the hypothesis that a new type of unit of verbal thinking—scientific concepts (according to Vygotsky)—appears in people from traditional cultures as the result of schooling. Vygotsky considered the difference between everyday and scientific concepts to be qualitative. They differ from each other both in their psychological features and in origin and direction of development. Correspondingly, we would have expected qualitative differences between the results of subjects attending school and those not attending school in the experiments in which essential properties of units of verbal thinking were studied.

In view of the heterogeneity of thinking, possible qualitative differences in units of thinking would have to appear in the experiments not in the sense that subjects who attended school and those who did not always solve problems differently. It is obvious that those who attended school by no means always think in scientific concepts, regardless of the fact that they might do so. In classification experiments carried out in Europe and America, depending on experimental material, instruction and possibly other factors, adult educated subjects use either semantic, functional or perceptive methods of classification (for example, Goldstein and Gelb, 1925; Goldstein and Scheerer, 1941; Stadler and Windheuser, 1977; Skeen et al., 1983; Frumkina and Mikheev, 1985). If we look at the instructions which were usually given a subject in studies of cross-cultural differences and changes in classification that occur under the influence of schooling from this point of view, it becomes clear that those attending school were not pushed into using the semantic method of classification characteristic for science. Investigators wishing to be "fair" with respect to traditional subjects avoid experimental problems and instructions that might be difficult for them to understand. This sometimes turns into "unfairness" with respect to schooled subjects. For example, there is no doubt that if in experiments on finding similarity, the instruction required the subjects not to name what is common in two objects, but to name the word that would stand for both objects, the schooled subjects would have a better chance to demonstrate their ability for generalizing and for its semantic basis. It would also be necessary to avoid a possible coincidence of functional and semantic classification and basis ("soup and bread are food"). Possibly the difference between subjects who had attended school and those who had not would be clearly apparent in cases where the problem would be guaranteed to be solved correctly only by subjects reliably oriented in interconceptual relations.

However, the results of subjects who had attended school are not as important in the design of the hypothesis that interests us. Critical from this point of view are the results of subjects from traditional groups. Will we find in them traits that indicate that the units of thinking used have properties that Vygotsky considered typical only for scientific concepts? Yes and no. According to available data, subjects from traditional groups do not define concepts. In experiments on finding similarity, they refer to concepts of a higher order significantly less frequently than educated subjects. In experiments on classification, they use the taxonomic (semantic) method of grouping less frequently than subjects who attended school. They verbalize the basis of the solutions of experimental problems to a significantly lesser degree and less frequently in all experiments. In general, we may say that operating with "superempirical" (interconceptual) relations is typical to a much lesser degree for traditional subjects than for those who had attended school. Operating with interconceptual relations and considering concepts in the context of their relations is characteristic primarily for science, for scientific information and for solving scientific problems. It is obvious that the development of units of verbal thinking must be functionally justified, that is, operations must exist that are possible only for "new" units, but not for those existing previously.

From the point of view of the hypothesis under discussion, however, something else is more important. In some experiments subjects from traditional groups exhibit features of units of verbal thinking that Vygotsky considered to be characteristic only for scientific concepts. They distinguish the concept and the referent so that this distinction cannot be considered characteristic exclusively for concepts applied in science. Traditional subjects sometimes also establish superempirical relations between concepts.

Evidently, Vygotsky's typology requires revision in at least three aspects. First, it was developed on material from children's thinking and may be applied with respect to the historical development of thinking only *mutatis mutandis*. That adults from traditional cultures distinguish concepts and referents indicates this plainly. In addition to science, there may be other spheres of activity that engender the same features of units of verbal thinking. Second, the typology lacks correlation with concrete types of activity (see also 2.3.3). For example, the properties of scientific concepts must be more precisely derived from the peculiarities of science as a type of activity and the functional significance of any of these properties in science must be disclosed in greater detail. Third, we know little about how the peculiarities of science mentioned here manifest themselves in the information assimilated in school and in solving school problems, that is, in those factors that presumably engender thinking in scientific concepts in people in school.

On the whole, the available experimental material confirms that changes in the units of verbal thinking that occur under the influence of schooling proceed in the direction from everyday toward scientific concepts (according to

Vygotsky). Thus far, however, it does not allow us to say whether corresponding qualitative changes occur. We know nothing about the dynamics of this process. Meanwhile, the available data do not compel us to reject the hypothesis on qualitative differences in units of verbal thinking. Specifically, various thinking processes may lie behind operating with "superempirical" relations in schooled subjects and those who had not attended school. Why is there such a sharp increase in verbalization, that is, realizing thinking operations, which many authors note unanimously? It is hardly an epiphenomenon. It is quite possible that realizing certain aspects of concepts allows the subjects who attended school to be easily oriented in interconceptual relations, which may not be the case in traditional subjects although their responses in some experiments do not differ from the responses of educated subjects. Only further experiments and varying the experimental material will confirm such assumptions or compel their rejection.

3.3. Why Schooling Changes Thinking. The Connection between Changes in Thinking and Changes in Verbal Texts and Self-Consciousness. We have considered the results of subjects who had attended school and those who had not in certain experiments in which units and operations of verbal thinking were studied. In doing this, we proceeded from the assumption that since science differs substantially from other types of activity, then with the dissemination of scientific information and habits of solving scientific problems, the acquisition of which makes up the basic content of schooling of the European type, certain changes in verbal thinking must occur which may be predicted on the basis of what is known about the peculiarities of scientific information and problems. Correspondingly, proceeding from the differences between science and other types of activity, we can explain certain essential differences in experimental results of subjects who had attended school and those who had not.

Meanwhile in current psychological literature, as we have seen (1.5), other ideas are prevalent on what specifically the aspects or components of schooling are that can in a short time evoke changes in the thinking of people from traditional cultures.

In this section, we will first consider the problem of the extent to which existing experimental data confirm the various ideas about the concrete factors which change thinking in school. Then we will turn to the problem of the correspondence between the differences in the verbal thinking of people from different cultures, established in experimental studies, and the differences in verbal texts. Finally, we will touch on the problem of the connections between the historical development of verbal thinking and self-consciousness.

3.3.1. Two Hypotheses of Vygotsky on Factors Engendering Thinking in Scientific Concepts. Earlier (1.3) we mentioned that Vygotsky derived two different hypotheses concerning the factors that transform thinking in school.

According to the first, becoming literate is one such factor. This hypothesis is a particular case of Vygotsky's general hypothesis that the emergence (and correspondingly in the case of ontogenesis, the acquisition) of new sign systems mediating higher mental functions plays a decisive role in the development of these functions. This hypothesis was shared by many investigators (for example, Bruner, see 1.5.1; Goody and Watt, 1963; Goody, 1977; Greenfield, 1972; Olson, 1975; and Donaldson, 1985). Briefly, this hypothesis may be stated as follows. Written language is more removed from reality than spoken language: the spoken word represents an object while the written word represents a spoken word that represents an object. For this reason, the units of written language are more abstract than the units of spoken language. Also, in written language, the words themselves become an object of activity and cognition, which rarely occurs in spoken language. The writer must, at least when he is acquiring literacy, think about how one word or another is written, which word is better to use in a given concrete case, how to make up a sentence with the words, etc. In other words, the word itself must be realized, and Vygotsky regarded the realization of concepts (meanings of words) separately from their referents as an essential characteristic of scientific concepts. Finally, in written language, the words are as if extracted from the context of the objective and included in a verbal context. In the verbal context, the words may be manipulated in various ways, which cannot be done with their referents, and these manipulations may cooperate in the development of the logical structures of thinking.

Such arguments supporting the transforming effect that the acquisition of literacy has on verbal thinking seem convincing at first glance. However, if we think about the fact that if we stop with this hypothesis, we will have to explain, <u>with</u> <u>this</u> <u>single</u> <u>factor</u>, the <u>whole</u> uniqueness of scientific concepts and their potential operations, described by Vygotsky, then the hypothesis clearly begins to appear inadequate. Of all the characteristic traits of thinking in scientific concepts, enumerated several times above, only one follows, of necessity, from the hypothesis described: awareness of the word as a reality *sui generis*. The rest appear as possible, but not obligatory consequences of becoming literate. Naturally, preference must be given to an explanation in which all the characteristic traits of thinking in scientific concepts will appear as indispensable, obligatory consequences of schooling.

Until recently, no studies had been done in which the effect that the acquisition of literacy has on thinking was studied "in pure form"—as a rule, in school, children, like adults from traditional cultures, acquire the rudiments of scientific knowledge simultaneously with reading and writing, and for this reason, it seems impossible under normal circumstances to separate empirically the effect of each of the factors on thinking. Scribner and Cole (1978, 1981) were the first to study the thinking of literate people who had not been in contact with scientific knowledge. The study was done with the Vai tribe in Liberia. In about 1830, the Vai invented their own system of syllabic writing which some of the men of this tribe use even now in correspondence, in business records, journals, etc. The process of acquiring this system of writing occurs outside school and is not accompanied by the acquisition of scientific knowledge. Scribner and Cole did extensive comparative studies of thinking and memory in five groups of the population: 1) illiterate; 2) having command of the Vai system of writing; 3) having command of the Arabic system of writing; 4) having command of both these systems; 5) having command of the English system. The subjects of groups 3 and 4 studied in an Islamic school, the subjects of group 5, in a European-type school. Experiments on classification, on solution of syllogistic problems, on remembering objects, and on Piaget's nominal realism were used. A comparison of the results of the first two groups of subjects showed that literacy in itself does not generate the substantial differences in thinking that were found in many studies in the thinking of subjects attending and those not attending school, beginning with the work of Luria. As if this were not enough, literate subjects who had not attended school (group 2), had no greater ability to identify and realize elements of speech than did those who were illiterate.

In the preceding section of this chapter, we saw that illiterate subjects were able to distinguish between the word and its referent. By the same token, the "necessity falls away" of exactly that particular effect on thinking that would actually be expected from acquisition of literacy.

All of this casts doubt on the correctness of the idea, widespread in psychology, pedagogy, the history of culture, and in the political ideology of developing countries, that acquisition of literacy in itself is a factor that produces substantial changes in thinking processes.

Not having found the assumed strong effect of literacy on cognitive processes, the authors posed the question: does acquiring literacy have any consequences for cognitive processes? They established experimentally that literate subjects solve riddles better, are better at combining separate syllables and words they hear into words and sentences, and remember syllables better (we must note that Vai writing is syllabic). Differences were also found in communication habits, for example, in knowing how to state the rules of a game or point out the way to a farm. The consequences of literacy for cognitive processes were, in this way, much more specific than the hypothesis under consideration would allow us to assume.

After the detailed studies of Scribner and Cole, the hypothesis on the transforming effect of the acquisition of literacy on thinking can be rejected. Even if we assume that what is important is not literacy in itself, but what is written and how it is written, that is, the concrete functions of written language, it becomes clear that these functions proceed not from literacy itself, but from other components of culture that also may affect thinking in a direct, "oral" way, that is, bypassing literacy.

Thus, there is literacy that is not accompanied by scientific thinking. Of course, the converse question is also of great interest: is scientific thinking possible without literacy? We know, in any case, that in formative experiments, the inception of scientific thinking has been formed in children who did not yet know how to read and write. Still open is the culturological problem as to whether the presence in a culture of a system of writing is a necessary condition for the emergence of scientific thinking as has been asserted, for example, in Goody and Watt (1963) and Goody (1977). In any case, after the work of Scribner and Cole, one thing is obvious: a system of writing is not a sufficient condition for this.

According to the second hypothesis of Vygotsky, from which we proceeded in the present chapter, thinking changes in the course of schooling because in school children master specific—scientific—knowledge and methods of solving specific—scientific—problems. Above, we tried to show that the features of thinking in scientific concepts, enumerated by Vygotsky, are functionally related specifically to these factors.

It must be noted that if the hypothesis on the transforming effect that the acquisition of literacy has on thinking is frequently and extensively discussed in Vygotsky's work, the second hypothesis is presented there basically by implication. In one place, he connects the development of the structure (form) of thinking with changes in the content of thinking, in what is being thought of: "When we study how man makes the transition to thinking with the help of concepts, we find the necessary enabling condition for the content of man's thinking to attain its higher development. In the development of content, we observe stages which would be impossible without an understanding of the form that corresponds to them. And, conversely, we note that each new step in the development of higher forms of thinking becomes possible only with a new step in the development of the content which confronts thinking with problems that are ever broader in scale" (Stenographic report..., 1930, p. 327). Vygotsky does not consider in any great detail the problems of the determining role of acquiring scientific knowledge in the development of thinking. At the same time, in one of his works, he discusses a problem as specific as the role of various school subjects in a child's formation of scientific concepts: "... The development of a scientific concept and the specific weight of this process in the area of various subjects, for example, arithmetic and language, on the one hand, and social science and natural science, on the other, are different, of course. In arithmetic, the child acquires a certain kind of thinking regardless of the material involved in solving the problem. In social science and natural science, the material is the actual reality that the concept reflects. For this reason, it seems to me that the path of development of a scientific concept in arithmetic and the path of its development in social science may be somewhat different" (Vygotsky, 1935, p. 115). Here the nature of the knowledge and skills acquired, and not the acquisition of literacy, is specifically the factor controlling the development of scientific concepts. Also, it is not a chance circumstance that Vygotsky speaks of <u>scientific</u> concepts (and not, let us say, about arbitrary, realized, abstract, etc. concepts). Vygotsky's students and followers consider specifically the second hypothesis to be typical of his ideas. Expounding Vygotsky's position, Leont'ev and Luria (1956, p. 20) write: "Schooling differs qualitatively from learning in the broad sense. In school, the child is confronted with a specific problem: to master the basics of the sciences, that is, of systems of scientific concepts." El'konin and Davydov (1966, p. 37) hold to the same point of view: "Original with L. S. Vygotsky is not the general position on the developmental role of schooling, but the fact that he saw as the source of this role, the <u>content</u> of the acquired knowledge, the acquired scientific, and not empirical concepts which also require a special form of training" (cf. Ibid., p. 4). In the introduction to the Russian edition of the book of J. Bruner et al., <u>Studies</u> in <u>Cognitive</u> <u>Growth</u>, Davydov notes: "The special role of written language in the mental development of a child is well known. However, ... Bruner loses sight of the important circumstance that it is not language in itself, even written language, but the specific <u>content</u> of school information, expressed with the help of language, that has a decisive effect on the mental development of the child" (Davydov, 1971, p. 13).

Vygotsky's second hypothesis seems to us to be more sound theoretically than other extant hypotheses concerning the factors in school that have an effect on thinking. B. Rogoff in her review paper (1981) on cross-cultural studies, in which the connections between schooling and development of cognitive processes were studied, identifies the following factors in school that presumably have an effect on thinking:

1) explicitly formulated general rules play an important role in schooling and direct the students in an independent search for the rules on the basis of which concrete problems of one type or another can be solved;
2) while children in traditional cultures are taught predominantly by demonstration and participation in the activity of adults, schooling occurs basically verbally, and outside everyday activity and material context;
3) in school, children are taught specific habits which they then apply, for example, in solving experimental problems, which sometimes engenders substantial differences in experimental results of subjects attending and those not attending school (for example, remembering various material as an independent activity and the corresponding giving of meaning to initially unrelated material, defining concepts, etc.);
4) training in literacy with consequences enumerated above.

We will bypass literacy training and concentrate on the first three factors. It is natural to ask: what is the source of these factors, these traits characteristic for schooling? What binds them together? It is easy to see that they are all primarily connected with the circumstance that children in school are taught scientific knowledge and solving scientific problems. In principle, the child can be taught to behave in a fitting manner, to draw, plant vegetables, chop wood, to recognize the existing value system, to tell stories, and so on without turning for this to explicit formulation of general rules, to detailed verbalization, to defining concepts according to certain rules, etc. These types of activity do not presuppose that a person would necessarily proceed in each concrete case from a learned general rule, etc. In science, on the other hand, just as in teaching scientific facts (5) and the ways of solving scientific problems, the factors enumerated by Rogoff appear to be absolutely indispensable.

To the extent that existing experimental data confirm the role of the factors cited by Rogoff in the transformation of thinking, they also confirm Vygotsky's hypothesis. But the potentials of this hypothesis have by no means been exhausted by the current experimental studies. Obviously, on the basis of data on the pecularities of science as a form of activity and on corresponding traits of schooling, it would be possible to derive an entire systematic hypothesis on the differences between the thinking of people who had attended school and those who had not. In the present work, we have limited ourselves to those characteristic traits of thinking that Vygotsky himself included in the concept, "thinking in scientific concepts."

Two reservations concerning the changes evoked by schooling in people from traditional cultures follow from the ideas of Vygotsky and Leont'ev. We have tried to consider them above in the interpretation of experimental data to the extent that the existing experimental material allows this.

First, there is no basis for expecting that all thinking must change entirely under the influence of schooling and that subjects attending school must apply the type of thinking specific to science that they acquired in solving any experimental and ordinary problems. This follows from the idea of heterogeneity of thinking as it was formulated above (2.2).

Second, Vygotsky was interested not so much in the differences between the thinking of people who had attended school and those who had not as in the process of the change in thinking resulting from schooling. This process remains practically uninvestigated in current comparative studies of people from various cultural groups.

3.3.2. Cross-Cultural Differences in the Processes of Verbal Thinking and in Verbal Texts. While many investigators doubted and continue to doubt the existence of any serious differences in the thinking processes of people in various cultures, no one, it seems, doubts that there are differences in the texts of different cultures. Above (2.1.5.) we tried to substantiate the idea of the functional correspondence between the features of thinking processes used in one form of activity or another and the features of texts produced in those forms of activity.

Is it possible to detect in experimental studies differences between the texts of traditional and "modern" cultures corresponding to differences in the results of subjects attending and those not attending school? We have seen that the differences in thinking are, to a large extent, connected with the presence of reflection in subjects attending school and its absence in subjects from traditional groups. Where the former think of concepts and connections between them, of the problem itself and methods of solving it, the latter, evidently, think only of external, objective reality that comprises the referent of the concepts used and which is the subject of the problem. Can we then say that in verbal texts of "modern" cultures we find reflection and in texts of traditional cultures we do not? Naturally, in the case of "modern" cultures, we must be interested primarily in scientific texts, since they presuppose reflection much more obviously than, let us say, artistic or religious texts.

R. Horton (1967) in his well-known work presents a basic analysis of common and different traits of modern science and systems of thinking of traditional cultures. Horton finds substantial common traits which had not been previously seen with such clarity. In systems of thinking of traditional cultures, as in modern science, in explanations of phenomena, an attempt is made to reduce diversity to identity, to explain the complex through the simple. In both cases, analogy is used; in both cases, theoretical thinking is resorted to only when the problem cannot be solved by common sense, etc.

Horton believes that ethnologists usually do not note these common traits because in African thought, spirits, gods, etc. occupy the place of impersonal scientific categories—personified categories, however, fulfill the same function as categories of modern science. (Many authors connect the transition from personified categories to nonpersonified within the framework of European culture with the emergence of philosophy in Greece. "Milesian ... philosophers reject personification of natural phenomena and by the same token effect a transition from the image (religious-mythological) representation to an abstract concept, more precisely, to theoretical thinking. ... This transition ... meant the discovery of a new picture of the world in which phenomena are explained through their natural conditionality and it meant a new approach to explaining the origin of the visible world itself as a whole" (Kessidi, 1972, 122).)

Against the background of common traits, Horton identifies one substantial difference. Modern science continuously assumes the presence of alternative points of view, different explanatory systems, while in any traditional culture, there is only a single system of thinking, without alternative, which embraces all the knowledge and beliefs that exist in the culture. According to Horton, this circumstance has a decisive significance. If there are alternative systems of thinking in a culture, then it is possible to argue about which of them is better and more correct, which corresponds more closely to the reality it describes and explains. Only in a culture in which there are alternative systems of thinking is it possible and imperative for a methodology to emerge that permits a study and evaluation of the systems' correspondence to certain laws and of methods used in the systems to describe and explain reality, that is, of the systems themselves, and not just the reality described and explained with their aid. For example, modern botany studies not only the plants themselves, but also how the different systems classify plants, how they explain the emergence of and change in species, etc. In other words, modern science is self-conscious. If, however, only a single system of thinking exists in a culture, it cannot have self-consciousness: in principle it is not possible to think about such a system since all the knowledge is within it, it cannot be criticized, considered to be good or bad, right or wrong; for this, the presence of at least one alternative system is required.

As far as we know, investigators of the so-called ethnosciences have not made a general systematic comparison of such systems with modern sciences. In any case, ethno-botanical and ethnozoological classifications are frequently very rich and detailed. Ethnographers sometimes experience difficulties in assimilating them, which surprises people in the cultures in which the studies are being done. The following may be listed as the basic characteristics that distinguish modern science from ethnosciences: 1) if in ethnosciences, the main concern is describing and classifying, in modern science, the main concern is explaining; 2) for modern science, as distinct from ethnosciences, the presence of competing descriptive and explanatory systems is characteristic; 3) singlebase classification, general explanatory laws and absence of contradiction (within each separate system) is required of descriptive and explanatory systems in modern sciences; 4) the presence of explicit, universal judgments to which there are no exceptions is characteristic for modern science; 5) in modern science, some pieces of knowledge are frequently derived from others according to certain formal rules. Without in any way pretending that this is a complete list, against this background, we would like to identify one principal difference between ethnosciences and modern science: in ethnosciences there is apparently no knowledge of the rules of classification, consciously developed criteria and principles of classification, just as there are no rules for deriving one piece of knowledge from others. An ethnozoologist cannot make judgments such as Lamarck makes in his Philosophy of Zoology: "Everywhere in nature, where man strives to acquire knowledge, he must use special means ..., that which I call artificial devices in natural sciences, devices which should by no means be confused with laws and actions of nature itself ... Nature has created no such thing; and, instead of fooling ourselves, confusing our creations with its creations, we must admit that classes, orders, families, genera, and names are means of our invention ..." (Lamarck, 1935, pp. 30, 32). A study of ethnobotanical classification systems shows that people in traditional societies cannot state the criteria for classification and do not define the concepts they use in classification (Raven et al., 1971). Only the plants themselves are realized, but not concepts of them and no connections between concepts, that is, no thinking about plants.

If we proceed from the views of Horton, it becomes clear why there are sciences (ethnosciences or folk sciences) in traditional cultures concerning the external world, but no sciences about thinking itself and its relation to reality. Ethnobotany, ethnozoology, and ethnoastronomy exist, but not ethnologic, ethnoepistemology, or "ethnopsychology" as sciences of the cognitive processes. What is striking in works on so-called African philosophy (see, for example, Onyewuenyi, 1976/77; Griaule, 1965) is the absence of epistemological problematics.

Thus, there is a basis for assuming that classification systems in traditional societies are constructed on the basis of realizing only the objects and phenomena of the external world, while modern science also includes information on thinking, on concepts, and on rules of operating with concepts in structuring scientific information. Evidently, teaching of these various systems of knowledge also occurs in different ways and affects the thinking of the child in different ways. Perhaps we can assume that the child's acquisition of a single system, a system without alternatives, of traditional information on the external world does not lead to his realizing his own thoughts, while the formal aspect of teaching in a European school is specially directed toward the child's realizing his own thinking and errors in it, toward his acquiring the rules of thinking.

This conclusion corresponds directly to the fact that reflection is absent from the thinking of subjects from traditional cultures and groups, as has been established in experimental studies. A person does not begin to reflect over his own thinking, to evaluate and verify the course of his thinking if he has not acquired from the culture the knowledge that there are right and wrong thinking, right and wrong conclusions. Obviously, in any culture, a child or adult may be told that the content of his conclusions or assertions does not match reality or disagrees with what others think, but this, naturally, is not the same thing as pointing out to a person the logical contradiction in his thinking. In order to think about thinking and to perform thinking operations requiring reflection, certain concepts of the knowledge about thinking are necessary which the individual evidently cannot generate "for his own sake." Apparently, people from traditional cultures acquire such concepts and information for the first time only in school. Of great interest is the problem, never studied at all, of the form in which they acquire this knowledge and the form in which it functions in general in the thinking of an educated person. In recent years, work on these problems has started in child psychology in studies of so-called metacognition (see the review, T. Tulviste, 1984). The data accumulated have already provided a basis for a generalization like: "... much of cognitive development consists not in increasing or improving knowledge of the environment, but in increasing (metacognitive) awareness of one's own cognitive processes" (Moshman and Timmons, 1982).

Naturally, the reasons for the initial appearance in history of the knowledge of thinking are also of great interest. Horton points out that for traditional cultures, nonacceptance of foreign systems of thinking is typical. For this reason, contacts between traditional cultures are not enough for the people to begin to compare different systems: because of ethnocentrism, they believe their own system to be justified a priori. As prerequisites for interaction of different systems of thinking, Horton (1967, p. 180–185) identifies: l) presence of written documents indicating that people in the given culture had different beliefs earlier; 2) the development of heterogeneous societies; 3) travel, commerce, etc. In ancient Greece, several different cultures, equal at the outset, were united, which led to the existence within the framework of a single culture of several alternative systems of thinking. According to Horton, this may well be the explanation for the appearance of knowledge about thinking, about the relation between thinking and external reality.

As we know, the appearance of explicitly formulated rules of thinking in ancient Greece is connected with a whole series of social and cultural factors of various orders (for example, with the appearance of ancient democracy and individual responsibility for crimes, which led to the need to argue for one's own point of view and to refute others; with the appearance of a phonetic system of writing, etc.). For us something else is more important now. On the basis of the correspondence, described here, between the thinking processes of people in certain cultures and the verbal texts of these cultures, we may assert that reflection as a feature of thinking processes apparently first arose in ancient Greece (or in the ancient cultures of the Far East). In other words, the "higher" type of thinking that Vygotsky called thinking in scientific concepts and Piaget called thinking in formal operations and which is usually considered as a "natural" component of human thinking, derived from physiological or general biological factors, is the result of a unique sociocultural situation that developed in ancient Greece. Consequently, its causes and explanation must be sought not in the brain and in the natural phenomena in general, but in comparatively recent history. This is not the usual method of explanation in psychology. It became possible owing to the "humanities" approach to specifically human ("higher") mental processes and owing to the application in the psychology of thinking of the method of cross-cultural comparison. Every person knows that scientific, reflective thinking within the framework of European cultures first appeared in ancient Greece (see, for instance, Snell, 1946; Vernant, 1969; Kessidi, 1972; Gaidenko, 1980), but this was considered only as a cultural, not a psychological "event." It was not connected with the features of thinking processes as material for studying the psychology of thinking.

The appearance in ancient Greece or in the Far East of reflective thinking as a mental process requires detailed study and presents an interesting problem for historical psychology; in solving this problem, we will be able to and will need to depend on data from modern cross-cultural studies. The main difference between the appearance of thinking in scientific concepts in ancient Greece and in other cultures is obvious: if it appeared in Greece due to some combination of sociocultural circumstances not yet described precisely, then in other cultures, its main generative factor was and is schooling.

It would be extremely interesting to compare the effect on thinking processes of different reflective systems of thinking and the corresponding types of schooling. Thinking in scientific concepts (or, in any case, reflective thinking) appeared not only in Greece, but also in certain cultures of the ancient Far East. Various methods of the conscious realization of thinking may exist, and, accordingly, of monitoring it. These differences can also be subjected to experimental study, but data of this type are very sparse thus far (see, however, the data on the effect of Islamic education on thinking in Scribner and Cole, 1981).

Thus, comparing certain experimental data with the results of Horton's comparative analysis of the features of verbal texts of traditional and "modern" cultures is a basis for the assertion that there is actually a correspondence between the features of thinking processes and the verbal texts. This is evidence for the possibility, in principle, of making judgments on the basis of texts about the specifics of the course of thinking processes when direct study of these processes is ruled out.

3.3.3. Changes in Thinking and in Self-Consciousness.

Some authors note the differences in self-consciousness between subjects attending and those not attending school. P. Greenfield, studying the Piagetian phenomena in Wolof children (Senegal), writes: "An interesting problem arose when it came to asking the unschooled children to justify their answers to this question. A previous experiment had shown that whereas the question, 'Why do you think or say that thus and such is true?' would meet with uncomprehending silence, the question, 'Why is thus and such true?' could often be answered quite easily. ... It would seem that the unschooled Wolof children are lacking in Western self—consciousness: they do not distinguish between their own thought or a statement about something and the thing itself. Thought and the object of thought seem to be one" (Bruner et al., 1971, p. 279).

Luria studied self-consciousness of people from traditional cultures in a different way. He was interested in the extent to which adult subjects could analyze their own mental qualities, the traits of their own character (Luria, 1974, p. 150). It developed that traditional subjects almost never do this, but attending short literacy courses is enough to cause the appearance of subjects' judgments of their own character, mentality, etc. in the protocols of conversations with them. As an example, we will provide the protocol of a conversation with an 18-year-old, barely literate woman from an isolated Central Asian village (Ibid., pp. 151–152): "After a long conversation on the characteristics of people, about their individual differences, the question was asked:

—What shortcomings do you recognize in yourself, what would you like to correct?—Everything is all right with me. I myself have no shortcomings, but if I see shortcomings in others, I see them... What about me? ... I have only one dress and two smocks, those are all my shortcomings.
—No, I'm not asking you about that! Tell me what kind of person you are now and what kind would you like to be. No doubt there is some difference?
—I want to be better, now I am bad, I have few clothes, it's not proper to go about in another village like this.
—And what do you mean by "to be better?"
—I mean I want to have more clothes.
—And what shortcomings does your sister have?
—She is still small, young, she can't speak very well... But how should I know, you know, I'm here and she's in another village... I have a brother, he studied very well, he doesn't have to be corrected at all.

The connection between acquiring scientific information, methods of solving school (scientific) problems, on the one hand, and the appearance of developed self-consciousness, on the other, is clearly not accidental. Historians of culture connect the appearance of both science and developed self-consciousness with ancient Greece (for example, Snell, 1946; Barbu, 1960). (What is more, as we know, a rebirth of both these phenomena was characteristic for the Renaissance period.) Here, we should keep in mind that the dynamics of the interconnected appearance of scientific thinking and self-consciousness in Greece was substantially different from its dynamics in people from present-day traditional cultures. In Greece, developed self-consciousness appeared due to diverse sociocultural circumstances. It is clear that self-consciousness changes when the social system changes: for example, when a single individual (and not the tribe) becomes the subject of social relations, when people begin to consider him as personally responsible for his actions, as their only "author"; when he begins self-consciously to choose a profession corresponding to his own inclinations and abilities, etc. It is less obvious why developed self-consciousness appears in school as a result of acquiring scientific knowledge while general social conditions do not at all require that the individual should single himself out from others and become conscious of his own mental processes and the traits of his personality.

As far as we know, thus far there has been no systematic study of the change in self-consciousness in children and adults from traditional cultures under the influence of schooling. We limit ourselves here to only a few remarks on this.

We may assume that schooling causes changes in self-consciousness for two different, but interrelated reasons.

We have seen above that solving scientific problems, including school problems, assumes a person's awareness of certain aspects of his own thinking while solving problems that are practical, ideological, etc. does not assume this. For this reason, we may say that schooling extends the circle of components of a person's own "I" of which he is conscious: this includes processes of thinking (and, evidently, memory, although manifestations of so-called metamemory have thus far been rarely studied in cross-cultural investigations). This change in self-consciousness seems to be obligatory since it is impossible to imagine solving scientific problems without reflection.

Another possible reason for changes in self-consciousness consists of the following: science, apparently more than any other kind of activity, requires a person to compare his own point of view with that of others. This is the result of the essence of scientific activity where value of assertions or theories is determined by how much better than already existing theories they explain a phenomenon. In science, for substantiating one's solution of a problem, one cannot cite the fact that "we always thought so (or did this)." If in other kinds of activity, it is frequently possible to depend on the opinions of others, in solving a scientific, or even a school problem, one must find the answer independently. It may be correct even when all others hold a different opinion. It is difficult to say how and to what extent this feature of science is reflected in schooling. In any case, the logical correctness as a criterion for evaluating judgments makes a person more independent, less dependent on the opinions of others, than other criteria. And comparing oneself with others comprises, as we know, an important component of self-consciousness.

Of course, only empirical studies can reveal the actual mechanisms of the effect of schooling on self-consciousness. In conclusion, I would like to note that in developing countries, both scientific thinking and developed self-consciousness are now appearing in the people en masse. Unexploited possibilities exist here for direct empirical study of processes similar in certain substantial aspects to those that occurred in ancient Greece 2500 years ago.

3.4. Conclusions. In order to find the weak places in our present general ideas about the connections between culture and thinking, it would be useful to turn our attention to the experimental results that surprise us.

These include, first, the circumstance that adults who had not attended school do not solve the simplest syllogistic problems, from the point of view of an educated person, if the reality involved in the problems is not familiar to them. The reason for surprise is evidently that we, with no adequate basis, consider our own thinking in all its essential traits, to be "natural" and universal human thinking. Solving the problem consists not in minimizing the significance of results obtained, but in acknowledging the method of thinking that subjects attending school use in these experiments as a particular case of human thinking. These results, like many other facts established in comparative experimental studies, show that thinking of people in "modern" cultures depends to a much greater degree than was assumed on the important role that science and school have for a long time played in European culture. We always knew that such a relationship exists, but only after comparative study of the thinking of people from different cultures and cultural groups did it become clear that even an "elementary" syllogistic conclusion owes its appearance and existence to science and school.

No less surprising are the results of studies on classification (see 3.2.5) and on problem solving (for example, Wason and Johnson–Laird, 1972; Podgoretskaya, 1980) that indicate that in the thinking of people who had attended school, there is much that is in no way connected with our ideas about logic as an essential property of the thinking of an educated person.

Taken as a whole, these two groups of data create a paradox. On the one hand, in its origin, the thinking of people in "modern" cultures seems to be connected with science to a much greater degree than has been assumed. On the other hand, in its nature, it seems to be scientific to a much lesser degree than we have thought. It is easy to see that this paradox reflects a contradiction not between the two indicated groups of experimental data, but between our general ideas about the nature of "our" thinking which we believe, on the one hand, to be natural and universal and, on the other, to be logical and scientific.

The paradox vanishes if we admit a much greater than heretofore dependence of thinking on culture, on activity, on those problems that people must solve. Then we will be left with very little basis for believing the thinking of people who had attended school to be "natural" and universal and for reducing it to one of its quite specific types, to thinking in scientific concepts.

The attempt undertaken in this chapter to interpret the results in identical experiments of subjects who had attended school and those who had not led us to the following basic conclusions:

1. The differences in experimental results of these two groups of subjects may be predicted and explained if we proceed from the peculiarities of science as a type of activity and scientific problems as problems of a special type.
2. There are certain bases for believing that schooling engenders a new type of verbal thinking in people from traditional cultures which might expediently be described as thinking in scientific concepts (according to Vygotsky). This type of thinking differs from other types both in its functions and in its structure (according to units and operations).

3. This new type of thinking does not abolish or replace previously existing types of thinking functionally corresponding to other types of activity and problems.
4. The differences in thinking of subjects who had attended school and those who had not correspond to certain differences in their self-consciousness and in verbal texts of the cultures to which they belong.

CHAPTER 4

Linguistic and Activity Relativity of Thinking

According to the hypothesis of linguistic relativity, best known now in the form of the Sapir–Whorf hypothesis, a person's representation of the world, his behavior and cognitive processes are subject to some influence of the lexical and grammatical features of the particular language he speaks. Since human thinking, memory and perception are mediated by language, and human languages differ substantially from each other, presumably there are differences in these processes among people who speak different languages (Carroll, 1964, p. 218, for example). In this chapter, we will deal primarily with the differences in cognitive processes, not with how the different languages analyze reality.

The Sapir–Whorf hypothesis has more of the status of an ideological assertion than of a hypothesis in the strict sense of the word. On this point, R. M. Frumkina (1980, p. 198) writes: "The Sapir–Whorf hypothesis, which has generated an extensive bibliography and even now has its proponents and opponents, was never formulated very clearly. There is no formulation of this hypothesis that could be considered 'canonical.' Various authors for whom the Sapir–Whorf hypothesis served as a point of departure for their work modified Whorf's formulation either to correspond to their own understanding of Whorf's basic position or on the basis of their sphere of interests. And in each case, it turned out that to some extent the proposed modifications were quite 'correlated' with Whorf's formulations. In this sense we ... may say that Whorf formulated this hypothesis in the form of a 'fuzzy concept'."

Our purpose is not to present a new modification of the Sapir–Whorf hypothesis or to systematize it (see the systematization carried out by Fishman, 1960), and especially not to verify it. Our purpose is much more modest. Various scholars have done numerous experiments directed toward confirming some particular hypotheses flowing from the Sapir–Whorf hypothesis. We will compare some of the differences these studies found in the cognitive processes of people speaking different languages with the differences in thinking of people from various cultures and cultural groups established in comparative studies of verbal thinking, due not to language, but to differences in activity between the cultures. Then we will consider certain linguistic aspects of cross-cultural differences in thinking that are due to activity.

4.1. A Comparison of the Differences in Thinking Due to Features of Language and Differences Due to Features of Activity. As we know, the Sapir–Whorf hypothesis was at first corroborated by speculative arguments. Proceeding from the features of language, assumptions were made about the features of cognitive processes without subjecting them to empirical confirmation since their justifiability seemed self-evident. An example from the literature: the grammar of the Nootka Indian language (Vancouver Island) requires that if someone is spoken of, the speaker must without fail include information on whether or not the person spoken of is left-handed, bald, short, astigmatic and has a good appetite. Because of the features of the grammar of the language, these data must inevitably be conveyed in speech regardless of whether they are significant within the given context of communication or not. Languages we are more familiar with place no such requirement before the speaker. Correspondingly, we may assume that the perception of a person by a Nootka Indian would be much richer in content than that of people who speak other languages. But this assumption was not confirmed empirically and was not demonstrated. Empirical verification is nevertheless essential. The fact that people speaking other languages do not need to convey in their speech similar details concerning a person spoken of does not at all mean that they do not note these details. For example, in Russian, one cannot use the past tense to say that a person did something if it is not known whether the person was a man or a woman. [Translator's note: in Russian, past tense verbs have gender endings.] One may do so in Estonian and, as a rule, gender is not indicated since the grammar of the language does not require this. However, it does not follow from this that an Estonian does not notice a person's gender.

Beginning with the 1950s, some hypotheses on the features of cognitive processes based on features of language were subjected to empirical confirmation, including studies by experimental psychologists. The direction of the hypotheses in these works was always the same: from language to cognitive processes. Proceeding from the features of the vocabulary or grammar of a language, the investigators looked for features of perception, memory and thinking. In many (although not in all) cases, corresponding features in cognitive processes were found. We will briefly consider some of the experimental studies which have become almost classical in their sphere (1).

R. Brown and E. Lenneberg (1954) proposed that since in memory of color, verbal memory (memory of color designations) operates together with visual memory, colors that can be easily named in a given language must be remembered better than others. Experiments were done with subjects speaking English. Easily named colors were defined in the following way: the subjects were asked to name the colors of 24 chips presented to them, and the colors that all the subjects named with the same word were identified as being easily named. Then a test was carried out to determine whether the easily named colors are remembered better than the others. The subject looked at four colored chips for 5 seconds, they were then removed and he was asked to find corresponding colors among 120 various colors. The correlation between the ease of naming a color and correctness of recognizing was not very high. If, however, there was a pause between looking at the chips and the presentation of the colors for recognition, the correlation increased significantly (in long-term retention of color in the memory, the role of verbal memory is greater than in short-term retention). It was thus possible to fix empirically the influence of the features of vocabulary on recognition as one of the processes of memory.

Since different languages divide the color spectrum in different ways, the ease of naming certain colors in them is not identical. If the ease of naming and memory are related, as the experiment described indicated, then people who speak in languages that divide the spectrum differently must remember and recognize one color or another with varying success, depending on the presence of a name for a corresponding color in their languages.

The correctness of such a hypothesis was demonstrated in the experiments of Lenneberg and Roberts (1956). The subjects were three groups of Zuni Indians. One group knew only their native language, another knew their native language and English, and the third knew only English. The Zuni language does not distinguish yellow and orange; in English, they are distinguished. The investigators expected that the subjects speaking only the Zuni language would experience more difficulty in recognizing these colors than subjects speaking two languages or speaking only English. The hypothesis was confirmed.

Lantz and Stefflre (1964) developed a new criterion for ease of naming (codability) based on ease of communication. Memory may be considered as a person's communicating with himself. It was proposed that if a person can successfully describe certain colors to another person, then he can name them very well for himself and, correspondingly, remember them very well with the help of words. Lantz and Stefflre identified as easily named those colors that one subject could describe verbally to another in such a way that the second person would recognize them. This criterion did not propose the naming of any color with one word—after the inspection, the subject could use as many words as he wanted in his description. It developed that with this criterion, the correlation between ease of naming and success in recognition was substantially higher than when the criterion was identical one-word naming of a certain color by many subjects. In the work of other authors who used the new criterion of codability, a close connection was also discovered between ease of naming and recognition of colors. After Lantz and Stefflre, Cole and Scribner stress that from the point of view of memory and other cognitive processes, it is apparent that features of the language itself and its statics (in this case, vocabulary) are not as important as features of <u>using</u> the language. It is not very important whether one individual word or another exists in a language. It is important that the subject was able to name the given reality—with one word or with several words.

The results described above and those of certain other investigators are a basis for claiming that cognitive processes of people speaking in languages with different lexical content actually have corresponding features.

Carroll and Casagrande (1958) demonstrated experimentally that the grammatical features of language may also influence cognitive processes. We know that in free classification of objects, children begin to make up groups on the basis of color earlier than on the basis of form. In other words, for small children, color is a more "important" trait of an object than form, but with age, this relation changes. In the language of Navajo Indians, verbs designating manipulation of objects are used with various suffixes depending on what the form of the objects being discussed is. In order to speak correctly, the speaker must pay attention to the form of objects. Carroll and Casagrande proposed that since English does not require this of the speaker, there is a basis for assuming that in children speaking the Navajo language, the transition from dominance of classification on the basis of color to dominance of classification on the basis of form must occur earlier than in English-speaking children. The results of the experiment confirmed the hypothesis. This demonstrated the influence of features of grammar on the development of thinking.

Hypotheses on the influence of the features of language on cognitive processes were not confirmed in all studies, but here it is enough for us that the presence of such an influence was confirmed in many cases. Other experimental studies undertaken to confirm the Sapir–Whorf hypothesis basically define more precisely the sphere of the justifiability of the connections indicated and certain other connections between language and cognitive processes.

Thus, we can say that features were discovered in cognitive processes that correspond to features of specific languages. Some features of the vocabulary of a language facilitate recognition and some features of grammar accelerate a recognized change in the development of thinking in the child.

However, the differences between cognitive processes of people speaking different languages, found in the experimental work described, cannot be called substantial from the point of view of studying cognitive processes. They cannot be described in the basic categories of the psychology of cognitive processes or psycholinguistics and clearly are not of a qualitative character. All people can, within the framework of their physiological abilities (2), recognize any colors. All children make a transition from classification on the basis of color to classification on the basis of form no matter which language they speak. Of much greater interest would be the differences in the course of the cognitive processes themselves, in the methods of perception, thinking and remembering. It would be interesting if people speaking one language would think or remember not sooner or more easily, but differently from the way people do who speak another language.

We might expect that the Sapir–Whorf hypothesis would lead to the discovery of substantial differences between cognitive processes of people speaking different-languages. However, this did not happen. On the basis of available experimental data, we cannot say that different types of cognitive processes correspond to different languages.

But do we have a right to expect that there are substantial differences in peoples' cognitive processes? Is it possible that such differences were not found in the works described because, on the whole, all people think and remember identically? In the preceding chapter, we saw that such differences do exist— primarily between the thinking of people who had attended school and those who had not. But these differences were due to differences not between languages, but between types of activity and methods of preparing children for the activity. By analogy to linguistic relativity, diversity in cognitive processes due to activity may be called activity relativity.

4.2. The Connections between Features of Activity, Language, and Thinking. The Sapir–Whorf hypothesis is based on an unstated assumption that some "one kind" of thinking corresponds to every language. Luria (1974, pp. 13–15) writes: "... In the work of the school of 'linguistic relativism,' a simplified idea of direct parallelism between language and thinking can be clearly traced ... diversity of content which might stand behind every word was ignored ... completely different forms of information on phenomena may be hidden behind identical vocabulary ... one and the same word may represent absolutely nonidentical systems of relations, that is, the meaning of words itself is developing." The results of studies of the development of verbal thinking and formation of concepts in the child, like the results of comparative experimental studies of thinking in people in different cultures and cultural groups are evidence that such correspondence does not exist. In any language, it is possible to think with methods qualitatively different and distinct from each other. And the differences due to activity, as we have seen, are much more substantial than those connected with differences between languages. Data presently available indicate that scientific thinking carried out in any arbitrarily chosen language has much more in common with scientific thinking in other languages than with common sense, with poetic or mystical thinking in the same language.

As distinct from the differences in cognitive processes corresponding to language differences, activity differences in cognitive processes are indispensable (from the point of view of theory). There is no need for people speaking different languages to think differently although they may think differently. On the other hand, activity differences in thinking are unavoidable since no one type of thinking is applicable to solving all problems. Scientific thinking cannot replace common sense or poetic thinking, and, vice versa, whereas functionally, thinking in English can scarcely not replace thinking in German.

In 2.3, we considered the typology of verbal thinking developed by Vygotsky. In this typology, which encompasses both units and operations of verbal thinking, the different types differ from each other in method of using the word in thinking. One and the same word is used differently in scientific thinking and in different types of complex thinking, for example, in everyday thinking (common sense) and in poetic thinking. Thus, if linguistic relativity is linked with linguistic statics, with features of its vocabulary and grammar, then activity relativity in higher cognitive processes is also linked with language, not with its statics, but with its dynamics—the use of language.

In modern linguistics, the use of language is also studied—specifically, studies are being made of the functions of language in culture. Hymes (1974) believes that the traditional representation, stemming from Herder, that the world consists of units of the type, "one ethnos—one language," is one-sided and inadequate. Any ethnos, any individual has a corresponding whole repertoire of "ways of speaking." "Ways of speaking" encompass speech styles, contexts of speech, and rules pertaining to style and context.

Correspondingly, Hymes makes a distinction between the classical linguistic relativity connected with the statics of language and functional relativity. In comparing the structures of languages, Sapir and Whorf proceeded from the premise that all languages fulfill the same functions. Hymes (1975a, p. 232) believes that "the role of language may be different in different language collectives and that, on the whole, functions of language in a society are a problem that should be studied and not accepted as a postulate ... If this is so, then the cognitive significance of any language depends not only on structures, but also on models of application." Earlier, the functions of language in a culture were evaluated basically in considering the phenomenon of multilingualism in which different languages fulfill different roles in the culture. But the problem of function of language also arises in monolingualism: "If in a multilingual situation, inquiry is made as to which of the languages, or codes, has a certain role, then in a monolingual situation, one might ask, <u>does</u> the given language have a certain role and if it does, then to what degree?" (Hymes, 1975a, p. 245).

For the psychology of cognitive processes, functional linguistic relativity is of great interest. We have seen (2.3) that it is expedient to interpret different types of verbal thinking as different methods of using the word in thinking. However, since verbal thinking has its origin in the interiorization of external speech, then it is reasonable to propose that there must be a correspondence between different styles of speech and types of verbal thinking. (We know that the structure of internal speech differs from the structure of external speech, but there is something common to both in their structure and in their functions—the problems that small children solve in external speech, older children solve [frequently using the same method] within the framework of internal speech.) In connection with this, the question arises as to the extent to which the functions of language in a culture which have been identified in linguistic research correspond to types of thinking found in studies of verbal thinking done in experimental psychology.

Hymes (1975b, p. 67) enumerates the following functions of language in a culture: expressive, directive, poetic, contact, metalanguage, referential, and contextual. Thus far these functions have not been studied in detail.

Linguistics and psychology of thinking now proceed from different aspects of culture. While Hymes enumerates the functions of language in <u>social intercourse</u>, the types of thinking described in psychology correspond, as we have seen, to different types of <u>activity</u>. Among the functions mentioned by Hymes, only the poetic may be directly ascribed to a specific type of activity. For the psychology of thinking at present, for example, linguistic and semiotic description of the specifics of using language in scientific information and in scientific texts would have more meaning.

What the approaches of Vygotsky and Hymes have in common is that in both cases socially normed methods of using language are studied: in Vygotsky, in thinking, and in Hymes, in social intercourse. In the experiments on color recognition considered above, the use of language was not studied as a separate problem—the dynamics of language was simply contrasted with its statics. We saw that the ease of naming colors correlated to a greater degree with successful recognition when the "dynamic" criteria of Lantz and Stefflre were used than with the "statics" criteria of Brown and Lenneberg. Thus, we may assert that the use of language had a greater significance than the features of the language itself. But are we dealing here with socially normed methods of using language and with what kind specifically? This question still remains unanswered.

It is obviously not reasonable to limit ourselves to only contrasting classical and functional linguistic relativity. We might assume that there must be a correspondence between the static features of a language and those functions that the given language fulfills in the culture. For example, if one language is used in scientific activity and communication and another is not, then should there not be a correspondence between those functional differences and some kind of differences in the statics of the languages?

P. Kay (1977) connects the methods of using a language with the types of activity existing in one culture or another. Methods of using language, in their turn, influence the statics of the language. Thus, according to Kay, one of the tendencies in the historical development of language is that the grammatical relations become more and more explicit. Kay believes that this tendency corresponds to the appearance and spread of methods of using language which deal with realities with which the participants in the conversation are not equally familiar and in which it is not possible to rely on a general situation which would involve both the speakers and the realities spoken of. Progressive division of labor in a society makes mutual understanding between people more difficult in comparison with societies in which all the people are occupied in identical types of activity. Diversity in types of activity engenders so-called autonomous speech that has little connection with nonspeech channels of communication and does not presuppose the presence in the listener of preliminary knowledge of the reality concerned. According to Kay, the main trend in the development of the use of language consists in a movement from nonautonomous systems of communication to autonomous. Kay cites empirical data indicating corresponding differences in vocabulary and grammar of languages used in currently existing traditional cultures and languages used in cultures for which far-reaching division of labor and presence of literacy are characteristic.

Of course, the tendency in development of language described by Kay is not the only tendency, and it scarcely has had the same major significance at all stages of the historical development of language. But such an approach opens more interesting prospects for the study of the connections between language and cognitive processes than the classical hypothesis of Sapir and Whorf. Kay's ideas about the causal connections between language, activity and cognitive processes correspond much more closely to empirical data than the so-called deterministic variant of the Sapir–Whorf hypothesis. According to the latter, specifically, changes in language would have to involve changes in cognitive processes. But no existing data confirm the presence of such a causal connection. Brown's words remain valid: "I don't know of any attempts as yet to show that an independently defined linguistic pattern has either historical or biographical priority over the thought pattern it is supposed to determine" (Brown, 1958, p. 262).

We have seen that changes in methods of using language and in the language itself, just like changes in cognitive processes, may be deduced from changes in activity in the course of the historical development of a society. A causal connection proceeds not from language to cognitive processes, but from activity to language and to cognitive processes.

In psychology, the features of scientific thinking have been studied most of all. This is true not only in child psychology, but also in the comparative study of thinking of people in different cultures and cultural groups. In the case of scientific thinking, "pure" comparisons are possible—cultures exist which do not have modern science, meanwhile there are no cultures which do not have different types of practical activity, art or ideology. For this reason, it would be expedient to turn our attention to those changes in language that are due to the introduction of schooling and modern scientific information into a culture. For example, in scientific activity, verification of all conclusions by comparing them with reality is inconceivable. Conclusions are verified by explicit or implicit application of knowledge of the laws of deduction. Since other types of activity evidently do not require such a method of verification of conclusions, then with the spread of schooling and scientific information, words must appear in the language ("logically," for example) that allow evaluation of the logical correctness of a conclusion (or existing words must acquire a new, additional meaning).

In experiments undertaken to confirm the Sapir–Whorf hypothesis, concrete hypotheses were always constructed on the basis of features of language and then confirmed with material from behavior and cognitive processes. This direction was suggested by the representation on the direction of causal connections: from language to thinking and activity. These studies did not lead to the discovery of any substantial differences in cognitive processes. Since another idea about causal connections may be considered more correct—from activity to language and cognitive processes—it would be reasonable to try to turn the design of empirical studies head over heels and use the features of certain types of activity as a basis for developing a hypothesis on vocabulary and grammar of languages used in given types of activity. It is possible that in this way we might find more substantial differences in the statics of different languages that would correspond to the features of activity and cognitive processes than the differences which have been used thus far in planning experimental studies.

It is completely normal that the course of thinking as a process is determined by activity, and not by language. In psychology, thinking is defined and studied mainly as problem-solving. Problems, however, are made up by activity, not by language. For this reason, the substantial differences between the thinking of people in different cultures and cultural groups correspond not to the languages which they speak, but to the types of activities in which they are engaged. Since in any culture, there are various types of activity that place different problems before a person, and since no single type of thinking is suitable for solving all problems, no single type of thinking, but various types of thinking correspond to any language (with the single exception of a situation in some culture in which there was only one sphere of activity for one language, while for all other spheres another language was used).

In this chapter, we made an attempt to show that features of cognitive processes depend much more on activity than on language. In other words, activity relativity is more significant that linguistic relativity. But how can we explain the continuous lively interest in linguistic relativity regardless of the shakiness of the factual basis of the hypothesis?

From the very beginning (starting with Humboldt), assertions concerning linguistic relativity were directly connected with ideological claims, with the desire to establish originality and uniqueness of thinking of the speakers of one language or another, or with the romantic search for alternatives to "European" thinking.

Fishman indicates even more remote ideological sources for the hypothesis of linguistic relativity: "Humboldtian ethnolinguistics ... has ancient and complex roots in folklore of many peoples. No doubt the connection between originality of a people and its language appeared long ago in the history of European and Near Eastern civilization. Ancient Greeks used the word, 'barbarians,' (those who say ba-ba, that is, speak an unintelligible language) with respect to those whom the gods did not endow with the Greek language, and ancient Hebrews believed that their language is a sacred resource without equal, created before the creation of the world and presented to them as a special gift of God. There is no doubt that linguistic consciousness, linguistic pride, faith in one's own linguistic exclusivity and, emanating from this, the untranslatability of one's own or someone else's higher language were often a part of ethnocentrism and the world view of many ancient and modern nations. Whorf's hypothesis was an attempt at a scientific approach to linguistic-behavioral phenomena pertaining to this imprecisely defined area, which until recently had been subject mainly to the strong influence of beliefs and emotions, and an attempt to provide an objective evaluation of these phenomena" (Fishman, 1960). Thus, assertions on the all-embracing uniqueness of the thinking of people speaking a certain language are an argument for the "we—they" oppositions. From social psychology, we know (see Porshnev, 1973, for example) that to preserve any social or ethnic group, it must be opposed to other groups and that it evaluate itself as being better in some way than other groups. If we add to the obvious differences between languages the assertion that, because of the uniqueness of their language, members of one ethnic group think and behave differently from members of other ethnic groups, then we have here a strong argument for the "we—they" opposition. In the modern world, the weight of any argument increases if it is recognized as being "scientific." Obviously, linguistic relativity has significantly more possibilities for being an argument for the "we—they" opposition than does activity relativity. We think that this is specifically what explains the lesser popularity of the ponderable phenomenon of activity relativity.

4.3. Conclusions. Verbal thinking, its units and operations are determined by activity. For this reason, the hypotheses on substantial features of thinking may be derived on the basis of studying features not of languages, but those types of activity in which thinking is applied and those problems that are being solved.

One and the same language and its lexical and grammatical features are used differently in different types of activity. The differences between respective types of verbal thinking are more substantial than the differences due to features of languages. As sociolinguistics and psycholinguistics undertake studies of the functions of language and features of its usage in various types of activity, new possibilities are discovered for psychological study of types of verbal thinking.

CONCLUSION

On the basis of the arguments presented and experimental data, we can assert that thinking in traditional cultures differs in certain aspects, sometimes qualitatively, from thinking in "modern" cultures. These differences are due to the circumstance that types of activity in which people in one culture or another are engaged and problems which they solve are partially different. On the other hand, universal types of verbal thinking correspond to common types of activity. Since scientific information and schooling are spreading rapidly in many countries where they were previously unknown, we must hurry to study the differences in thinking of people from different cultures and cultural groups that are due to these factors.

The thinking of people in "modern" cultures is more diverse, more heterogeneous, than we usually think. In addition to scientific thinking, it includes other types of verbal thinking, whose study and purposeful development have received too little attention thus far. Meanwhile, the features of thinking in these cultures are conditioned by science to an even greater degree than we are accustomed to think. Like the thinking of people in traditional cultures, it is not "natural" human thinking, but corresponds to certain types of activity in which it is used. All types of verbal thinking are subject to elucidation through culture and history, and more precisely, through activity and its historical development.

Verbal thinking in its units and operations has changed, is changing and will change to the extent that human activity changes and the problems that need to be solved change. One of the aspects of the cultural-historical development of thinking is that people begin to be aware of their thinking and control it. Since the psychology of thinking elucidates the patterns of the processes of thinking, in this aspect, it may, obviously, assist in its development to some extent.

Finally, I must say that in this book, a sphere of science is discussed in which the basic empirical work was done in the last 10 years. The number of studies is growing rapidly. We can only hope that the data presented here and the inferences and assumptions will help to elucidate new facts and facilitate the appearance of more adequate inferences and assumptions.

Notes

Chapter 1

1. With mental development, thinking becomes ever more differentiated from perception and action and, in comparison with perception, its role increases. In "primitives," however, perception dominates; their emotions are stronger than those of Europeans, and this impedes the development of thinking: "... because of the general antagonism between activities of simpler abilities and ... more complex ... dominance of lower life interferes with higher mental life" (Spencer, 1876–1877, p. 89). The results of experimental studies done later showed that actually there is no cross-cultural difference in sharpness of senses. The problem Spencer raised of change in interfunctional relations in the course of mental development is being discussed even now in the study of both sociogenesis and ontogenesis of the mind.

2. Similar hypothetical, not to say arbitrary, reconstructions of the possible course of the development of various beliefs based on the assumption of the essential identity of thinking operations in any cultures and any historical epochs constitute a large part of the first volume of Spencer's Principles of Sociology.

3. For example, "The aboriginal Australians customarily held to be one of the most 'primitive' peoples on earth, have a kinship terminology and a method of counting kinship based on it so complex that for many years it defied the attempts of students to analyze it. It puts to shame our own simple series of kinship terms where we do not even distinguish between paternal and maternal grandparents or older or younger brother and call literally dozens of relatives by the same word, 'cousin'" (Herskovits, 1955, p. 360). This example in the present context is good in that Spencer deduces growing complexity of conceptual systems from complexity of the environment and, from the point of view of common sense, this may seem convincing. In the given case, however, the object (biological kinship) remains unchanged through history, and corresponding conceptual systems are undoubtedly becoming simplified. Here it is obvious that complexity of the conceptual system depends not on complexity of the object as such, but on the extent to which people in one culture or another need to classify a given material and designate its elements.

4. J. Smith (Smith, 1972) showed that precisely this famous example of "prelogical" thinking, under lively discussion in the literature even now, is

partially based on a misunderstanding: most likely, the Bororo had in mind specifically that <u>after</u> <u>death</u> they turn into araras. However, other similar examples may be cited, the authenticity of which is undoubted (Ibid., and Salmon, 1978). Also compare the analysis of the Holy Trinity proposed by Leach (Leach, 1976, pp. 67–70).

5. Probably the appearance of this idea in Levy–Bruhl is connected not only with a rejection of "flat evolutionism," but also with the circumstance that Durkheim rejected the idea of evolutionists that all human societies take the same path of historical development in a certain order. Durkheim wrote: "There is no basis for the assumption that different types of people develop in the same mode; they take various paths. Human development must be represented not in the form of a straight line, but as a tree with various and multiple branches" (cited from Sorokin, 1920, p. 285).

6. He writes: "Only at the beginning of the 20th century did works appear that systematized the many ethnographic data accumulated earlier on the qualitative uniqueness of the thinking of peoples that are on relatively low rungs of socioeconomic and cultural development (Levy–Bruhl, Weule et al.). In spite of the unsatisfactory quality of the theoretical interpretations of the factual material presented, these works were significant in that they showed the insupportability of the position on the immutability of laws of the human mind and introduced into the study of thinking the idea of qualitative changes which thinking undergoes in the course of historical development" (Leont'ev, 1964, p. 87. See also Leont'ev, 1931, p. 55).

7. Both of these assertions in their time were widespread: almost all authors believed that thinking of "primitives" is extraordinarily emotional and that "underdevelopment" of thinking in them is compensated for by an exceptionally good memory. Compare this with the ideas of Spencer on the relation of perception and thinking in peoples in various cultures.

8. If Levy–Bruhl usually contrasts common sense and scientific thinking, taken together, with "prelogical collective representations," then in this excerpt, on the contrary, he contrasts scientific thinking with that which is used in "everyday practice."

9. Both deficiencies, limiting the number of possible types of thinking to only two without any real basis and the ambiguity of categories used in describing the types of thinking, are present not only in the typology of Levy–Bruhl, but in almost all existing typologies of verbal thinking. See Tulviste, 1981c, and 2.3.1 in this book.

10. In as categorical a form as in Vygotsky, this idea was presented at that time in the works of M. M. Bakhtin: "We cannot deduce consciousness directly from nature as naive mechanistic materialism and modern objective psychology have attempted and still attempt to do ... Consciousness is made up of and functions in symbols created in the process of social contacts of an organized collective. Individual consciousness is nurtured by symbols, grows from them and reflects their logic and their pattern in itself" (Voloshinov, 1930, p. 17). Accordingly, "the conscious mind is a social-ideological fact accessible to neither physiological nor any other natural-science methods ... the psychic phenomenon can be explained only by social factors" (Ibid, p. 28). For the influence of Bakhtin's ideas on Vygotsky, see Ivanov, 1973, pp. 21–22, 24–25. Also compare A. N. Leont'ev's "It was exactly the humanitarian (particularly semantic and semiotic) culture that was adopted by Vygotsky in his years of work on The Psychology of Art that helped him not to yield to reflexological schemes ..." (1982, p. 32).

11. On this point, see, for example, Leont'ev, 1982, pp. 25, 28; Yaroshevskii, 1984, p. 333.

12. The general attitude of Levi–Strauss toward history and the historical approach is expressed here. Concerning this, see the special work of C. Parain (1975). Parain (p. 364) justifiably writes that "in Levy–Strauss' book La Pensée Sauvage, attention to history seems more like a concession than evidence of the author's serious convictions."

13. S. Clarke develops a similar argument: "It is on the basis of the asserted character of the mind that the myth is reduced to a formal structure, that structure being explained as an effect of the mind. When it is asserted that the structures which appear reveal the character of the unconscious mind, this assertion can be no more than a tautology, for it is on the basis of the assumed character of the mind that the structures were identified as constitutive of myth (Clarke, 1977, p. 745)."

14. M. Harris compares Levi–Strauss's postulating mental structures precisely with postulating instincts, in particular, by psychoanalysts: "This search for elementary mental 'structure' is nothing but a return to the practice of explaining sociocultural phenomena by means of conveniently posited instincts. For a universal instinctual dread of sleeping with one's mother, Levi–Strauss substitutes a universal mental duality of self and other. The methodological error is identical" (Harris, 1969, p. 492).

15. Having a high opinion of the contribution of Levi–Strauss to the study of archaic thinking, M. M. Mukanov and N.I. Chistyakova write: "From the point of view of the psychologist, the research of Levi–Strauss is most valuable in that it shook our faith in the conception of Levy–Bruhl on prelogical thinking and demonstrated the identity of the thinking of the 'savage' with that of modern man."

16. In other work, Bruner also writes that "even if a teacher uses oral language, this language nevertheless develops outside the context of direct action. Both of these types of speech activity (that is, written speech and oral speech of the teacher - P.T.) are highly abstract" (Bruner, 1977, p. 381; also compare Bruner et al., 1971, p. 336).

17. For example, when some results of experimental study of thinking done in the Kpelle tribe in Liberia indicated differences between "basic" cognitive processes of subjects attending school and those not attending, Cole et al. rejected this conclusion. They write: "At present we are not willing to accept this inference. We prefer to pursue the hypothesis that members of the nonliterate groups studied in those experiments can reason hypothetically, but that they fail to see the applicability of such reasoning in our experimental tasks" (Cole et al., 1971, p. 231). The evidence follows: references to some ethnographic and experimental data indicate the presence in the subjects of "hypothetical reasoning." The concept of "hypothetical reasoning," which the authors apply with respect to such different processes as syllogistic conclusion from premises when the materials in question are unknown to the subject from personal experience and assumptions expressed in court, seems unfortunate to us. But here Cole and his coauthors prefer not a movement in the direction of a typology of tasks, situations and processes of thinking more suitable for the study of the object studied, but a rejection of the conclusion that follows from experimental data but contradicts the idea of universality of "basic" cognitive processes. As a result, the data of the experiments in this case are left without appropriate interpretation.

Chapter 2

1. Leont'ev (1982, p. 28) writes: "... Internal logic of the development of Vygotsky's theory brought it in earnest to the problems of interiorization, analyzed in detail by the French psychological school at the same time. But there was an essential difference in the understanding of interiorization by that school and by L. S. Vygotsky. The French school understood interiorization in the way that certain forms of social consciousness are implanted from without into the <u>primordially existing</u>

and primordially asocial individual consciousness (E. Durkheim) or elements of external social activity or social cooperation are introduced into it (P. Janet). For Vygotsky, however, consciousness is formulated only in the process of interiorization—there is no primordial asocial consciousness either in phylogenesis or in ontogenesis."

2. It is another matter that we must not judge all the thinking of people who created and used the texts on the basis of only any one type of text. Regardless of the many reservations of Levy–Bruhl, he was frequently understood specifically as if he had maintained that all thinking of "primitives" is entirely prelogical.

3. H. Gardner justifiably indicates that "... though Piaget has claimed to study the development of the mind, he has embraced a surprisingly narrow end state for cognition. In Piaget's view, mature cognition is no less, and no more, than the domain of logical-rational thought: accordingly, his end state is the competent scientist. Piaget has consequently paid little heed to adult forms of cognition removed from the logic of science: there is scant consideration of the thought processes used by artists, writers, musicians, athletes ..." (Gardner, 1979, p. 76).

4. H. Werner joins this argument: "The theory of a qualitative difference between primitive and advanced mentality has been rejected for the simple reason that enough evidence for primitive behavior can be found in our own culture. But developmental psychology does not deny the fact that there is a good deal of primitive activity in western civilization; on the contrary, since this is so clearly demonstrable within our own sphere, this fact is one of our strongest proofs of the existence of qualitatively different levels of functions" (Werner, 1948, p. 18).

5. R. Brown writes about concepts: "...concrete and abstract are relative judgments that can only be applied within a hierarchy of categories... The only absolute of abstraction ... is the all inclusive category—everything or perhaps the Universe. The only absolute of concreteness is the unique spacetime point. Everything in between is either concrete or abstract according as it is contrasted with a superordinate or a subordinate" (Brown, 1968, p. 266).

6. As an alternative, we indicate the point of view of R. Goldman regarding religious thinking. Goldman writes: "... religious thinking is no different in mode and method from non-religious thinking. Religious thinking is a shortened form of expressing the activity of thinking directed towards religion, not a term meaning separate rationality" (Goldman, 1964, pp. 3–4;

cf. also p. 10). In other words, religious thinking is determined only by its object. Such a position seems to be unfortunate for the obvious reason that the objects of religious thinking may serve equally well as objects of other types of thinking: scientific, artistic, common sense, etc.

Chapter 3

1. We must admit that only later was our attention called to the fact that molybdenum is not a precious metal.

2. Tables 2–6 were taken from T. Tulviste, 1985.

3. Regardless of this, the problem of why schooled subjects exhibit only thinking in scientific concepts almost exclusively in some experiments (for example, in solving simple syllogistic problems) and not in others is of great interest.

4. S. Ball and R. Simpson, using a standard experiment, showed that participation in renaming objects led to a decrease in the degree of nominal realism in all American pupils who participated in the experiment (Ball and Simpson, 1977). We still do not know why the same result is not achieved when preschoolers name their dolls, participate in the selection of a name for their newborn brothers and sisters, etc.

5. That is, in teaching the facts specifically as <u>scientific</u>. In principle it is possible to teach a child to <u>believe</u> that the Earth moves around the Sun, and so forth.

Chapter 4

1. We do not propose to present a review of these works. See the reviews of Cole and Scribner, 1977, pp. 57–80; Lloyd, 1972, pp. 36–44.

2. See Bornstein (1973) on the systematic differences in physiological abilities to distinguish colors.

References

S. E. Ball and R. A. Simpson, "Shifts from nominal realism in grade school children as a function of participating in a naming task", *Journal of Psychology*, 1977, 96:217–221.

Z. Barbu, *Problems of Historical Psychology*. New York: Grove Press, 1960, 222 pp.

F. C. Bartlett, "Psychological methods and anthropological problems", *Africa*, 1937, 10:401–420.

J. W. Berry and P. R. Dasen (eds.) *Culture and Cognition: Readings in Cultural Psychology*. New York: Harper & Row, 1973, 487 pp.

J. A. Blackburn, "The influence of personality, curriculum, and memory correlates on formal reasoning in young adults and elderly persons", *Journal of Gerontology*, 1984, 39:207–209.

F. Boas, *The Mind of Primitive Man*. Moscow, Leningrad: GIZ, 1926, 1926, 154 pp. (Russian translation).

M. H. Bornstein, "Color vision and color naming: a psychophysiological hypothesis of cultural difference", *Psychological Bulletin*, 1973, 80:257–285.

M. D. S. Braine, "On the relation between the natural logic of reasoning and standard logic", *Psychological Review*, 1978, 85:1–21.

J. S. Brook, "A test of Piaget's theory of nominal realism'", *Journal of Genetic Psychology*, 1970, 116:165–175.

R. Brown, *Words and Things*: New York. Free Press, 1968, 398 pp.

R. Brown and E. H. Lenneberg, "A study of language and cognition", *Journal of Abnormal and Social Psychology*, 1954, 49:454–462.

J. Bruner, "The Psychology of Cognition (Going Beyond the Information Given).", Moscow: Progress, 1977, 414 pp. (Russian translation).

J. Bruner, R. Oliver, and P. Greenfield (eds.), *A Study of the Development of Cognitive Activity*, Moscow: Pedagogika, 1971, 392 pp. (Russian translation).

J. Bruner, Vygotsky's zone of proximal development: The hidden agenda, In: B. Rogoff and J. V. Wertsch (eds.): *Children's Learning in the "Zone of Proximal Development"* (New Directions for Child Development, No. 23). San Francisco: Jossey–Bass, 1984, pp. 93–97.

J. Bruner, Vygotsky: a historical and conceptual perspective, In: J. V. Wertsch (ed.): *Culture, Communication and Cognition: Vygotskian Perspectives*, Cambridge: Cambridge University Press, 1985, pp. 21–34.

A. V. Brushlinskii, *A Cultural-Historical Theory of Thinking (Philosophical Problems in Psychology)*, Moscow: Vysshaya Shkola, 1968, 104 pp. (In Russian) .

E. A. Budilova, *Sociopsychological Problems in Russian Science*, Moscow: Nauka, 1983, 232 pp. (In Russian).

N. A. Butinov, Levi–Strauss and the problems of social organization of Australian aborigines, In: *Ethnography Abroad. Historiographic Notes*, Moscow: Nauka, 1979, pp. 114–148 (In Russian).

N. A. Butinov, Levi–Strauss, ethnographer and philosopher, In: *C. Levi–Strauss. Structural Anthropology*. Moscow: Nauka, 1983, pp. 422–466 (In Russian).

J. B. Carroll (ed.) *Language, Thought, and Reality: Selected Writings of Benjamin Lee Whorf*, Cambridge, Mass.: MIT Press, 1964, 278 pp.

J. B. Carroll and J. B. Casagrande, The function of language classifications in behavior, In: E. E. Macoby, T. M. Newcomb, and E. L. Hartley (eds.): *Readings in Social Psychology*, New York: Holt, Rinehart & Winston, 1958.

A. K. Chase and J. R. von Sturmer. "Mental man" and social evolutionary theory, In: G. E. Kearney, P. R. deLacey and G. R. Davidson (eds.): *The Psychology of Aboriginal Australians*, Sydney: Wiley, 1973, pp. 3–15.

T. V. Chernigovskaya and V. L. Deglin, *The problem of internal dialogism (neurophysiological study of language competence)*, Uchen. Zap. Tartusk. Gos. Un-t, No. 641 (Structure of Dialog as a Principle in the Work of the Semiotic Mechanism, Works on Sign Systems, 17) Tartu, pp. 33–44 (In Russian).

N. Chomsky, *Language and Thought*, Moscow: Izd-vo MGU. 1972, 122 pp. (Russian translation.)

S. Clarke, "Levi–Strauss's structural analysis of myth", *Sociological Review,* 1977, 25:743–774.

S. Clarke, *The Foundations of Structuralism: a Critique of the Structuralist Movement*, Brighton, Sussex: Harvester Press, 1981, 264 pp.

M. Cole, An ethnographic psychology of cognition, R. Brislin, S. Bochner and W. Lonner (eds.) In: *Cross-cultural Perspectives on Learning*, Beverly Hills Calif.: Sage, 1975, pp. 157–175.

M. Cole, Foreword, In: A. R. Luria: *Cognitive Development: Its Cultural and Social Foundations*, Cambridge, Mass., London: Harvard University Press 1976, pp. XI–XVI.

M. Cole and S. Scribner, *Culture and Thought, A Psychological Study*, Moscow Progress, 1977.264 pp. (Russian translation) .

M. Cole, Society, mind, and development, In: *The Child and Other Culture Inventions*, F. S. Kessel and A. W. Siegel (eds.), New York: Praeger, 198? pp. 89–114.

M. Cole, The zone of proximal development: where culture and cognition create each other, In: J. V. Wertsch (ed.): *Culture, Communication, and Cognition Vygotskian Perspectives*. Cambridge: Cambridge University Press, 198? pp. 146–161.

M. Cole and J. S. Bruner, Preliminaries to a theory of cultural differences, In: *Seventy-first Yearbook of the National Society for the Study of Education*, Chicago, 1972, pp. 161–179.

M. Cole, J. Gay, J. A. Glick, and D. W. Sharp, *The Cultural Context of Learning and Thinking: an Exploration in Experimental Anthropology*, New York: Basic Books, 1971, 304 pp.

M. Cole and B. Means, *Comparative Studies of How People Think: An Introduction*, Cambridge, Mass., London: Harvard University Press, 1981, 208 pp.

M. Cole, D. W. Sharp and C. Lave, "The cognitive consequences of education: some empirical evidence and theoretical misgivings", *Urban Review*, 1976, 9:218–233.

D. E. Cooper, "Alternative logic in 'primitive thought'" *Man*, 1975, 10:238–256.

M. Crick, "Anthropology of knowledge", *Annual Review of Anthropology*, 1982, 11:287–313.

V. V. Davydov, New studies in the field of child psychology, In: *A Study of the Development of Cognitive Activity* Moscow: Pedagogika (J. Bruner, R. Olver, and P. Greenfield, eds.), 1971, pp. 5–13. (In Russian).

V. V. Davydov, *Types of Communication in Teaching*, Moscow: Pedagogika, 1972, 424 pp. (In Russian).

J. Dewey, *Psychology and Pedagogy of Thinking*, 2nd ed. Berlin: GIZ RSFSR. 1922, 196 pp. (Russian translation).

M. Donaldson, *Thinking Activity of Children*, Moscow: Pedagogika, 1985, 192 pp. (Russian translation).

E. Durkheim, Sociology and the theory of cognition, In: New Ideas in Sociology, *Second Volume, Sociology and Psychology*, St. Petersburg: Obrazovanie, 1914, pp. 27–67 (In Russian).

E. Durkheim, *The Elementary Forms of Religious Life*, London: Allen & Unwin, 1976, 456 pp.

E. Durkheim and M. Mauss, *Primitive Classification*, Chicago: University of Chicago, 1963, 96 p.

D. B. El'konin and Davydov, V. V., eds., *Capabilities of Acquiring Knowledge according to Age (Lower School Classes)*, Moscow: Prosveshchenie, 1966, 442 pp. (In Russian).

C. R. Ember, "Cross-cultural cognitive studies", *Annual Review of Anthropology*, 1977, 6:33–56.

R. H. Ennis, "An alternative to Piaget's conceptualization of logical competence", *Child Development*, 1976, 47:903–919.

J. St. B. T. Evans, "On the problems of interpreting reasoning data: logical and psychological approaches", *Cognition*, 1972, 1:373–384.

J. St. B. T. Evans, "Linguistic determinants of bias in conditional reasoning", *Quarterly Journal of Experimental Psychology*, 1983, 35A:635–644.

J. St. B. T. Evans, J. L. Barston, and P. Pollard, "On the conflict between logic and belief in syllogistic reasoning", *Memory & Cognition*, 1983, 11:295–306.

J. A. Fishman, "A systematization of the Whorfian hypothesis", *Behavioral Science*, 1960, 5:323–339.

J. H. Flavell, Metacognitive aspects of problem solving, In: *The Nature of Intelligence*, Hillsdale, N.J.: Erlbaum, L. B. Resnick (ed.), 1976, pp. 231–235.

J. H. Flavell, Cognitive monitoring, In: *Children's Oral Communication Skills*, New York, Academic Press, W. P. Dickson (ed.), 1981, pp. 35–60.

I. G. Frank-Kamenetskii, Primitive thinking in the light of Japhetic theories and philosophy, In: *Language and Literature*, Vol. 3, Leningrad, 1929, pp. 142–148 (In Russian).

R. M. Frumkina, Linguistic hypothesis and experiment (on the specifics of hypothesis in psycholinguistics), In: *Hypothesis in Modern Linguistics*, Moscow: Nauka, 1980, pp. 183–216 (In Russian).

R. M. Frumkina and A. V. Mikheev, "Freedom" and "norms" in experiments on free classification, In: *Linguistic and Psycholinguistic Structures of Speech*, Moscow, 1985, pp. 66–77 (In Russian).

P. P. Gaidenko, *The Evolution of the Concept of Science* (Establishment and Development of the First Scientific Programs), Moscow: Nauka, 1980, 568 pp. (In Russian).

P. Ya. Gal'perin and D. B. El'konin, Toward an analysis of the theory of J. Piaget on the development of thinking in children, In: J. H. Flavell: *The Genetic Psychology of Jean Piaget*, Moscow: Prosveshchenie, 1967, pp. 596–621 (In Russian).

H. Gardner, "Developmental psychology after Piaget: An approach in terms of symbolization", *Human Development*, 1979, 22:73–88.

C. Geertz, *The Interpretation of Cultures: Selected Essays*, New York: Basic Books, 1973, 470 pp.

J. Glick, Cognitive development in cross-cultural perspective, In: *Review of Child Development Research*, Vol. 4, Chicago: Chicago University Press, F. D. Horowitz (ed.), 1975, pp. 595–648.

A. A. Goldenweiser, *Early Civilization: An Introduction to Anthropology*, New York: Knopf, 1922, 428 pp.

R. Goldman, *Religious Thinking from Childhood to Adolescence*, London: Routledge & Kegan Paul, 1964, 276 pp.

K. Goldstein and A. Gelb, "Uber Farbamnesie nebst Bemerkungen uber das Wesen der amnestischen Aphasie uberhaupt in der Beziehung zwischen Sprache und dem Verhalten zur Umwelt", *Psychologische Forschung*, 1925, 6:127–186.

K. Goldstein and M. Scheerer, "Abstract and concrete behavior: An experimental study with special tests", *Psychological Monographs*, Vol. 53, 1941 (Whole No. 239).

J. Goody, *The Domestication of the Savage Mind*, Cambridge: Cambridge University Press, 1977, 180 pp.

J. Goody and I. P. Watt, "The consequences of literacy", *Comparative Studies in Society and History*, 1963, 5:304–345.

P. M. Greenfield, "Oral or written language: the consequences for cognitive development in Africa, the United States and England", *Language and Speech*, 1972, 15:169–178.

P. M. Greenfield and J. S. Bruner, "Culture and cognitive growth", *International Journal of Psychology*, 1966, 1:89–107.

M. Griaule, *Conversations with Ogotemmeli, An Introduction to Dogon Religious Ideas*, London: Oxford University Press, 1965, 230 pp.

J. Grinevald, "J. Piaget on Levi–Strauss: an interview with Jean Piaget", *New Ideas in Psychology*, 1983a, 1:73–79.

J. Grinevald, "J. Levi–Strauss' reaction: an interview with Claude Levi–Strauss", *New Ideas in Psychology*, 1983b, 1:81–86.

L. L. Gurova, *Psychological Analysis of Problem Solving*, Voronezh: Izd-vo Voronezhsk. Un-ta, 1976, 328 pp. (In Russian).

C. R. Hallpike, "Is there a primitive mentality? ", *Man*, 1976, 11:253–270.

C. R. Hallpike, *The Foundations of Primitive Thought*, Oxford: Clarendon Press, 1979, 516 pp.

M. Harris, *The Rise of Anthropological Theory: a History of Theories of Culture*, New York: Crowell, 1969, 806 pp.

M. Henle, "On the relation between logic and thinking", *Psychological Review*, 1962, 69:366–378.

M. J. Herskovits, *Cultural Anthropology*, New York: Knopf, 1955, 569 pp.

R. Horton, "African traditional thought and Western science", *Africa*, 1967, 37:50–71, 155–187.

R. Horton, Levy–Bruhl, Durkheim and the scientific revolution, In: *Modes of Thought: Essays on Thinking in Western and Non-Western Societies*, London: Faber & Faber, R. Horton and R. Finnegan (eds.), 1973, pp. 249–305.

D. Hymes, Speech and language: on the origins and foundations of inequality among speakers, In: *Language as a Human Problem*, New York: Norton, M. Bloomfield and E. Haugen (eds.), 1974, pp. 45–71.

D. Hymes, Two types of linguistic relativity (with examples from ethnography of American Indians), In: *New Developments in Linguistics, No. 7. Sociolinguistics*, Moscow: Progress, 1975a, pp. 229–298 (Russian translation).

D. Hymes, Ethnography of speech, In: *New Developments in Linguistics, No. 7, Sociolinguistics*, Moscow: Progress, 1975b, pp. 42–95 (Russian translation).

V. V. Ivanov, Binary structures in semiotic systems, In: *Systemic Studies, 1972 Annual*, Moscow: Nauka, 1972, pp. 206–236.

V. V. Ivanov, "The significance of M. M. Bakhtin's ideas on the symbol, the utterance, and the dialogue for modern semiotics", *Uchen. Zap. Tartusk.*

Gos. Un-t, No. 308 (Works on Sign Systems, 6). Tartu, 1973, pp. 5–44 (In Russian).

V. V. Ivanov, C. Levi–Strauss and the structural theory of ethnography, In: C. Levi–Strauss, *Structural Anthropology*, Moscow: Nauka,1983, pp. 397–421 (In Russian).

V. V. Ivanov, Yu. M. Lotman, A. M. Pyatigorskii, and B. A. Uspenskii, Points on the semiotic study of cultures (as applied to Slavic texts), In: *Semiotics and the Structure of a Text*, Wroclaw: Wydawnictwo Polskiej Akademii Nauk, 1973, pp. 9–32 (In Polish).

G. Jahoda, Theoretical and systematic approaches in cross-cultural psychology, In: *Handbook of Cross-cultural Psychology*, Vol. 1, Boston: Allyn & Bacon, H. C. Triandis and W. W. Lambert (eds.), 1980.

W. James, *Pragmatism*, St. Petersburg: Shipovnik, 1910, 242 pp. (Russian translation).

I. L. Janis and F. Frick, "The relationship between attitudes toward conclusions and errors in judging logical validity of syllogisms", *Journal of Experimental Psychology*, 1943, 33:73–77.

C. N. Johnson and M. P. Maratsos, "Early comprehension of mental verbs: Think and know", *Child Development*, 1977, 48:1743–1747.

C. N. Johnson and H. M. Wellman, "Children's developing understanding of mental verbs: Remember, know, and guess", *Child Development*, 1980, 51:1095–1102.

P. N. Johnson–Laird, "Ninth Bartlett Memorial Lecture: thinking as a skill", *Quarterly Journal of Experimental Psychology*, 1982, 34A:1–29.

R. Kammann and L. Streeter, "Two meanings of word abstractness", *Journal of Verbal Learning and Verbal Behavior*, 1971, 10:303–306.

P. Kay, Language evolution and speech style, In: *Sociocultural Dimensions of Language Change*, New York: Academic Press, C. G. Blount and M. Sanchez (eds.), 1977, pp. 21–33.

J. G. Kennedy, *Herbert Spencer*, Boston: Twayne, 1978, 163 pp.

F. Kh. Kessidi, *From Myth to Logos (Coming into Being of Greek Philosophy)*, Moscow: Mysl', 1972, 312 pp. (In Russian).

F. Klix, *Awakening Thought (At the Source of Human Intellect)*. Moscow: Progress, 1983, 302 pp. (Russian translation).

Laboratory of Comparative Human Cognition, Cognition as a residual category in anthropology, *Annual Review of Anthropology*, 1978, 7:51–69.

Laboratory of Comparative Human Cognition, "What's cultural about cross-cultural cognitive psychology?", *Annual Review of Psychology*, 1979, 30:145–172.

Laboratory of Comparative Human Cognition, "Culture and cognitive development", In: *Mussen Handbook of Child Development*, Vol. 1, New York: Wiley, W. Kessen (ed.), 1983.

J.-B. Lamarck, *The Philosophy of Zoology, Vol. 1*, Moscow, Leningrad: Biomedgiz, 1935, 332 pp. (In Russian) .

D. Lantz and V. Stefflre, "Language and cognition revisited", *Journal of Abnormal and Social Psychology*, 1964, 69:472–481.

E. Leach, *Levi–Strauss*, London: Fontana/Collins, 128 pp.

E. Leach, *Culture and Communication: the Logic by Which Symbols Are Connected. An Introduction to the Use of Structural Analysis in Social Anthropology*, Cambridge: Cambridge University Press, 1976, 106 pp.

A. Lefford, "The influence of emotional subject matter on logical reasoning," *Journal of General Psychology*, 1946, 34: 127–151.

G. W. Leibniz, New experiments in human understanding of the author of the system of predetermined harmony. In: *G. W. Leibniz, Works, Vol. 2*, 1983, pp. 47–545 (Russian translation).

E. H. Lenneberg and J. Roberts, "The language of experience: a study in methodology," *International Journal of American Linguistics*, 22:(Memoir 13), 1956.

A. N. Leont'ev, *Development of Memory (Experimental Study of Higher Psychological Functions)*, Moscow, Leningrad: Uchpedgiz, 1931, 277 pp. (In Russian).

A. N. Leont'ev, "Thinking," *Voprosy filosofii*, 1964, No. 4:85–95. (In Russian).

A. N. Leont'ev, *Problems in Mental Development*, 3rd ed., Moscow: Izd-vo MGU, 1972, 576 pp. (In Russian).

A. N. Leont'ev, *Activity, Consciousness, Personality* (In Russian), Moscow: Politizdat, 1975, 304 pp. (English translation: Englewood Cliffs: Prentice-Hall, Inc., 1978).

A. N. Leont'ev, Introduction. The creative path of L. S. Vygotsky, In: *L. S. Vygotsky, Collected Works, Vol. 1*. Moscow: Pedagogika. 1982, pp. 9–41 (In Russian).

A. N. Leont'ev and A. R. Luria, The psychological views of L. S. Vygotsky, In: *L. S. Vygotsky, Collected Psychological Studies*, Moscow: Izd-vo APN RSFSR, 1956, pp. 4–36 (In Russian).

O. Leroy, *La Raison Primitive. Essai de Refutation de la Theorie du Prelogisme*, Paris: Librairie Orientaliste Paul Geuthner, 1927, 316 pp.

C. Levi–Strauss, *The Savage Mind*, Chicago: University of Chicago Press, 1966, 290 pp.

C. Levi–Strauss, *Das Ende des Totemismus*, Frankfurt a.M.: Suhrkamp, 1968, 142 pp.

C. Levi–Strauss, *The Elementary Structures of Kinship*, Rev. ed. London: Eyre & Spottiswoode, 1969, 542 pp.

C. Levi–Strauss, "Structuralism and ecology," *Social Science Information*, 1973, 12:7–23.

C. Levi–Strauss, *Structural Anthropology*, Moscow: Nauka, 1983, 536 pp. (Russian translation).

198

L. Levy–Bruhl, *Primitive Thinking*, Moscow: Ateist, 1930, 340 pp. (Russian translation).

L. Levy–Bruhl, "A letter to E. E. Evans-Pritchard," *British Journal of Sociology*, 1952, 3:117–123.

L. Levy–Bruhl, *The Notebooks on Primitive Mentality*, New York: Harper & Row, 1975, 204 pp.

B. B. Lloyd, *Perception and Cognition: A Cross-cultural Perspective*, Harmondsworth: Penguin, 1972, 190 pp.

Yu. M. Lotman, "The Phenomenon of culture," *Uchen. Zap. Tartusk. Gos. Un-t*, No. 463. (Semiotics of Culture, Works on Sign Systems, 10), Tartu, 1978, pp. 3–17 (In Russian).

Yu. M. Lotman, Brain, text, culture, the artistic intellect, In: *Semiotics and Information Science*, No. 17,Moscow, 1981a, pp. 3–17 (In Russian).

Yu. M. Lotman, "Rhetorics," *Uchen. Zap. Tartusk. Gos. Un-t*, No. 515 (Structure and Semiotics of the Artistic Text, Works on Sign Systems, 12), Tartu, 1981b, pp. 8–28 (In Russian).

Yu. M. Lotman, "Asymmetry and dialogue," *Uchen. Zap. Tartusk. Gos. Un-t*, No. 635 (Text and Culture, Works on Sign Systems, 16) Tartu, 1983, pp. 15–30 (In Russian).

Yu. M. Lotman and Z. G. Mints, "Literature and mythology," *Uchen. Zap. Tartusk. Gos. Un-t*, No. 546 (Semiotics of Culture, Works on Sign Systems, 13) , Tartu, 1981, pp. 35–55 (In Russian) .

Yu. M. Lotman and B. A. Uspenskii, "Myth, name, culture," *Uchen. Zap. Tartusk. Un-t*, No. 308 (Works on Sign Systems, 16) Tartu, 1973, pp. 282–303 (In Russian) .

A. R. Luria, 1959. Development of speech and formation of mental processes. In: *Psychological Science in the USSR. Vol. 1.* (In Russian.) Izdvo APN RSFSR. Pp. 516–577.

A. R. Luria, Psychology as an historical science (on the problem of the historical nature of the psychological processes, In: *History and Psychology*, Moscow: Nauka, 1971, pp. 36–62 (In Russian).

A. R. Luria, *On the Historical Development of Cognitive Processes. Experimental Psychological Studies*, Moscow: Nauka, 1974, 172 pp. (In Russian).

A. R. Luria, On the problem of psychological orientation of physiology, In: *Problems in Neuropsychology*, Psychological Studies, Moscow: Nauka. 1977, pp. 9–27 (In Russian).

A. R. Luria, *Stages on the Road Travelled (A Scientific Autobiography)*, Moscow: Izd-vo MGU (E. D. Khomskaya, ed.), 1982, 182 pp. (In Russian).

U. Masing, "De hermeneutica," *Communio Viatorum*, 1973, No. 1–2:1–29.

McDougall, L. Levi–Strauss in fairyland, In: *The Realm of the Extra-Human: Agents and Audiences*, The Hague, Paris: Mouton, A. Bharati (ed.), 1976, pp. 31–49.

E. M. Meletinskii, *The Poetics of Myth*, Moscow: Nauka, 1976, 408 pp. (In Russian).

E. M. Meletinskii, Mythology and folklore in the works of Levi–Strauss, In: *Levi–Strauss, Structural Anthropology*, Moscow: Nauka, 1983, pp. 467–522 (In Russian).

N. Minick, "The socialization of cognition: a preface to theoretical, conceptual, and methodological developments," Manuscript, 1980.

J. J. B. Morgan and J. T. Morton, "The distortion of syllogistic reasoning produced by personal convictions," *Journal of Social Psychology*, 1944, 20:39–59.

D. Moshman and M. Timmons, "The construction of logical necessity," *Human Development*, 1982, 25:309–323.

M. M. Mukanov, "A Psychological Study of Intellect from the Historical Ethnic Aspect," Author's abstract of Doctoral Dissertation, Moscow, 1980. (In Russian).

M. M. Mukanov, "Distinguishing between invariant and variable factors as an alternative to the representation of L. Levy–Bruhl on pre-logical thinking," *Psikhologiya*, Alma-Ata, 1981, No. 11:94–11. (In Russian).

M. M. Mukanov and N. I. Chistyakova, C. Levi–Strauss on the identity of the thinking in primitive and modern man, In: *Genetic and Social Problems of Intellectual Activity*, Alma-Ata, 1975, pp. 7186 (In Russian).

R. Needham, Introduction, In: E. Durkheim and M. Mauss, *Primitive Classification*, Chicago: University of Chicago Press, 1963, pp. vii–xlviii.

U. Neisser, *Cognitive Psychology*, New York: Appleton-Century-Crofts, 1967, 352 pp.

R. Olson, "The languages of experience: On natural language and formal education," *Bulletin of the British Psychological Society*, 1975, 28:363–373.

I. Onyewuenyi, "Is there an African philosophy?" *Journal of African Studies*, 1976/77, 3:513–528.

A. Paivio, I. C. Yuille, and S. A. Madigan, "Concreteness, imagery, and meaningfulness values for 925 nouns," *Journal of Experimental Psychology*, 1968, 76(1) Pt. 2.

C. Parain, Structuralism and history, In: *Structuralism: Pro and Con. Collection of Articles* (Moscow: Progress, 1975, pp. 361–376 (Russian translation).

V. V. Petukhov, Analysis of L. Levy-Bruhl's conception of "primitive thinking," In: *New Developments in Psychology*, 2nd ed., Moscow: Izd-vo MGU, 1977, pp. 3–22 (In Russian).

J. Piaget, *Le Jugement et le Raisonnement chez l'enfant*, Neuchatel, Paris: Delachaux & Niestle, 1924, 344 pp.

J. Piaget, *Speech and Thought in the Child*, Moscow, Leningrad: Uchpedgiz, 1932, 412 pp. (Russian translation).

J. Piaget, *Collected Works in Psychology*, Moscow, Prosveshchenie, 1969, 660 pp. (Russian translation).

J. Piaget, *Structuralism*, New York: Harper Torchbooks, 1971, 154 pp.

J. Piaget, *The Child's Conception of the World*, Frogmore: Paladin, 1973, 444 pp.

N. A. Podgoretskaya, *A Study of the Devices of Logical Thinking in Adults*, Moscow: Izd-vo MGU, 1980, 150 pp. (In Russian).

A. A. Popov, *Nganasans* (Tavgi Samoyeds), Vol. 1, Moscow, Leningrad: Izd-vo AN SSSR, 1948, 128 pp. (In Russian).

A. A. Popov, *Nganasans: Social Organization and Beliefs*, Leningrad: Nauka, 1984, 152 pp. (In Russian).

B. F. Porshnev, *Oppposition as a Component of Ethnic Self-Consciousness*, Moscow: Nauka, 1973, 15 pp. (In Russian), (Ninth International Congress of Anthropological and Ethnographic Sciences, Chicago, September, 1973, Presentations of the Soviet Delegation).

V. Ya. Propp, *Folklore and Reality. Collected Articles*, Moscow: Nauka, 1976, 326 pp. (In Russian).

P. H. Raven, B. Berlin, and D. E. Breedlove, "The origins of taxonomy," *Science*, 1971, 174 :1210–1213.

A. P. Riftin, "Categories of the Visible and Invisible Worlds in Language (Preliminary Outline)," *Uchen. Zap. Leningr. Gos. Un-t*, Seriya Filol. Nauk, 1946, No. 10:136–152. (In Russian).

B. Rogoff, Schooling and the development of cognitive skills, In: *Handbook of Cross-cultural Psychology, Vol. 4*, Boston: Allyn & Bacon, H. C. Triandis and A. Heron (eds.), 1981, pp. 233–294.

B. Rogoff and J. Lave (eds.), *Everyday Cognition: Its Development in Social Context*, Cambridge, Mass., London: Harvard University Press, 1984, 314 pp.

S. L. Rubinshtein, The problem of consciousness and activity in the history of Soviet psychology, In: S. L. Rubinshtein: *Principles and Ways of Developing Psychology*, Moscow: Izd-vo AN SSSR, 1959, pp. 249–255 (In Russian).

S. L. Rubinshtein, Problems in psychology in the works of Karl Marx, In: *S. L. Rubinshtein: Problems in General Psychology*, Moscow: Pedagogika, 1973, pp. 19–46 (In Russian).

L. S. Sakharov, "Methods of studying concepts," *Psikhologiya*, 1930, 3(1):3–33.

M. H. Salmon, "Do Azande and Nuer use a non-standard logic?," *Man*, 1978, 13:444–454.

S. Scribner, Recall of classical syllogisms: a cross-cultural investigation of error in logical problems, In: *Reasoning: Representation and Process in Children and Adults*, Hillsdale, N.J., Erlbaum, R. J. Falmagne (ed.), 1975, pp. 153–173.

S. Scribner, Modes of thinking and ways of speaking: Culture and logic reconsidered, In: *Thinking: Readings in Cognitive Science*, Cambridge: Cambridge University Press, P. N. Johnson–Laird and P. C. Wason (eds.), 1977, pp. 483–500.

S. Scribner and M. Cole, "Literacy without schooling: Testing for intellectual effects," *Harvard Educational Review*, 1978,48: 448–461.

S. Scribner and M. Cole, *The Psychology of Literacy*, Cambridge, Mass., London: Harvard University Press, 1981, 336 pp.

B. I. Sharevskaya, "Against the anti-Marxist distortions in interpreting problems of primitive thinking and primitive religion," *Sovetskaya Etnografiya*, 1953, No. 3:9–26. (In Russian).

D. Sharp, M. Cole, and C. Lave, "Education and cognitive development: The evidence from experimental research," *Monographs of the Society for Research in Child Development*, 1979, 44(1,2) (Serial No. 178).

F. N. Shemyakin, The theory of Levy–Bruhl in the service of imperialistic reaction, In: *Philosophical Notes, Vol. 5, Problems in Psychology*, Moscow, Leningrad: Izd-vo AN SSSR, 1950, pp. 148–175 (In Russian).

Zh. I. Shif, *Development of Scientific Concepts in the Pupil. A Study of the Problem of Mental Development of the Pupil in the Teaching of Social Sciences*, Moscow, Leningrad: Uchpedgiz, 1935, 80 pp. (In Russian).

J. A. Skeen, B. Rogoff, and S. Ellis, "Categorization by children and adults in communication contexts," *International Journal of Behavioral Development*, 1983, 6:213–220.

R. R. Skemp, "Reflective intelligence and mathematics," *British Journal of Educational Psychology*, 1961, 31:45–55.

J. Z. Smith, "I am a parrot (red)," *History of Religions*, 1972, 11:391–413.

B. Snell, *Die Entdeckung des Geistes. Studien zur Entstehung des Europaischen Denkens bei den Griechen*, Hamburg: Claaszen & Goverts, 1946, 264 pp.

P. Sorokin, *System of Sociology*, Vol. 1, *Social Analysis*, Chapter 1, Teaching on the structure of simplest (clan) social phenomena, Petrograd: Kolos, 1920, 360 pp. (In Russian).

H. Spencer, *Principles of Psychology*, St. Petersburg: I. I. Bilibin, 1876, Vol. 1–4 (Russian translation).

H. Spencer, *Principles of Sociology*, St. Petersburg: I. I. Bilibin, 1876–1877, Vol. 1–2, 900 pp. (Russian translation).

M. Stadler and A. Windheuser, "Untersuchungen uber instruktionsinduzierte Denkstile," *Zeitschrift fur experimentelle und angewandte Psychologie*, 1977, 24:324–351.

Stenographic Account of the First All-Union Congress on Human Behavior, Leningrad, Moscow: Gosmedizdat, 1930 (In Russian).

T. Tamm, The appearance in ontogenesis of the ability to solve syllogisms, In: *Proceedings of the Republic Conference of the Students' Scientific Society, 1977, Part 4, Psychology*, Finno-Ugric Languages,Tartu, pp. 61–68.

T. Tamm and P. Tulviste, "Theoretic syllogistic reasoning: Regressing when not used?," *Acta et Commentationes Universitatis Tartuensis*, 522, "Problems of Cognitive Psychology,"Tartu, 1980, pp. 50–59.

R. Thouless, "Effect of prejudice on reasoning," *British Journal of Psychology*, 1959, 50:289–293.

R. Thurnwald, *Ethno-psychologische Studien an Sudseevolkern auf dem Bismarck-Archipel und den Salomo-Inseln*, Leipzig: J. A. Barth, 1913, 164 pp. (Beihefte zur Zeitschrift fur angewandte Psychologie und psychologische Sammelforschung, 6).

R. Thurnwald, Psychologie des primitiven Menschen, In: *Handbuch der vergleichenden Psychologie, Vol. 1, Die Entwicklungsstufen des Seelenlebens*, Munchen: Reinhardt, G. Kafka (ed.), 1922, pp. 145–320.

S. A. Tokarev, Sources of Ethnographic Knowledge (to the Middle of the Nineteenth Century), Moscow: Nauka,1978, 164 pp. (In Russian).

P. Tulviste, "The Sociohistorical Development of Cognitive Processes (Based on Data of Experimental-Psychological Studies in Other Countries)," Candidate's Dissertation in Psychology, Moscow, 1975. (In Russian).

P. Tulviste, "Toward the interpretation of parallels between ontogenesis and the historical development of thinking," *Uchen. Zap. Tartusk. Gos. Un-t*, No. 411. (Works on Sign Systems, 8), Tartu, 1977, pp. 90–102 (In Russian) .

P. Tulviste, The theoretical problems of the historical development of thinking, In: *Principles of Development in Psychology*, Moscow: Nauka, 1978, pp. 81–104 (In Russian).

P. Tulviste, "On the origins of theoretic syllogistic reasoning in culture and in the child," *Acta et Commentationes Universitatis Tartuensis*, 474, "Problems of Communication and Perception," Tartu, 1978, pp. 3–22.

P. Tulviste, "On the origins of theoretic syllogistic reasoning in culture and the child," *Newsletter of the Laboratory of Comparative Human Cognition*, University of California, San Diego, 1979, 1:73–80.

P. Tulviste, The problem of typology of verbal thinking, In: *The Scientific Works of L. S.. Vygotsky and Modern Psychology, Proceedings of the All-Union Conference*, Moscow,1981a, pp. 154–157 (In Russian).

P. Tulviste, 1981b, Comparative study of children's thinking in various cultures, In: *Readings on Age and Pedagogical Psychology, Works of Soviet Psychologists, 1946–1980*, Moscow: Izd-vo MGU, pp. 189–193 (In Russian).

P. Tulviste, P. 1981c. Is there verbal thinking specific to children? *Voprosy Psikhologii*, No. 5:34–42. (In Russian).

P. Tulviste, "Is there a form of verbal thought specific to childhood?," *Soviet Psychology*, 1982, 21:3–17.

P. Tulviste and A. Lapp, "Could Margaret Mead's methods reveal animism in Manus children? A partial replication study in a European culture," *Acta et Commentationes Universitatis Tartuensis*, 474, "Problems of Communication and Perception," Tartu, 1978, pp. 23–30.

T. Tulviste, "Origin of reflection in thinking: A review of the studies in child and cross-cultural psychology," *Uchen. Zap. Tartusk. Gos. Un-t*, No. 691.

(Cognitive Processes, Works in Psychology), Tartu, 1984, pp. 64–78. (In Russian).

T. Tulviste, "Determination of Reflection in Verbal Thinking," Candidate's Dissertation in Psychology, Moscow, 1985. (In Russian).

T. Tulviste and P. Tulviste, The correspondence between the nature of units and operations in verbal thinking: Experimental confirmation of Vygotsky's hypothesis, In: *Linguistic and Psycholinguistic Structures of Speech*, Moscow, 1985, pp. 109–115 (In Russian).

E. B. Tylor, *Primitive Culture*, Moscow: Sotsekgiz, 1939, 568 pp. (Russian translation) .

J.-P. Vernant, Mythe et Pensee chez les grecs, Etudes de Psychologie Historique, 2nd ed, Paris: Maspero, 1969, 331 pp.

V. N. Voloshinov, *Marxism and the Philosophy of Language. Basic Problems in the Sociological Method in Linguistics*, 2nd ed., Moscow, 1930,157 pp. (In Russian).

L. S. Vygotsky, "The problem of planning research on pedology of national minorities," *Pedologiya*, 1929, No. 3:367–377. (In Russian).

L. S. Vygotsky, *Mental Development in Children during Learning*, Moscow, Leningrad: Uchpedgiz, 1935, 133 pp. (In Russian).

L. S. Vygotsky, *Collected Studies in Psychology*, Moscow: APN RSFSR, 1956, 520 pp. (In Russian).

L. S. Vygotsky, *Development of Higher Mental Functions. Nonpublished Works*, Moscow: Izd-vo APN, 1960, 500 pp. (In Russian).

L. S. Vygotsky, *Collected Works*, Vol. 1, 1982a, 488 pp.; Vol. 2, 1982b, 504 pp.; Vol. 3, 1983, 368 pp.; Vol. 4, 1984, 434 pp. (In Russian).

L. S. Vygotsky and A. R. Luria, *Studies in the History of Behavior. The Ape, the Aborigine, the Child*, Moscow, Leningrad: GIZ, 1930, 232 pp. (In Russian).

A. F. C. Wallace, "Culture and cognition," *Science*, 1962, 135:351–357.

P. C. Wason and P. N. Johnson–Laird, Psyschology of Reasoning: Structure and Content, Cambridge, Mass., London: Harvard University Press, 1972, 264 pp.

H. Werner, *Comparative Psychology of Mental Development*, New York: International Universities Press,1948, 564 pp.

K. Weule, The Culture of "Uncultured" Peoples, St. Petersburg: Soikin,1913, 100 pp. (In Russian).

K. Weule, *Die Kultur der Kulturlosen: ein Blick in die Anfange menschlicher Geistesbetatigung*, Stuttgart: Kosmos, 1921.

R. Williams, "Nominal realism in the child of the seventies? A replication," *Journal of Genetic Psychology*, 1977, 130:161–162.

P. Worsley, Groote Eylandt totemism and Le totemism d'aujourd'hui, In: *The Structural Study of Myth and Totemism*, London: Tavistock, E. Leach (ed.), 1967, 141–159.

W. Wundt, *Reden und Aufsatze. 2. Aufl.* Leipzig: Kroner,1914, 400 pp.

M. G. Yaroshevskii, Afterword, In: *L. S. Vygotsky: Collected Works, Vol. 6.* Moscow: Pedagogika, 1984, pp. 329–347 (In Russian).

R. L. Zimmerman, Levi–Strauss and the primitive, In: *Claude Levi–Strauss: The Anthropologist as Hero*, Cambridge, Mass., London: MIT Press, E. N. Hayes and T. Hayes (eds.), 1970, pp. 215–234.

SUBJECT INDEX